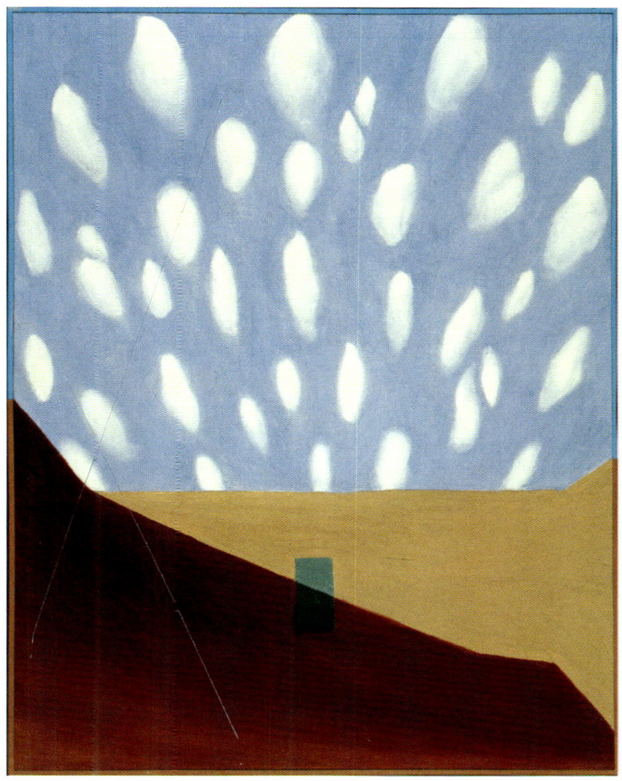

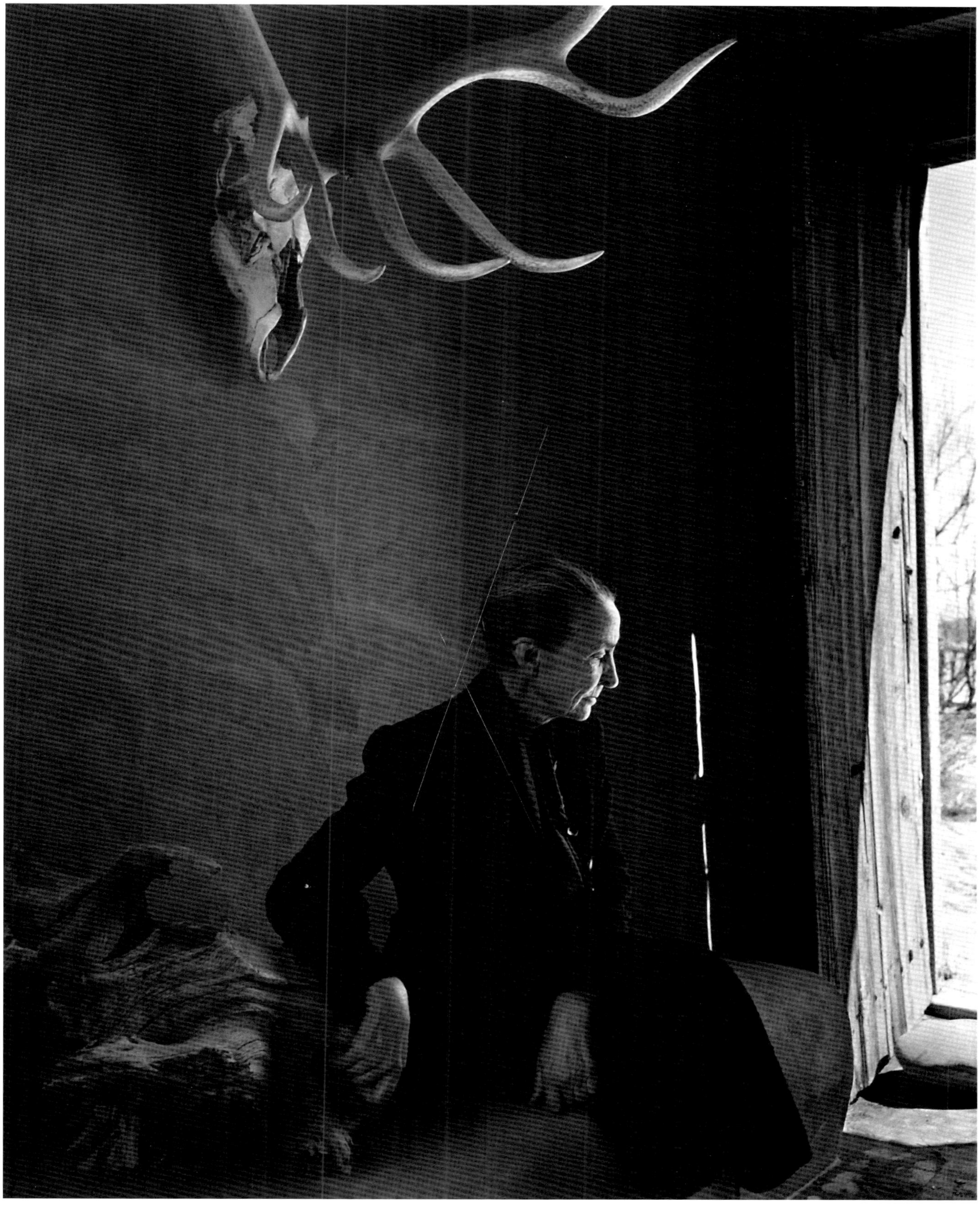

Yousuf Karsh, *Georgia O'Keeffe*, 1956, silver gelatin print. Collection of Mississippi Museum of Art, Jackson. Gift of Mississippi Chemical Corporation. 2005.018. © 1956 Yousuf Karsh.

Georgia O'Keeffe

COLOR AND CONSERVATION

René Paul Barilleaux and Sarah Whitaker Peters

René Paul Barilleaux, Editor

Essays by
Sarah Whitaker Peters
Dale Kronkright
Judith C. Walsh

The Annie Laurie Swaim Hearin Memorial Exhibition Series

Mississippi Museum of Art
Jackson

in association with
Penn State University Press

Georgia O'Keeffe: Color and Conservation is published on the occasion of a traveling exhibition of the same title organized by René Paul Barilleaux and Sarah Whitaker Peters, assisted by Robin C. Dietrick, originating at the Mississippi Museum of Art, Jackson, February 4-May 29, 2006. Subsequent venues are the Georgia O'Keeffe Museum, Santa Fe, New Mexico, June 16–September 10, 2006, and the Memorial Art Gallery of the University of Rochester, New York, September 30–December 31, 2006.

The Mississippi Museum of Art gratefully acknowledges the support of the Robert M. Hearin Foundation, without which this book and the *Georgia O'Keeffe: Color and Conservation* exhibition would not have been possible.

Support for *Georgia O'Keeffe: Color and Conservation* is also provided in part by funding from Trustmark National Bank.

The Mississippi Museum of Art and its programs are sponsored in part by the city of Jackson and The ArtsAlliance of Jackson & Hinds County. Support is also provided in part by funding from the Mississippi Arts Commission, a state agency, and in part by the National Endowment for the Arts, a federal agency.

Library of Congress Cataloging-in-Publication Data

Barilleaux, René Paul.
Georgia O'Keeffe : color and conservation / René Paul Barilleaux and Sarah Whitaker Peters ; René Paul Barilleaux, editor ; essays by Sarah Whitaker Peters, Dale Kronkright, Judith Walsh.
p. cm
Catalog of an exhibition at the Mississippi Museum of Art, Jackson, Feb. 4-May 29, 2006; Georgia O'Keeffe Museum, Santa Fe, June 16-Sept. 10, 2006; Memorial Art Gallery, Univ. of Rochester, N.Y., Sept. 30-Dec. 31, 2006.
"The Annie Laurie Swaim Hearin memorial exhibition series."
Includes bibliographical references.
ISBN 1-887422-11-0 (hardcover : alk. paper)
1. O'Keeffe, Georgia, 1887-1986--Exhibitions. 2. Art--Conservation and restoration--Exhibitions. I. Peters, Sarah Whitaker. II. O'Keeffe, Georgia, 1887-1986. III. Mississippi Museum of Art. IV. Georgia O'Keeffe Museum. V. University of Rochester. Memorial Art Gallery. VI. Title.

N6537.039A4 2006
759.13--dc22

Distributed by Penn State University Press.

Copyedited by Kathy L. Greenberg.

Image rights and reproduction coordinated by Robin C. Dietrick.

Designed by Heidi Flynn Allen, Flynn Design.

Prepress and scanning by All Systems Colour.

Printing by Everbest Printing Company Ltd., Hong Kong/China.

MISSISSIPPI MUSEUM *of* ART

COVER: *In the Patio VIII*, 1950. oil on canvas, 26" x 20". Collection of Georgia O'Keeffe Museum, Santa Fe, New Mexico. Gift of The Burnett Foundation and The Georgia O'Keeffe Foundation. 1997.05.08. Photograph: Malcolm Varon. © Georgia O'Keeffe Museum.

CONTENTS

ABOUT ANNIE LAURIE SWAIM HEARIN

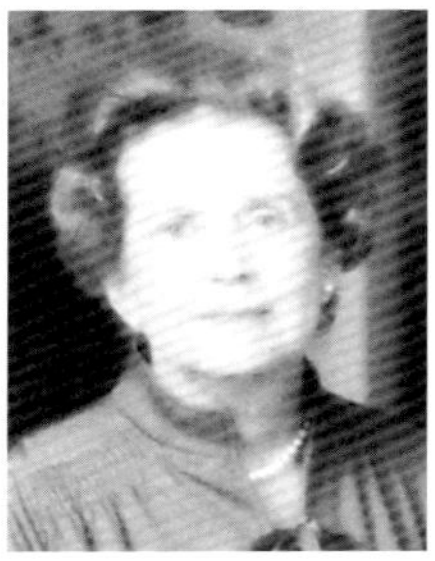

Georgia O'Keeffe: Color and Conservation is the eighth presentation in a series presented by the Mississippi Museum of Art and the Robert M. Hearin Foundation to honor the memory of Annie Laurie Swaim Hearin.

Mrs. Hearin was born and educated in Alabama but spent her adult life in Jackson, devoting herself to her family and her community. She was active in many community organizations, including serving as president of the Junior League of Jackson. Mrs. Hearin found special satisfaction in her friends, family, and involvement in the Mississippi Museum of Art.

The impact of Mrs. Hearin's years of service has been far reaching. A generous contributor and trusted adviser, she served the Museum on its Board of Trustees and as president of its Gallery Guild. She was instrumental in the Museum's decision to establish a restaurant in its facility; not content to be an adviser and policy setter, Mrs. Hearin contributed numerous hours supporting the restaurant as a waitress and as day chairman of the volunteers until her death. She and her husband, Robert M. Hearin (now deceased), were also critical in the founding of the Impressions Gallery, a hands-on gallery for young people at the Museum. In addition, Mrs. Hearin helped establish the Mississippi Museum of Art Foundation, Inc., acting as a charter member of its board. Her concern for the Museum was not only for strong programming, but also for its long-term health and its potential to benefit the community for many years beyond her life.

Her two children, Robert M. Hearin, Jr., and Annie Laurie Hearin McRee, continue the legacy begun by their mother and are active supporters of the Museum. Previous exhibitions in the Annie Laurie Swaim Hearin Memorial Exhibition Series include *Dutch and Flemish Seventeenth Century Paintings: The Harold Samuel Collection*, *Edgar Degas: The Many Dimensions of a Master French Impressionist*, *Italian Paintings from Burghley House*, *Our Nation's Colors: A Celebration of American Painting*, *The American West: Out of Myth, Into Reality*, *Passionate Observer: Eudora Welty among Artists of the Thirties*, and *Paris Moderne: Art Deco Works from the Musée d'Art Moderne de la Ville de Paris*.

The Mississippi Museum of Art is grateful for the life of Mrs. Hearin, the example she left for us all, and the Robert M. Hearin Foundation's generosity in establishing this series for the enjoyment of generations to come.

ACKNOWLEDGMENTS

Betsy Bracley

The eighth presentation of the Annie Laurie Swaim Hearin Memorial Exhibition Series, *Georgia O'Keeffe: Color and Conservation* is the culmination of work by an impressive group of people. The Mississippi Museum of Art is proud of the wonderfully productive relationship between its own René Paul Barilleaux and Sarah Whitaker Peters, collaborators on this publication and co-curators of the accompanying exhibition. Their intelligent and sensitive probing of the relationship between artist Georgia O'Keeffe and her personal conservator, Caroline Keck, makes this an exciting contribution to O'Keeffe's scholarship. Mrs. Keck's gracious consent to share her correspondence with O'Keeffe is a tribute to the late artist's ability to form lasting, substantive, and meaningful friendships.

Readers will find the insights of Dale Kronkright, chief consulting conservator at the Georgia O'Keeffe Museum, especially captivating, and we appreciate his dedication to this project. Judith C. Walsh, paper conservator for the National Gallery of Art, Washington, D.C., also provides a provocative perspective on O'Keeffe's efforts to ensure that future generations would have the pleasure of viewing her work.

For her continued assistance and extensive knowledge, we are grateful to Barbara Buhler Lynes, curator at the Georgia O'Keeffe Museum, Santa Fe, New Mexico, and director of the Georgia O'Keeffe Museum Research Center, Santa Fe. Without her help this book and the complementary exhibition would not have been possible. Likewise, Agapita Judy Lopez, director at the Georgia O'Keeffe Foundation, Abiquiu, New Mexico, provided valuable ongoing assistance to this project.

Our colleagues—George King, director of the Georgia O'Keeffe Museum, Grant Holcomb, director of the Memorial Art Gallery of the University of Rochester, New York, and Marie Via, director of exhibitions at the Memorial Art Gallery, made the collaboration of the traveling exhibition a delight. Many thanks also for the generosity of our colleagues and friends who agreed to share their valued artworks for the accompanying exhibition.

The creation of this publication and the subsequent exhibition was transformed from a vision to reality by the smart, efficient, and caring work of a wonderful team: Mississippi Museum of Art Registrar Robin C. Dietrick combined intelligence with a generous work ethic; copyeditor Kathy L. Greenberg perfected and re-perfected publication documents; and book designer Heidi Flynn Allen of Flynn Design once again transformed a scholarly work into an aesthetic experience with integrity and skill.

Finally, without the loving legacy of Annie Laurie Swaim Hearin and the generosity of her trustees at the Robert M. Hearin Support Foundation, many would miss this rare opportunity to share in the life and work of one of America's masters.

LENDERS TO THE EXHIBITION

AMON CARTER MUSEUM FORT WORTH, TEXAS

BALTIMORE MUSEUM OF ART MARYLAND

COLORADO SPRINGS FINE ARTS CENTER, TAYLOR MUSEUM COLORADO

FITCHBURG ART MUSEUM MASSACHUSETTS

GEORGIA O'KEEFFE MUSEUM SANTA FE, NEW MEXICO

GERALD AND KATHLEEN PETERS SANTA FE, NEW MEXICO

MEMORIAL ART GALLERY OF THE UNIVERSITY OF ROCHESTER NEW YORK

MEMPHIS BROOKS MUSEUM OF ART TENNESSEE

MISSISSIPPI MUSEUM OF ART JACKSON

MUSEUM OF FINE ARTS, BOSTON MASSACHUSETTS

MUSEUM OF FINE ARTS, MUSEUM OF NEW MEXICO SANTA FE

MUSEUM OF FINE ARTS, ST. PETERSBURG FLORIDA

NATIONAL GALLERY OF ART WASHINGTON, D.C.

NEW ORLEANS MUSEUM OF ART LOUISIANA

PANHANDLE-PLAINS HISTORICAL MUSEUM CANYON, TEXAS

PRIVATE COLLECTION

THE GEORGIA O'KEEFFE FOUNDATION ABIQUIU, NEW MEXICO

THE MUSEUM OF MODERN ART, NEW YORK NEW YORK

THE NEWARK MUSEUM NEW JERSEY

THE UNIVERSITY OF MISSISSIPPI UNIVERSITY

INTRODUCTION

René Paul Barilleaux

To create a fresh and original look at an iconic painter such as Georgia O'Keeffe is a challenge. Countless examinations of the work of masters like O'Keeffe offer a wide range of interpretations and evaluations aimed at diverse audiences, from the serious scholar to the casual art appreciator. Yet there remain unexplored aspects of any artist's creative output and professional career that provide a new and exciting opportunity for in-depth investigation. This publication, *Georgia O'Keeffe: Color and Conservation*—coupled with a traveling exhibition of the same title—brings to the public a significant yet previously uninvestigated aspect of O'Keeffe and her concerns with the craft of her art.

The conservation of paintings remains in a largely secretive realm, for the most part distant from the typical museum visitor and even further from the minds of most artists. Georgia O'Keeffe, unlike the majority of her artist-colleagues, understood very well how shoddy craftsmanship and improper care could impact the long-term physicality of her paintings and pastels. A consummate craftsman, O'Keeffe took great care to achieve the same degree of success with the preservation of her art as she did with its creation. Until now, however, little has been exposed about how actively the artist participated in the ongoing professional conservation of her work.

The centerpiece of this book is a series of letters between the artist and her longtime conservator, Caroline Keck. Available to the public for the first time, these communications reveal previously unknown information about O'Keeffe's studio practices and working process. The letters also give highly personal voices to these two women, while the reciprocal nature of the correspondence closely chronicles the evolution of a relationship that spanned nearly forty years.

Sarah Whitaker Peters, who collaborated on this project, painstakingly transcribed O'Keeffe's distinctive penmanship and selected the letters for publication. She offers clues to their content in the form of introductions and annotations. In addition, Peters links the letters' historical record to current understandings of O'Keeffe's art in her research of the specific works about which O'Keeffe and Keck corresponded.

To further enhance the new insight that the O'Keeffe-Keck letters provide are three essays: an overview by Sarah Peters and texts by Dale Kronkright and Judith C. Walsh that focus specifically on the conservation of O'Keeffe's work today. Peters interweaves elements of the artist's biography (about which she herself wrote in *Becoming O'Keeffe: The Early Years*) with explorations of the artist's aesthetic concerns, attention to craft, and studio work. Dale Kronkright, chief consulting conservator at the Georgia O'Keeffe Museum, Santa Fe, New Mexico, extends Peters's discussion and the issues surrounding ongoing conservation of O'Keeffe's paintings into a contemporary realm. Likewise, Judith C. Walsh, paper conservator at the National Gallery of Art, Washington, D.C., complements existing knowledge on the conservation of the artist's pastels and the particular challenges they present. Together, the contributions of these three experts establish an entirely new body of scholarship on O'Keeffe's professional career.

In addition to the reproductions of paintings and pastels that are found throughout this publication, photographs of the artist in various settings add a human element to the art. A rare photograph of Caroline Keck, pictured with her husband and fellow conservator, Sheldon Keck, enhances the archival nature of the book, as do reproductions of two of O'Keeffe's letters displaying her unique (and often hard to read) handwriting. The book's final section illustrates pictures included in the three accompanying museum exhibitions.

Despite her ubiquity and near universal popularity, Georgia O'Keeffe remains an enigmatic and even controversial figure in the history of art. Because reproductions of O'Keeffe's work appear in diverse and sometimes unlikely locations, the artist herself is often misrepresented and her work misread. This book, together with the museum exhibition it accompanies, intends to enlighten both readers and viewers about a significant, yet unexplored, aspect of the art of one of the past century's most famous American creators.

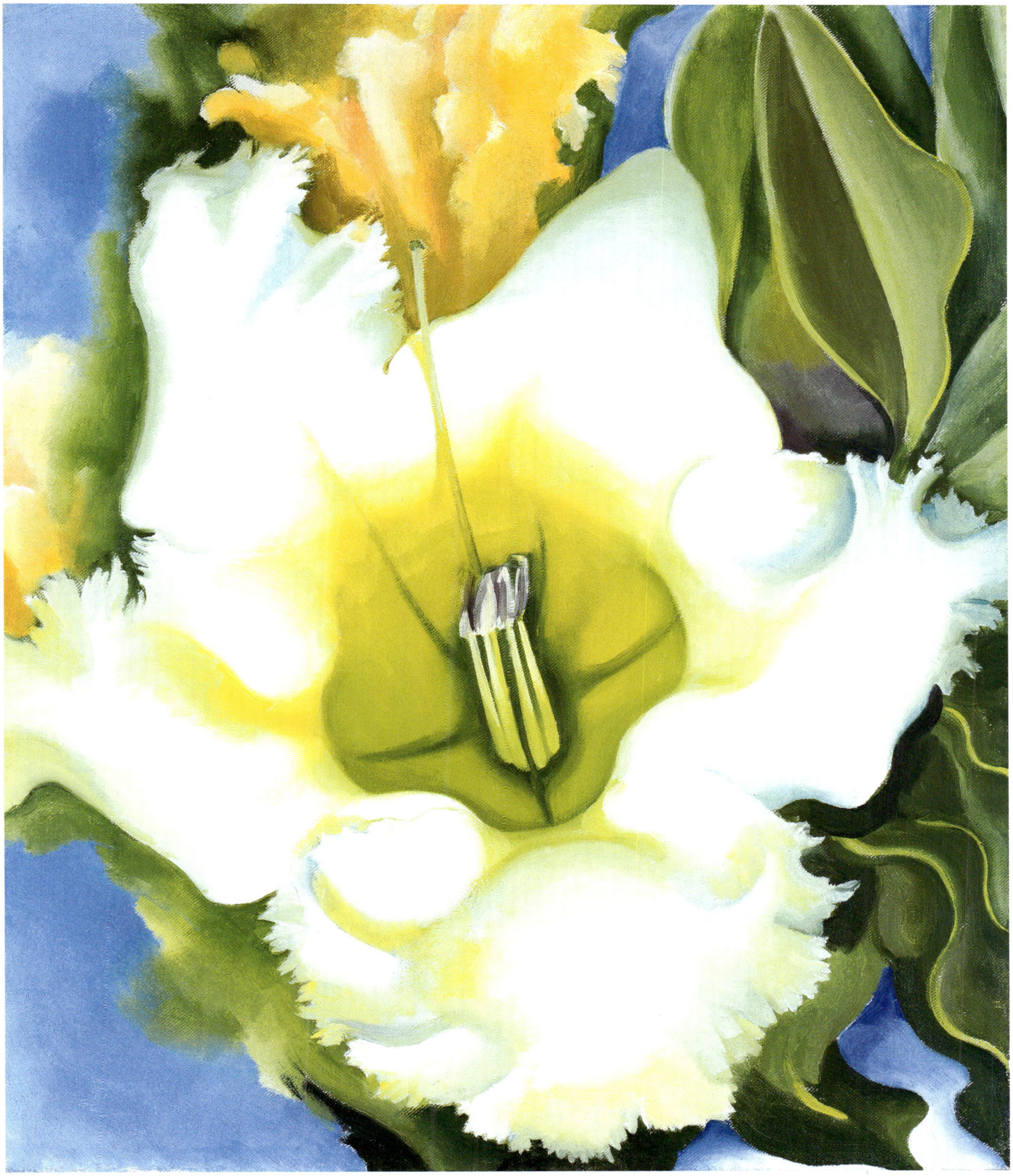

Cup of Silver Ginger, 1939. oil on canvas, 19" x 16". Collection of Baltimore Museum of Art, Maryland. Gift of Cary Ross. BMA 1940.122.

Georgia O'Keeffe

COLOR AND CONSERVATION

Sarah Whitaker Peters

Courtesy of Georgia O'Keeffe Museum Research Center, Santa Fe, New Mexico. Photograph: Malcolm Varon.

The idea for this groundbreaking project came from an almost unknown correspondence between Georgia O'Keeffe and her longtime conservator, Caroline Keck. Nothing quite like it exists in the history of art. There are ninety-seven letters extant written between 1946 and 1981—sixty by O'Keeffe and thirty-seven by Keck.

In 2001 the Georgia O'Keeffe Museum Research Center in Santa Fe, New Mexico, displayed the artist's painting materials for the first time ever.[1] She had kept them hidden from public view throughout her life. When I went to see them, Barbara Buhler Lynes, director of the Research Center, suggested that I also read a trove of letters that Keck had recently given to the Georgia O'Keeffe Foundation. I did and found them revelatory, even for veteran O'Keeffe scholars. These very personal letters contain descriptions of the ways and means both women employed to keep O'Keeffe's artistic intentions safe from the ravages of time.

Keck and O'Keeffe wrote with clarity and verve. Their acuity of mind, their pithy candor with each other, and their shared confidences about art and life, all convinced me that the letters should be published. Accordingly, I wrote to Keck, who was still working as a conservator in Cooperstown, New York. She answered that she had no objection to their publication. The foundation then graciously gave the Mississippi Museum of Art and me permission to do so.

Because these letters describe certain canvases before and after Keck's treatment of them, I thought it would be of value to gather together as many of these paintings as possible for an exhibition, with wall texts giving a brief history of how wear-and-tear damages were mitigated.[2] This way, viewers could better understand how crucial conservation is to keep pristine O'Keeffe's original color and line characteristics—and take new delight in seeing what a consummate craftsman she was.

René Paul Barilleaux, deputy director for programs at the Mississippi Museum of Art, was enthusiastic about organizing such an exhibition, and he immediately took on the daunting task of persuading museums and private collectors to lend their works. Any exhibition of an artist as famous as O'Keeffe presents a host of problems. There are far more requests than lenders can ever grant, since paintings are fragile and have to rest after touring. Many are spoken for years ahead and inevitably there are scheduling conflicts. We had our share of such disappointments; but some of those paintings that were unavailable for one reason or another have been reproduced in this book by kind permission of their owners, many of whom expressed regret at not being able to contribute to the show.

A special note of appreciation must go to Barbara Buhler Lynes, curator at the Georgia O'Keeffe Museum and director of its invaluable Research Center, as well as to the Georgia O'Keeffe Foundation and its director, Agapita Judy Lopez. The essays by two conservators of O'Keeffe's paintings, Judith C. Walsh, paper conservator for the National Gallery of Art, and Dale Kronkright, chief consulting conservator for the Georgia O'Keeffe Museum, are important contributions to the project and to the field. I am acutely conscious of an enormous debt to Judy and Dale for opening my mind to the history and craft of conservation. Particular gratitude is owed to Grant Holcomb, director of the Memorial Art Gallery in Rochester, New York, and to its director of exhibitions, Marie Via.

As co-curator, I would like to thank the entire staff of the Mississippi Museum of Art, especially my collaborator, René Paul Barilleaux, who has been a tower of strength from beginning to end. Others who have given me extremely generous help are Eumie Imm-Stroukoff, Gloria Lorenzo, Anne Fredericks, Susan Dodge-Peters Daiss, P. Gregory Schwed, Sandra Kisters of the Netherlands, Kathy L. Greenberg, and Robin C. Dietrick.

In the spring of 1945 James Johnson Sweeney, curator of the Museum of Modern Art, offered Georgia O'Keeffe the first retrospective ever granted to a woman artist. He told her that he would choose the paintings and write the catalogue essay. O'Keeffe accepted with an honest letter that expresses exactly what she was about as an artist when Caroline Keck met her:

> *I must say to you again that I am very pleased and flattered that you wish to do the show for me. It makes me feel rather inadequate .... For myself I feel no need of the showing .... When I say that ...—I should add that I think that what I have done is something rather unique in my time and that I am one of the few who gives our country any voice of its own—I claim no credit—it is only that I have seen with my own eyes and that I couldn't help seeing with my own eye—*[3]

O'Keeffe's aesthetic is a various one. She changed it according to mood and locale. It wasn't so much that her painting technique was experimental—she remained consistent to her early academic training at the School of the Art Institute of Chicago (1905-6) and the Art Students League of New York (1907-8). Rather, it was that she used her materials (always the best available) intuitively for different effects. Different places presented her with different ideas and problems to solve as a painter. She always liked that. In 1923 O'Keeffe (uncharacteristically) confided some of her thoughts on form making to Sherwood Anderson, sure that as a creative writer he would understand what she was saying:

> *I feel that a real living form is the natural result of the individual's effort to create the living thing out of the adventure of his spirit into the unknown—where it has experienced something—felt something—it has not understood—and from that experience comes the desire to make the unknown—known ... [S]ometimes it is all working in the dark—but a working that must be done—Making the unknown—known—in terms of one's medium is all absorbing .... The form must take care of itself—*[4]

Georgia Engelhard, a painter and niece of O'Keeffe's husband, Alfred Stieglitz, recollected in 1980 that

> *When OK painted small objects—flowers, leaves, clam shells, stones etc., she did paint from a model. The first paintings were usually small and then later she would develop the motif into something larger. She definitely worked from realism to abstraction on many occasions ... [W]hen we were on the Gaspé and [she] did the barn and cross series these were painted from nature—she would paint the most important sections [on the motif] and then finish the work later from memory. But many of her landscapes were NOT painted directly from nature—and they are largely the impressions that certain scenes made on her ...*[5]

O'Keeffe loved playing with opposing optical qualities like transparency and opacity. She had a passion for pattern as well. A student and teacher of Arthur Wesley Dow's essentially Japanese principles of picture making, she was familiar with his harmoniously spaced linear design composed of abstract arrangements of light and dark patterns, or *notan*. Dow's synthetic system of composition, which O'Keeffe described as "filling space in a beautiful way," became a lifelong underpinning for her particular brand of modernism. For the Stieglitz Circle artists, modernism meant what he liked to call

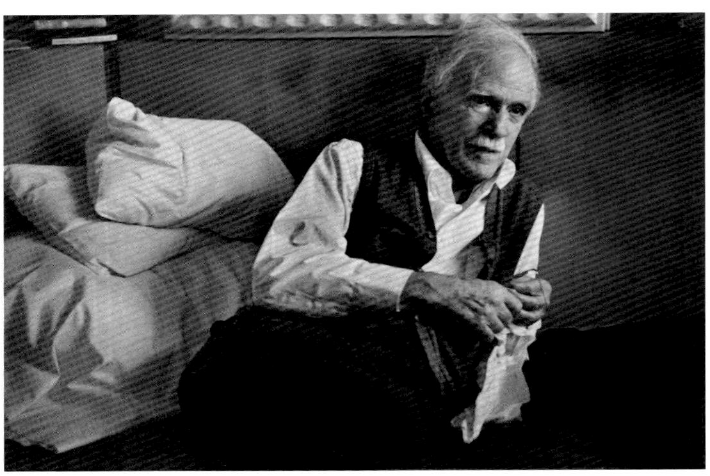

Henri Cartier-Bresson, *USA. New York City. 1946. Alfred Stieglitz, US photographer,* 1946, silver gelatin print. Courtesy of Magnum Photos.

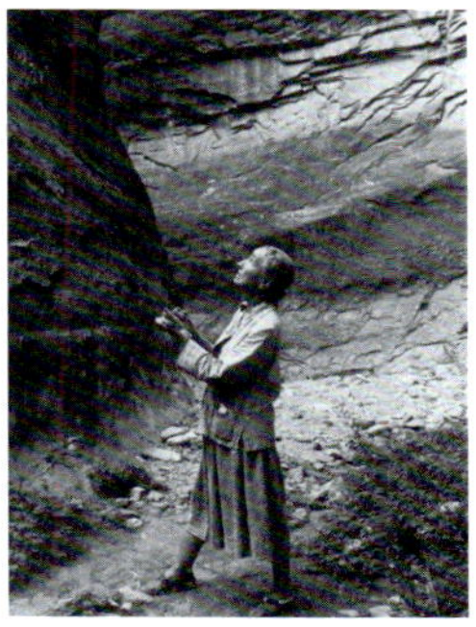

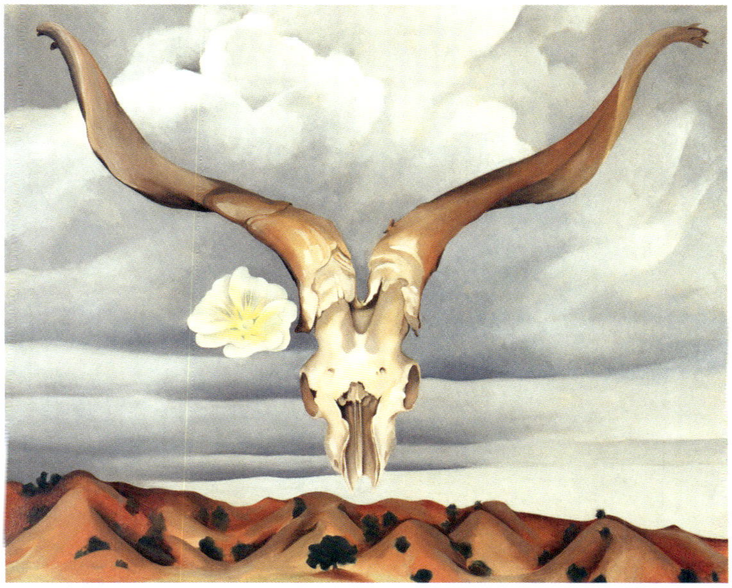

(Left) Todd Webb, *O'Keeffe Sketching in Glen Canyon*, 1961, silver gelatin print. Courtesy of Evans Gallery, Portland, Maine. *(Right)* *Ram's Head, White Hollyhock—Hills*, 1935, oil on canvas, 30" x 36". Collection of Brooklyn Museum of Art, New York. Bequest of Edith and Milton Lowenthal. 1992.11.28.

"the new"—in other words, the *original*. And O'Keeffe basically worked out of herself.

Consider also photography. Between 1919 and 1929, when O'Keeffe worked side by side with Stieglitz at Lake George, New York, and in New York City, she found a whole new set of aesthetic possibilities in the photographic process. Not for nothing had she watched him printing his negatives in their close quarters. Like Stieglitz, O'Keeffe believed the camera to be an instrument of "objective" truth (even though it isn't). Straight photography as practiced by Stieglitz and others around him offered her new artistic elements to extend or reinvent. It would take her abstraction in different directions, even while it lengthened her reach to record truth—from the close-up to the telephoto—although she never said so. Her secret, highly original synthesis of painting and photography would become increasingly sophisticated.[6]

In the long span of her landscapes (perhaps her chief claim to greatness), O'Keeffe painted in four major locales: the Texas panhandle, out of which came her rhapsodic, critically acclaimed watercolors of 1916-18; Lake George, where she and Stieglitz influenced each other's mediums so transformatively; New York City, where she used a wide array of photo optics, including convergence, halation, and flare to render her skyscrapers of the twenties; and New Mexico, the best loved of them all. This was the place that she found "naturally" photographic and the place where she once said, "I felt as grateful for my largest hurts as I did for my largest happiness."[7]

Although she used color, sometimes arbitrarily, to construct space and express her emotions, her painting always kept a powerful linear eloquence. Georgia Engelhard's letter emphasizes that she was "an excellent draftsman—which I feel is due to her conservative art training. I always feel that so many modern artists can't draw —but she certainly COULD." Barbara Buhler Lynes's 1999 *catalogue raisonné* reveals O'Keeffe to have been an obsessively hidden draftsman throughout her life as an artist. There are seven hundred and thirty drawings extant—including seventeen sketchbooks and her spontaneous notations in ballpoint pen and pencil—most of them completely unknown.[8] They show the crystalization of her ideas, and they show just how hard she worked to better herself in this traditional discipline of hand and eye. It was hardly accidental that O'Keeffe's legendary breakthrough as an original American modernist in 1915 happened with a charcoal stick on large pieces of white paper spread out on the floor. These images of reduced forms in nature, with their veiled uterine and phallic overtones, would remain as ghostly armatures in many of her subsequent compositions, whether abstract or realist.

Paul Rosenfeld noted in 1922 that "The color of O'Keeffe has an edge that is like a line."[9] She created her edges with the finest and most precise kind of brushwork. Found among her painting materials were hundreds of different-size brushes that she sometimes shaped

Consider also photography. Between 1919 and 1929, when O'Keeffe worked side by side with Stieglitz at Lake George, New York, and in New York City, she found a whole new set of aesthetic possibilities in the photographic process.

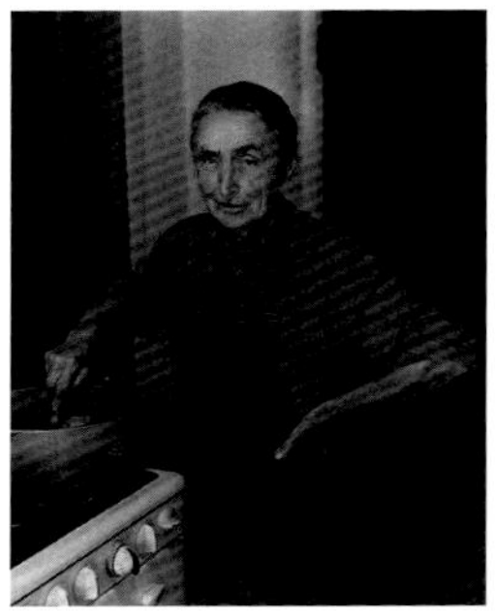

She was a meticulous craftsman in everything she chose to do—from cooking to making clothes and gardens to grinding her own pigments between glass (on occasion) for greater translucency to having a go at creating her own pastel sticks. She loved the very substance of color.

with scissors for greater precision. How the peaks and valleys of dissimilar canvas weaves resisted the pressure of her brushes never failed to interest her. The subtle syntax of her brush marks has a wide range—from the directional (following the outlines and angles of her forms) to the feathery in her broad fields of color.

O'Keeffe had been fascinated with textures and textiles from the time of her earliest acquaintance with Dow's teaching exercises —which stressed them—and was not above putting sand and stone in her paint to more accurately render the texture of adobe or rock.[10] Her old friend Ansel Adams, the photographer, once observed that "a lot of O'Keeffe's paintings in New Mexico are done from the stones she's just picked up in the desert."[11] She was a meticulous craftsman in everything she chose to do—from cooking to making clothes and gardens to grinding her own pigments between glass (on occasion) for greater translucency to having a go at creating her own pastel sticks. She loved the very substance of color.

Fiercely private about her methods of applying paint to canvas, O'Keeffe did not even allow her husband to watch her at work. She made an exception of Georgia Engelhard, who painted on location with her and observed that "[O'Keeffe] . . . painted out of her head more than on site . . . was very quick with her canvas—used colors straight [from the tube] with no turpentine . . . didn't overpaint much, [said] it caused cracks . . . often stretched her own canvases . . . used a separate brush for each color . . . . had a strong sense of the juxtaposition of colors . . . knew how to make white and green in such a way to make the white whiter and the green greener."[12]

Early in 1946, in preparation for the first exhibition of O'Keeffe's work at the Museum of Modern Art (May through July, with no catalogue because James Sweeney never found time to write one), assistant curator Dorothy Miller asked Caroline Keck, the museum's official restorer, to meet with the artist to talk about a surface finish for her paintings. According to Keck,

> *They were having a rough time HANDLING her art. The frames were no protection against fingermarks and fingermarks could not easily be removed because the paintings had no protective layer. Few artists realize the problems of hanging a show involved HANDLING. It's all very well to be idealistic and insist that paintings be moved with the hands flat out, pressure from the palms holding the weight, etc. That, however, is crap . . . and impossible to keep to even if those employed in the work cared about it. By appointment I went to the gallery and met her there. She showed me some paintings where she had used a wax finish (for a period, the FOGG [Museum] advised wax over varnish; actually NOT a good system, attracts more dirt than without wax) which she disliked. I did too. Then she showed me a handsome painting, "Black Abstraction" which a friend of Stieglitz's (who looked like Harpo Marx) had varnished, disastrously. His varnish was too thick, he stood the painting vertical too soon, the whole was orange/yellow, streaked and rilled, AWFUL. It so happened that I cleaned off this and without charge—and I wasn't sure the system would work—did it dry, friction with Damar resin and fingertips rotation. She knew as well as I did that black is probably the most sensitive paint of all. It could be that was what sold her on asking me to care for her paintings; but we did hit it off easily and I cancelled a lunch date to go with her across to their apartment for a two-some lunch and then back to talk more about care of her paintings.*[13]

(Above) Todd Webb, *O'Keeffe Making Stew, Ghost Ranch, New Mexico*, 1961. silver gelatin print. Courtesy of Evans Gallery, Portland, Maine.

Sweeney was considering fifty-seven of her works: forty-one to be lent by the artist herself, six from Stieglitz, and the rest from museums and private owners. The Museum of Modern Art already owned *Lake George Window* (1927).[14]

Keck continued,

> *I finally sold her on varnishing as a valuable compromise between an ideal surface reflection and prevention of unwanted alteration. She is one of only two artists . . . who actually stood by and forced a cleaning of a surface when [I] hesitated. The O'Keeffe, in this case, was a city night scene which had hung in a town penthouse and was coated with air-borne grime. It had not been varnished. The yellows (all those minutely lighted windows!) were instantly soluble even in water or pure petroleum benzine. When I declined to clean it, Georgia came to 87 State Street and stood over me while I CLEANED it on her insistence. She stated the yellows were solid paint (they were) and she preferred to have them lightly skinned rather than covered with a grey film. The cleaning was a vast visual improvement (as she smugly pointed out to me, saying: see, it wasn't too bad . . .) but I had goose pimples all the time I was doing it.*[15]

O'Keeffe's charge to Keck was to see to it that her pictures did not change, that her meticulous craftsmanship was kept immaculate (as their abundant correspondence documents). The artist didn't put her complete trust in many people or keep it there. But this remarkable relationship lasted until O'Keeffe's age and blindness eclipsed her craft aspirations. Honesty was their watchword. Keck rarely flinched from the painful task of describing and treating ruptured canvas threads, hand pressure marks from hanging, chip losses in the blues from travel, flaking edges due to mechanical damage, and uneven surfaces. She also had to cope with pigment problems like the treacheries of Mars green and the chalking tendencies of straight ultramarine.

> *The catch is [that] nothing stays the same. Airborne dust, atmospheric shifts, temperature, light, you name it. The best we can do is mitigate; arrange an easy removal of surface detritus, which is feasible if an isolation layer exists . . . One of the serious problems with O'Keeffe paintings is crackle in flat areas where the mere lines of cracking interferes with pictorial plane and interrupt an intended wholeness of pattern. Cracking comes from such a varied number of causes that it is almost impossible to preclude. LINING only helps until the crackle takes over again, as it is bound to.*[16]

Their relationship was a two-way street. O'Keeffe liked doing things for herself. She often asked for Keck's advice on such matters as varnish spray materials and the nailing of frames, but she didn't always take it. Her letters also contain specific requests for the "right" solvents and resin so she could make her own mixtures. She was as finicky in her craft practices as she was plain in her garb and domestic surroundings.

Keck thought O'Keeffe a fine technician and told her so. But she did not approve of some of O'Keeffe's practices.

> *I do think it only fair for you to make a point regarding her g d metal frames, made to her satisfaction . . . but the bane of any future conservator. They had a tight and precise fit. A LINED canvas simply would NOT fit back unless the frame were distorted. On this point, I never won; Georgia refused to have her pictures enclosed (as she put it) in a wooden fence. JESU . . . what I had to do to reframe a lined O'Keeffe!*[17]

Nor did Keck approve of O'Keeffe's handholds—pieces of cardboard attached to the back with half circles cut out—or how she would add a layer of priming to a prepared canvas of her own.

O'Keeffe's charge to Keck was to see to it that her pictures did not change, that her meticulous craftsmanship was kept immaculate (as their abundant correspondence documents).

It was this unique latter-day version of turn-of-the-century American tonalism that Keck saw almost immediately how to conserve. No one had been able to do it before, even O'Keeffe, who normally liked doing things for herself. (Until Keck used it successfully, O'Keeffe had not wanted to varnish for fear that her color would yellow.)

Keck also disliked the huge cloud canvases of the 1950s because they were almost impossible to protect. But her most constant complaints were about the detrimental effects caused by the all-too-frequent travel of O'Keeffe's paintings to exhibitions. Nevertheless, the trust and liking between them never faltered. As Keck wrote, "We were good friends. Mostly, she was highly amused over the issues between us when I blew my top."[18]

In 1938 Georgia O'Keeffe stated, "My achievement stands in color."[19] By what yardstick did she measure this achievement? She left behind no published writings on the effects of color, as had Wassily Kandinsky and Henri Matisse, the bellwethers of her modernism.[20] But we do have some picklocks. "The art of modernist painting equals the art of color," wrote New York critic Willard Huntington Wright in 1922.[21] In the same year O'Keeffe herself said, "I paint because color is a significant language to me."[22]

For her, as for Kandinsky and Matisse, the choice of paint color was intuitive. This does not mean that she was immune to color theories. On the contrary, ideas about how to cause specific emotions in the viewer with color had been in the air—and on the page with charts—ever since Michel-Eugène Chevreul published *De La Loi du Contraste Simultane des Couleurs* in 1839. By the turn of the century Charles Blanc's popularization of Chevreul's text, translated as *The Grammar of Painting and Engraving* (1873), had become a staple in American art schools. Color theory was definitely in the Zeitgeist.

Arthur Wesley Dow, O'Keeffe's great teacher, had identified modernism with music. It was through his influential teaching text, *Composition* (first published in 1899), that she learned about Whistler's radical use of musical nomenclature and the series concept—both of which she adopted. In 1918 she would title two of her color abstractions *Music—Pink and Blue* (*I* and *II*).

How much stock did O'Keeffe put in Kandinsky's widespread Symbolist ideas about the psychic and musical effect of colors? Probably a lot at first, particularly about blue—the only color she chose to work with right after her breakthrough abstract charcoals of 1915.[23]

> *The power of profound meaning is found in blue . . . . The inclination of blue to depth is so strong that its inner appeal is stronger when its color is deeper . . . . In music a light blue is like a flute, a darker blue a cello, a still darker blue a thunderous double bass.*[24]

Never willing to discuss her sources, she said only, "From experiences of one kind or another, shapes and colors come to me very clearly."[25]

Like Kandinsky, O'Keeffe seems to have had a synaesthetic gift. Synaesthesia (when the stimulation of one of the senses evokes the sensation of another—the best known being color-hearing) is a phenomenon still to be scientifically measured. But ongoing work in the neurosciences suggests strongly that it is real and not imagined or a contrived brain phenomenon.[26] Two things O'Keeffe has written would support this. While studying with Alon Bement at Columbia University's Teachers College in New York during 1914-15, she became interested in the idea that "music could be translated into something for the eye."[27] In 1917 she wrote Paul Strand, "I sang you three songs—in paint. I'd like you to hear them. I don't know why, but I would—it's all the same song sung different ways."[28]

Whatever else may be said on this topic, it is abundantly clear that the music/color analogy expanded O'Keeffe's senses and delighted her imagination. No one has ever improved on Paul Rosenfeld's masterly description of her color intentions and effects. A music critic, he was able to find concise language for what he saw. (Perhaps he too was synaesthetic.)

For her, as for Kandinsky and Matisse, the choice of paint color was intuitive. This does not mean that she was immune to color theories.

> *Fused in her painting there exist the tenderest, rose-petal gradations and widest, most robust oppositions of color. The most complexly varied contraries of tone are juxtaposed with a breathtaking freshness . . . . Through [O'Keeffe], polyharmonies of the compositions of Stravinsky and of Leo Ornstein seem to have begotten sisters in the sister art of painting . . . . Many modern painters have perceived the relativity of all color; have felt that every hue implies the presence in some form or other of its complement, its ideal opponent that gives it force; and have expressed these complements in their works . . . . Few, it seems, have been able to race the entire scale . . . to proceed in one small area of green from the Amazonian heat of green mottled with dusty yellow, to the bitter antarctic cold of green-blue . . . . And although she managed to run the entire gamut between heat and coolth* [sic] *of a tone, within a diminutive area, her scale makes no sacrifice of subtleties. Her most delicious gradations remain distinct and pure.*[29]

It was this unique latter-day version of turn-of-the-century American tonalism that Keck saw almost immediately how to conserve.[30] No one had been able to do it before, even O'Keeffe, who normally liked doing things for herself. (Until Keck used it successfully, O'Keeffe had not wanted to varnish for fear that her color would yellow.)

So keenly did O'Keeffe's eye see gradations of hue that she often ordered the same name colors from different manufacturers (mainly Winsor-Newton, Lucien Lefebre Foinet, Grumbacher, and Block X), in case there were differences between them. Dale Kronkright warns that not much is actually known about her color. The only evidence to date is what was left in her studio after she died. It therefore remains a topic for research.[31]

Twelve different hues of green were found in her studio: tubes of Thalo, veridian, celedon, cobalts and chromes, oxide of chromium, and Hookers Green. With such a large number of greens, did she consider it to be a primary color, as did Nobel Prize-winning chemist Wilhelm Ostwald (1853-1932)? Ostwald's *Letter to a Painter on the*

Theory and Practice of Painting was found in O'Keeffe's "Book Room" at Abiquiu. He regarded green (despite its mixture) to be perceptually autonomous, and his color circle of 1916 shows nine different greens. At the very least, it was a psychological primary for her and she was a virtuoso with it. Could O'Keeffe even have depicted *herself* as the color green, the way Matisse did with the color red?[32] Be that as it may, both artists were soundly trained in academic practice and both tried, with different strategies, to make color sing.[33]

Another surprising find in her studio after her death was approximately three hundred and twenty color chips. They were stored there in covered boxes, in different color groups, often with the old rubber bands still around them. The earliest ones in the collection are marked August 1, 1934. Many were dated and quite a few had specific notes on the back in her handwriting, such as "May 23-27/ Cobalt Blue H w/poppy oil/ Venice turpentine" and "oxide chromium/ poppy oil/ 2nd grinding." Some groups were made on the same day, with subtle differences in their translucency. By far the greatest number were from the 1930s; there were almost none from the 1940s. A new resurgence of making them came in the 1950s, after she moved to New Mexico permanently. Few exist from the 1960s and none at all after that. The chips were hand cut in different sizes (mostly 2 x 3 inches) from hardboard. Some were glazed, but most were not. The colors have remained quite true, probably because they were kept in the dark. (Found as well were color tests made on strips of canvas and sheets of paper.) From this astonishing array we can glean the rigorous structure of hues behind her images.

Another surprising find in her studio after her death was approximately three hundred and twenty color chips.

Her use of color chips seems like a collision between modern and academic practice. Where did she get this idea? She never said. The chips were another of her closely guarded secrets. One possibility would be Albert H. Munsell (1858-1918), who in the early 1900s tried to classify nature's colors so they could more accurately be reproduced on canvas by hue, value, and chroma. Munsell's system, with its "Color Tree" and painted samples (which he called "wafers"), was widespread in American art schools. Arthur Dow, himself a painter, had struggled for years with Munsell's "photometer" to standardize red, purple, blue, green, and yellow so he could reliably create color harmony. He failed. In his book *Composition* he maintained that color could be "taught like music," but he still found it "baffling." (Dow was no modernist, and the exercises in his book show clearly that for him line was dominant over color.)

With all of this paradoxical information, what are we to make of Georgia O'Keeffe's color chips—and when did she start to use them? The ones found in her studio were not ordered from the Munsell Color Company (which offered, as "scientific" teaching aids, one thousand one hundred and fifty different matte-finish color chips and one thousand four hundred and fifty glossy ones). She created her own. No others exist, so we can't tell if any were made before 1934. But her habit of figuring out color harmonies before putting them on canvas was not a new one. We know, for example, that she made drawings with specific color notes during the late 1920s. In her Beverly Spiral sketchbook of 1929-30 there is an untitled drawing of a tree with the following directions: "3 Ochre darker / 1 hottest, golden brown / 2 Ochre, very light / 3 Ochre, darker / 4 Ochre, blackish / 5 grey & green, 6 hottest (graphite)."[34]

O'Keeffe eschewed accident as carefully as did Ingres and Degas. In 1962 she told Katherine Kuh, "I rarely start anything that isn't pretty clear to me before I start. I know what I'm going to do before I begin."[35]

As for the chips themselves, all the ones we have were made in New Mexico. Barbara Lynes thinks that O'Keeffe may have started making them in order to have physical references to the actual hues

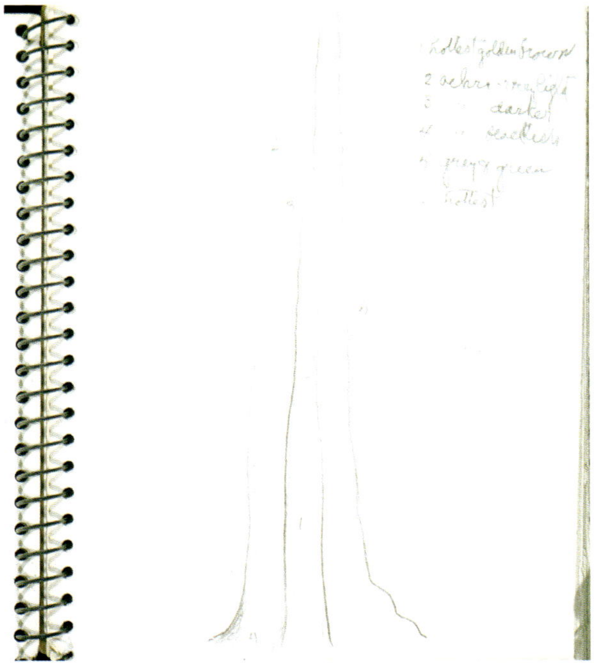

in her beloved New Mexico landscapes, and that they were intended for later use in her New York studio, where she often finished paintings begun on the Ghost Ranch or at Abiquiu.[36] (As long as Stieglitz lived, she wintered in New York.) This is entirely plausible, and it would confirm something that Keck wrote: "What I learned, living at [her] Ghost Ranch was that Georgia was a very realistic painter."[37] It would seem, then, that the chips were a kind of memory bank for later studio use, tangible visual notes taken on wide-ranging motifs, from her close Ghost Ranch environs to the remote "Black Place," which she discovered in 1942 and painted at least ten times.

Into this well-documented mix should be added chromotherapy: the belief that color can heal sickness.[38] Matisse was convinced that his pictures emitted "a beneficent radiation."[39] O'Keeffe, too, thought her color had curative powers. Proof of this exists in a 1926 letter she wrote to an ailing friend: "I am learning something . . . if I could put it clearly into form it would cure you—that is worthy of a laugh—but I'm sure it is true."[40] Although she never mentioned such a thing in the letters to her conservator, this belief offers yet another slant on why she took such pains to see that the original color characteristics of her paintings were protected.

Most of O'Keeffe's letters to Keck were written from Abiquiu, jotted by hand, often in haste, and often hard to read. Keck's, however, were neatly typed and mailed from Brooklyn, New York, where she shared a studio with her husband, Sheldon Keck (1910-93), the eminent restorer for the Brooklyn Museum of Art.[41] After 1963 Keck

Into this well-documented mix should be added chromotherapy: the belief that color can heal sickness. Matisse was convinced that his pictures emitted "a beneficent radiation." O'Keeffe, too, thought her color had curative powers.

Beverly Spiral sketchbook, *Untitled (Tree)*, 1929-30, graphite on paper, 4 7/8" x 3 7/8". Collection of The Georgia O'Keeffe Foundation, Abiquiu, New Mexico.

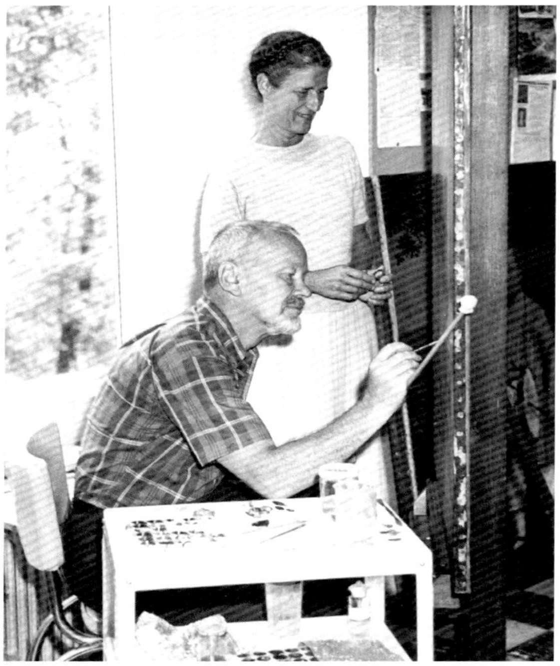

Unknown photographer, *Caroline and Sheldon Keck*, no date, silver gelatin print. Collection of Brooklyn Museum Archives, New York. Photograph Collection, People: Staff.

wrote from their home and studio in Cooperstown, New York. From 1969 to 1981 the Kecks ran the Cooperstown Conservation Program under the New York State Historical Association while continuing as consultant conservators to many national institutions—including the Guggenheim Museum and the Phillips Collection. They were also instrumental in founding the first masters program in art conservation at New York University's Institute of Fine Arts.

The O'Keeffe-Keck letters printed here have been chosen with two aims in mind: first, to let their words convey the respectful, meticulous hand-and-eye practice of preventive/corrective conservation, and second, to chart the growth of a remarkable friendship between two differently gifted, highly opinionated, and scrupulous craftsmen working separately in what Bernard Berenson once called "the kitchen of art." As their articulate exchanges make clear, they regarded each other as equals. Keck tried hard to remember that O'Keeffe was the client, but that never stopped her from speaking her mind—often heatedly. O'Keeffe didn't always take Keck's professional advice, even when she asked for it. But their mutual respect and regard, once earned, remained constant.

NOTES

1 *Juan and Anna Marie Hamilton made a gift of O'Keeffe's tangible personal property to the Research Center on December 18, 2000. All mentions here of O'Keeffe's art materials refer to objects in the center's collection.*

2 *Many of these are listed in Barbara Buhler Lynes,* Georgia O'Keeffe: Catalogue Raisonné, *2 vols. (Washington, D.C.: National Gallery of Art; New Haven, Conn., and London, England: Yale University Press; Abiquiu, N.M.: The Georgia O'Keeffe Foundation, 1999).*

3 *Georgia O'Keeffe to James Johnson Sweeney, June 11, 1945, in Jack Cowart, Juan Hamilton, and Sarah Greenough,* Georgia O'Keeffe: Art and Letters *(Washington, D.C.: National Gallery of Art; Boston, Mass.: New York Graphic Society, 1987), 241.*

4 *O'Keeffe to Sherwood Anderson, Lake George, New York, September 1923, in* Art and Letters, *174-75.*

5 *Letter to the author following a March 12, 1980, interview with Engelhard in Interlaken, Switzerland.*

6 *For more about the influence that photography had in forming O'Keeffe's mature style, see Sarah Whitaker Peters,* Becoming O'Keeffe: The Early Years *(New York: Abbeville Press, 1991; 2d ed., 2001), 183-275.*

7 *O'Keeffe to Mabel Dodge Luhan, September 1929, in* Art and Letters, *196.*

8 *For a survey of these drawings on paper, see Judith C. Walsh's essay in the* catalogue raisonné, *vol. 1, 25-26.*

9 *Paul Rosenfeld in* Vanity Fair *19 (October 1922): 122. The essay is reprinted in Barbara Buhler Lynes,* O'Keeffe, Stieglitz and the Critics, 1916-1929 *(Ann Arbor, Mich.: UMI Research Press, 1989), 175-79.*

10 *See* catalogue raisonné, Cebolla Church *(1945), 1103.*

11 *Peters,* Becoming O'Keeffe, *340, n. 70.*

12 *Letter to the author, March 12, 1980.*

13 *Letter to the author, March 2, 2003.*

14 *I am grateful to Sandra Kisters for this information.*

15 *Ibid.*

16 *Letter to the author, February 13, 2003.*

17 *Ibid.*

18 *Ibid.*

19 *Quoted in Bonnie G. Kelm and Ann C. Madonia, eds.,* Georgia O'Keeffe in Williamsburg *(Williamsburg, Va.: Muscarelle Museum of Art, 2001), 24.*

20 *For more on the influence of Kandinsky and Matisse on O'Keeffe's early modernism, see Peters,* Becoming O'Keeffe, *94-102, 119-23.*

21 *W. H. Wright, "The Future of Painting,"* Freeman *(November 1922): 256. Wright, brother of the Synchromist painter Stanton Macdonald-Wright, was well known to the Stieglitz Circle of artists.*

22 *O'Keeffe in* Manuscripts, *no. 4 (December 1922). Cited in Lynes,* O'Keeffe, Stieglitz and the Critics, *182.*

23 *Her correspondence with Anita Pollitzer in 1915 suggests that O'Keeffe first learned about Kandinsky's highly influential ideas in* Uber das Geistige in der Kunst *(translated as* The Art of Spiritual Harmony*) by reading about them in Arthur Jerome Eddy's* Cubists and Post Impressionism *(Chicago: A. C. McClurg, 1914).*

24 *Wassily Kandinsky,* The Art of Spiritual Harmony, *trans. Michael Sadleir (London and Boston: Constable and Company Ltd., 1914), 75-76.*

25 *O'Keeffe in John I. H. Baur,* Nature in Abstraction: The Relation of Abstract Painting and Sculpture to Nature in Twentieth-century American Art *(New York: Whitney Museum of American Art, Macmillan, 1958), 77.*

26 *On this, see Richard Cytowic,* The Man Who Tasted Shapes *(New York: J. P. Putnam Sons, 1993). John Gage in* Color and Meaning: Art, Science and Symbolism *cautions that synaesthesia—the very senses themselves—is, by and large, a product of cultural understanding. For Gage, color is a trope. (Berkeley, Calif.: University of California Press, 1999), 262-68.*

27 *Georgia O'Keeffe,* Georgia O'Keeffe *(New York: Viking, 1976), text opposite plate 14.*

28 *O'Keeffe to Strand, in an envelope postmarked June 12, 1917. Quoted, in part, in Peters,* Becoming O'Keeffe, *186-87. These three watercolors are numbers 189, 190, and 191 in the* catalogue raisonné.

29 *Paul Rosenfeld in* Vanity Fair *19 (October 1922), reprinted in Lynes,* O'Keeffe, Stieglitz and the Critics, *175-77.*

30 *For a definition and history of American tonalism, see Wanda M. Corn,* The Color of Mood 1880-1910 *(San Francisco, Calif.: M. H. de Young Memorial Museum, 1972), 1-12.*

31 *In the spring 2005 issue of the* Georgia O'Keeffe Museum News, *it was announced that the museum had received an award from the National Endowment for the Arts. These funds will make it possible for curators and conservators from five museums to work collaboratively to examine O'Keeffe's works and learn her studio practices, such as the kinds of paints she used, how they were applied, and how they shed light on the aesthetic of her work. The results will be published.*

32 *On this identification, see Jack Flam,* Matisse: The Man and His Art, 1869-1918 *(Ithaca, N.Y.: Cornell University Press, 1986), 499, n. 46.*

33 *Perhaps significantly, there are three books on Matisse in her Abiquiu library archive, including Alfred H. Barr's* Matisse: His Art and His Public *(New York: The Museum of Modern Art, 1951), inscribed to O'Keeffe from Barr.*

34 *See* catalogue raisonné, *1851.*

35 *O'Keeffe, quoted in Katherine Kuh,* The Artist's Voice: Talks with Seventeen Artists *(New York: Harper & Row, 1962), 194.*

36 *Lynes to the author, August 16, 2004.*

37 *Keck to the author, March 2, 2003. For an illustrated study of O'Keeffe's New Mexico colors—both realistic and arbitrary—see Barbara Buhler Lynes, Lesley Poling-Kempes, and Frederick W. Turner,* Georgia O'Keeffe and New Mexico: A Sense of Place *(Princeton, N.J.: Princeton University Press; Santa Fe, N.M.: Georgia O'Keeffe Museum, 2004).*

38 *For a succinct history of chromotherapy, see John Gage,* Color and Culture: Practice and Meaning from Antiquity to Abstraction *(Berkeley, Calif.: University of California Press, 1993), 206, 209.*

39 *On this, see John Elderfield in* Henri Matisse: A Retrospective *(New York: The Museum of Modern Art, 1992), 66.*

40 *O'Keeffe to Blanche Matthias, March 1926, in* Art and Letters, *117.*

41 *Caroline Kohn and Sheldon Keck met while training as conservators at the Fogg Art Museum in 1932-33.*

Painter and Conservator

A COLLABORATION

Dale Kronkright

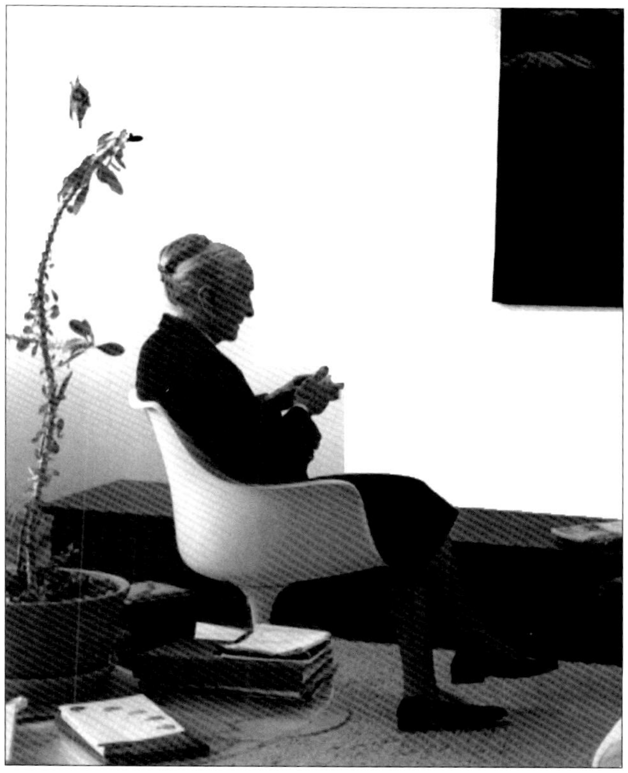

In the mid-1940s, when the Museum of Modern Art, New York, began the process of organizing a major retrospective of Georgia O'Keeffe's work, the artist had completed approximately eleven hundred works, of which about seven hundred were oil paintings. She knew that many of these oils had become covered with dirt and that they had also become soiled and damaged as a result of being transported to and from various places. Since the early 1930s, O'Keeffe had shipped her paintings back and forth from the two places in which she lived and worked—New York and New Mexico. Likewise, those that had been purchased by museums and private collectors had been included in and shipped to numerous exhibitions.

In cities, paintings that were not protected behind glass became grimy with a thin deposit of black coal and oil boiler soot. In travel, canvases that were slack in their stretchers billowed and vibrated against their stretcher bars, creating creases and cracks along the outer margins. Dirty hands and fingers from less-than-fastidious art handlers accidentally smudged, dented, and poked and, in the process, cracked and flaked her broad fields of evenly applied paint. The dirt, vibration, and shaking of the paintings in cars, trucks, and trains compounded these conditions.

These damages often occur with unglazed oil paintings that are decades old and that have been exhibited and moved frequently, and art conservators are often asked to clean and repair their surfaces. When conservators work on paintings by artists who are no longer living and who left no record of how they wanted their paintings to look, they have to infer the artist's original intentions from extensive

For the first time since the artist's death in 1986, we have a chance to discover how O'Keeffe felt about the appearance of her paintings and about their preservation.

(Above) Todd Webb, *Georgia O'Keeffe in her studio, Abiquiu, New Mexico*, 1977, silver gelatin print. Courtesy of Evans Gallery, Portland, Maine.

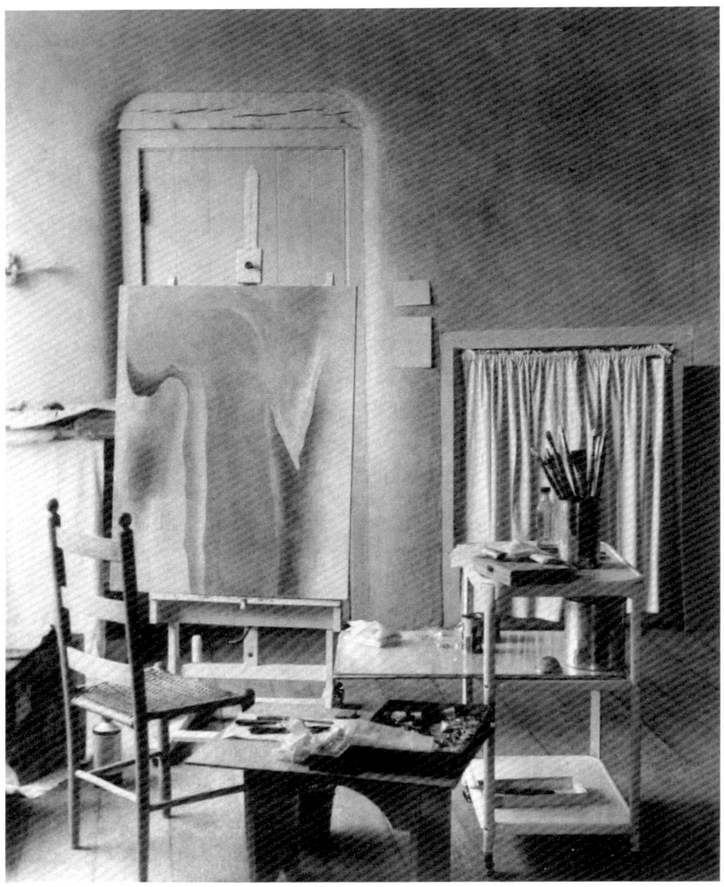

Todd Webb, *Studio, Ghost Ranch*, 1962, silver gelatin print. Courtesy of Evans Gallery, Portland, Maine.

O'Keeffe was perfectly willing to "throw it away" when damage or visual changes to materials obscured the qualities she felt were fundamental to the understanding of a painting.

analyses of the work. Georgia O'Keeffe was the exception in that she frequently corresponded with Caroline Keck, the conservator she engaged for more than forty years, beginning in 1946, about the care and preservation of her paintings.

For the first time since the artist's death in 1986, we have a chance to discover how O'Keeffe felt about the appearance of her paintings and about their preservation. O'Keeffe, the painter, and Keck, the conservator, exchanged hundreds of letters, many of which are published for the first time here, in which both the artist and the conservator expressed their ideas about caring for and conserving O'Keeffe's work. Moreover, these letters demonstrate that O'Keeffe was unusual in her commitment to caring for and conserving her paintings. The correspondence provides important, new information that documents what is perhaps the earliest collaboration between an artist and a conservator—both personal and professional. More importantly, for curators and conservators interested in the preservation of Georgia O'Keeffe's paintings, the letters represent a unique opportunity to understand the artist's developing sense of acceptable appearances and the influence of the conservator in shaping that aesthetic.[1]

By considering the circumstances that brought Keck and O'Keeffe together and by studying the ideas and sentiments conveyed in their correspondence over the decades, this essay intends to reveal a relationship that both enlightened the conservator's approaches to the repair of O'Keeffe's paintings and shaped the artist's expectations about how her paintings should look and best be preserved. Although the treatments any conservator applies to a work of art naturally alter the appearance of the object to one degree or another, the changes that occurred as a result of Keck's treatments clearly fell within the parameters of O'Keeffe's ideas about how she wanted her paintings to look. The dialogue between painter and conservator informed and resolved Keck's understanding of O'Keeffe's visual intentions for the technical expressions in paint we see across each canvas. For O'Keeffe, the dialogue appears to have cultivated a unique admiration and trust for Keck's skills and, more importantly, for her judgment and candor. This essay illustrates these ideas and characterizes the visual and technical qualities of O'Keeffe's paintings that O'Keeffe and Keck discussed in their many letters.

From both the letters and from other documentary sources, it is easy to conclude that O'Keeffe felt strongly about the acceptable appearance of her paintings. The *catalogue raisonné* identifies thirty-five of O'Keeffe's works in her personal collection that she eventually destroyed.[2] It is not certain how many of these were destroyed, because the condition of the paintings had either been damaged or deteriorated to the point that O'Keeffe felt they no longer represented what she had set out to achieve in their execution. But additional references certainly lead us to believe that many may have been destroyed for just that reason. Conservator Judith C. Walsh relates how Sheldon Keck, Caroline's husband and fellow conservator, told his conservation graduate students that O'Keeffe would destroy any of her paintings that she believed had "failed" owing to a problem with art materials.[3] In the 1970s O'Keeffe had conservator Felrath Hines, a longtime student and colleague of the Kecks, sand away and gesso-over several of her paintings that were on the verso of other finished works.[4] As Sarah Whitaker Peters demonstrates in this publication, O'Keeffe was perfectly willing to "throw it away" when damage or visual changes to materials obscured the qualities she felt were fundamental to the understanding of a painting.[5]

O'Keeffe might have felt similarly in 1946 when confronted by one of her own paintings at the Museum of Modern Art in New York. The museum was preparing a retrospective exhibition of O'Keeffe's works and had gathered paintings from both public and private collections. A friend of Stieglitz's had badly cleaned and varnished one of those pieces, and by some accounts O'Keeffe ordered the now glossy and evenly saturated painting destroyed. The assistant curator, Dorothy Miller, convinced O'Keeffe that she should at least discuss the problem with a New York conservator, Caroline Keck, whom the museum contracted from time to time for repair and care of its collection. Keck used many modern approaches to restore paintings, and there was a chance that the disfiguring varnish could be removed.

Keck's ability to read the language of O'Keeffe's materials and techniques, and to find ways to preserve and repair damages to them, grew with each passing year.

What began as a brief discussion between O'Keeffe and Keck continued into a daylong dialogue at the artist's New York apartment. Keck was allowed to remove the varnish and attempt to prove to O'Keeffe that a thinly applied varnish, made from one of the newly available, long-chain, copolymer acrylics, could be applied in a manner that would preserve the relationship between O'Keeffe's visual elements and still protect the paints from the vagaries of urban settings, long-distance transport, and careless handling. Keck did so, which greatly impressed O'Keeffe.

O'Keeffe found reasons to trust her paintings to few people during her career, and she relied on even fewer people for any length of time. Yet O'Keeffe trusted and sought out the advice and technical judgment of Caroline Keck for nearly forty years. They became close friends, enjoyed their disagreements, and sought each other's council. Certainly the conservator learned from O'Keeffe what the essential elements of the artist's materials and techniques were and how they were meant to relate to each other visually. Keck's ability to read the language of O'Keeffe's materials and techniques, and to find ways to preserve and repair damages to them, grew with each passing year.[6] She passed on her knowledge of O'Keeffe's preferences and intentions to a handful of her students in the 1960s and 1970s—in particular Felrath Hines, who continued treating soiled and damaged paintings for O'Keeffe while the Kecks established a conservation training program in Cooperstown, New York, and Jean Volkmer, who worked as conservator at the Museum of Modern Art in New York. In November 1960 Keck also shared her insights into O'Keeffe's preferences and studio techniques with Edmond de Beaumont, conservator at the Worcester Art Museum whose works she seems to have admired.[7]

Possibly for the first time in modern history, the *artist* was, in turn, influenced by her relationship with the conservator. From the beginning Keck convinced O'Keeffe that modern synthetic varnishes could be used to protect O'Keeffe's paintings without greatly compromising the gloss, saturation, and values of the paint. All varnish, even the thinly sprayed, low molecular weight, synthetic acrylic varnish that Keck used, changes these elements to a small degree. But O'Keeffe seemed to have accepted this change as one that did not compromise her aesthetic, knowing that it would protect and preserve her work. In fact, she believed in the process to the extent that in 1961 she ordered a compressor, spray-guns, and synthetic varnishing resins and solvents so that she could varnish her new paintings herself.

Keck also convinced O'Keeffe that cracks in the paint along stretcher bar creases and depressions resulting from dents and pokes were best diminished by infusing the cracks with a synthetic adhesive, then lining the verso of the canvas to a secondary canvas and mounting both to a hollow-core, dimensionally stable panel. Although this technique flattened the paint somewhat, O'Keeffe accepted this change and often suggested to Keck that her paintings needed lining and mounting when Keck did not find such treatment necessary.

Keck advised O'Keeffe about numerous other aspects of the craft, such as the rapid drying characteristics of Mars pigments and the poorly bound elements of commercial ultramarine blue in oil; the quality of various weaves of linen canvas; the necessity of properly stretching and backing a painting; and the proper methods to prepare a hardboard panel for oil painting. For the most part, O'Keeffe seemed to have incorporated this advice into her studio practices.

In Caroline Keck, O'Keeffe found a professional conservator who understood the complex technical elements in the artist's studio techniques and use of materials. Caroline Keck "got" Georgia O'Keeffe, especially in O'Keeffe's estimation. In 1950 O'Keeffe wrote to Keck, "It is a comfort to think of how careful you are. I want you to do what ever you think best for that painting."[8]

In 1960 Keck wrote to O'Keeffe, "I think you are impossible to inpaint, but then I always have thought so, it never looks like your work, the surface shows the difference between your personal use of a brush and color and someone elses. That is one of the reasons I find it criminal to damage the surface of your paintings . . . on your paintings everything not by you shows like a sore thumb."[9] In this note, Keck summed up the astonishing risk that damage to an O'Keeffe painting posed: the surfaces are composed of exquisitely executed, complex passages of brushwork, textures, and color that are nearly impossible to replicate.

Conservator Judith C. Walsh was the first to coin the phrase "The Language of O'Keeffe's Materials" in describing the varied but distinguishing virtuoso techniques and uses of materials O'Keeffe relied upon in creating works in charcoal, pastel, and watercolor.[10] It is not difficult to extend this metaphor to understand the artist's techniques in oils. Throughout her life (and as evident in the exhibition this publication accompanies) O'Keeffe presented a visual language of unique and distinct effects in paint that valued several important things: the ability to synthesize, simplify, and distill the visible world into concentrated relationships of painted forms created by carefully modulated passages of color; the skillful and seemingly effortless manipulation and command of materials; precision and economy of effort; and the ability to access the most subtle physical characteristics of light in paint. It is a language that conservator Keck was able to sense, beginning at their first meeting, and one that she was able to master despite its great complexity and subtleties. It is also a language that, given a little time, the viewer can begin to learn.

People often first sense that O'Keeffe's work in paint and pastel appears quite literal, suggesting what we might expect to see when looking at the actual object represented in the work. But more often O'Keeffe's paints simplify color within a representational setting to get at what, for her, must have been the most compelling sensibilities. In contrast to the appearance of actual objects, O'Keeffe's use of paint variously flattens, shifts, concentrates, and even re-imagines colors, subtly or forcefully edging the composition further into the world of abstraction.

In 1950 O'Keeffe wrote to Keck, "It is a comfort to think of how careful you are. I want you to do what ever you think best for that painting."

Moreover, understanding O'Keeffe's use of color as an artist is more complex than paying attention *only* to the colors in her visual vocabulary. In 1976, while filmmaker Perry Miller Adato filmed the artist evaluating photographic transparencies of her paintings for a forthcoming book,[11] O'Keeffe remarked, "It doesn't really matter if the color isn't absolutely right if the picture feels right when you finish the print."[12] O'Keeffe was not suggesting that she could easily accept a painting of hers where the colors weren't essentially correct. But to O'Keeffe, having the exact color reproduced was not as important as accurately portraying the *relationships* and *distinctions* between the colors in her paints.

Casting aside expectations when viewing O'Keeffe's work, we can discover the intricate painterly characteristics that she applied to the canvas with purpose, economy, and skill.[13] We can see that there are many qualities besides simple color that relate the compositional elements to each other. In looking at an entire exhibition of O'Keeffe's work, we can gather the impression that there are no accidents here, no circumstantial, streaked blending of colors, textures, or unintended and experimental shapes covered over with second thoughts.

Although O'Keeffe used the natural world and physical landscape as some of her most frequently occurring subjects, she did not attempt to paint everything she saw. She selected only those characteristics that best conveyed her experiences. Likewise, while painters theoretically have every color in the visible electromagnetic spectrum with which to work, O'Keeffe excluded most of them and mixed paints with specific characteristics, presumably because they gave her certain visual and emotional responses. Besides mixing exact proportions of hues from tubes of oil paint to create a particular color, O'Keeffe also selected a precise value (the degree of lightness or darkness), saturation (the degree to which a hue stands by itself or is muddied or obscured by other hues), opacity (the degree to which the paint reflects light like a solid object or transmits it like a translucent film), and gloss (the degree to which paint has a smooth, glass-like surface or a matte, dull, grainy surface).

> Over the many decades of her career and in the thousands of works she completed, the "language" of O'Keeffe's selective and deliberate manipulation of paint appears effortless despite its sophistication, complexity, and precision.

O'Keeffe's paints have deliberate textural qualities that scatter light in some passages while strongly pulling it in or reflecting it brilliantly at others. In many forms, there are short, scrubbing brush-strokes where paint appears to have the consistency of a stiff paste, holding the thousands of ridges formed by each brush hair, even as a fully cured, dry paint film. There are paints that appear to have been applied in thin, cream-like consistencies in long, linear brushstrokes with high ridges deftly pushed to the edge of the form. There are glass-like surfaces where brushstrokes have all but disappeared and where a palette knife has floated smoothly across a surface like ice. There are bright passages where O'Keeffe has rubbed the surface with fingers, a dry brush, or even a rag, removing all but a stain of paint and exposing the weave of the canvas below.

We can observe the evidence of the brush moving through stiff, paste-like paints with the same assuredness that O'Keeffe worked in thin, translucent glazes and passages painted with oils the consistency of smooth cream. O'Keeffe achieved stiff and sometimes ridged textures in paint not by the incremental addition of multiple paint layers, but rather by the deliberate formulation of her paints and grounds. With future technical analysis, conservators will hopefully begin to more fully document the skillful use of resins, solvents, drying media, fillers, and dry pigments that O'Keeffe mixed to achieve her skillfully applied variations in paint opacity and consistency.

In almost every passage of a Georgia O'Keeffe painting, we can see there is only one layer of paint over the white-primed canvas, often visible below. The compositional forms seldom overlap and their shapes and borders have not been altered during the execution of the work. There are even spaces between the forms where we see only white, primed canvas and perhaps a small smudge of graphite or charcoal from the underdrawing. Within each passage and color, the nuanced gradations of values and textures are, to be sure, complex, subtle mixtures of pigments and binders, but those mixtures are not blended on the canvas or within the forms. They clearly have been manipulated into their final appearance and body on the palette and then thinly applied, exclusively where required.

Over the many decades of her career and in the thousands of works she completed, the "language" of O'Keeffe's selective and deliberate manipulation of paint appears effortless despite its sophistication, complexity, and precision. But Caroline Keck understood that seemingly effortless effects were actually the result of endless practice, repetition, and critical evaluation. In 1967 Keck wrote, "Your paintings are altered, more than those of many other artists, when they are not maintained in their original state, and to keep them carefully requires respect and understanding in the part of people who presume to treat their damages."[14]

In a 1976 letter to Sarah Whitaker Peters, the eighty-nine-year-old artist described her process: "For me it was easy. I didn't work unless it was easy to work. When it was easy to work, I never thought of all the complicated things you accuse me of."[15] Many decades after the execution of the majority of her works, O'Keeffe's memory of her process was that she worked intuitively, directly, and without a lot of conscious internal debate. This is probably true of many of the actual compositions, but it wasn't always so. Painters are in the business of making tangible, physical things. They must have paint in order to work, and getting paints to behave and appear exactly as desired is difficult.

Evidence of O'Keeffe's systematic and sustained practices in the studio can be seen in the generous gift from Juan and Anna Marie Hamilton to the Georgia O'Keeffe Museum Research Center, including all of the studio materials O'Keeffe owned at the time of her death. In preparation for painting, O'Keeffe dedicated a great deal of time to developing precise qualities in her paints, experimenting with resin media, slow- and fast-drying oils, waxes, and thinners, and repeatedly hand-mulling pigments to increase their translucency and achieve the desired body. While working, she kept notes, facsimiles, and annotated textbooks that are now available for study.

O'Keeffe stored books at the two houses she owned in New Mexico. Those she kept at her Ghost Ranch house are in the collection of the Georgia O'Keeffe Museum Research Center, while those she kept in her Abiquiu house are in the care of the Georgia O'Keeffe Foundation.[16] Among the materials archived at the Georgia O'Keeffe Museum Research Center is a 1996 copy of an annotated studio practices book owned by O'Keeffe, *The Materials of the Artist and Their Use in Painting: With Notes on the Techniques of the Old Masters* by Max Doerner. Doerner, a German artist, scientist, and professor at the Academy of Fine Arts in Munich, first published the book in German in 1921. It was translated and published in English for the first time in 1934.

O'Keeffe owned at least two copies of the book; the first 1934 edition was given to her by her husband, Alfred Stieglitz, who inscribed it to her on November 20, 1934, five days after her birthday. O'Keeffe made over one hundred penciled marginal marks and underlines in the first four chapters regarding grounds, pigments, and binders in oil paintings, with very few annotations in the following six chapters regarding tempera, pastel, watercolor, mural painting, and the techniques of the Italian, Dutch, and Flemish masters. O'Keeffe also owned a copy of the second 1949 edition, now in the library at the Georgia O'Keeffe Foundation house in Abiquiu, that contains more annotations, again only in the first four chapters on oil painting materials. The notes in both copies suggest that O'Keeffe worked for decades to master a systematic command of the multiple visual characteristics achievable in oil paints.

> We can be fairly certain that O'Keeffe's creation of color chips is related to her reading of the 1934 edition of Doerner's book, as many of the materials listed on the backs of the chips are underlined and annotated by artist.

In 1934, about the same time that O'Keeffe received the first copy of Doerner's book, she began making test coupons of paint mixtures on cut-up rectangles of primed, canvas-covered paperboard.

Today, when we examine a painting by O'Keeffe and consider its appearance and preservation, we must realize that we are likely looking at a painting whose appearance falls somewhere on an interesting historical continuum.

She organized these paperboard coupons by hue or color in small boxes, bundling the coupons of a given hue with rubber bands. Some of the color chips are dated, and on nearly all of the backs she inscribed a summary of the oil tube colors, extra binders, extra thinners, and multiple grindings under a glass muller that she used to reach the final effect in body, color, saturation, opacity, and gloss. These chips were kept in her studio and actively referred to while she painted well into her later career, as a 1951 letter to Stieglitz's nephew, William Howard Schubart, reveals.[17]

We can be fairly certain that O'Keeffe's creation of color chips is related to her reading of the 1934 edition of Doerner's book, as many of the materials listed on the backs of the chips are underlined and annotated by artist. Barbara Buhler Lynes has pointed out that there is an interesting convergence of compelling forces surrounding O'Keeffe's work immediately following 1934. These are O'Keeffe's first years in the intensely painted desert formations at Ghost Ranch. The overwhelming light, colors, textures, and forms in and around the Ghost Ranch may have done more than capture O'Keeffe's attention. It is possible that these landscapes may have challenged the artist in new ways, initiating a search for adaptable canvas grounds, new and more extensively amendable pigments, binders and additives.[18]

It is interesting to think that O'Keeffe may have been challenged to discover new ways of depicting in paint the surface textures, contours, multiple planes of focus, and intensity that she had not previously encountered in Taos and Alcalde during the preceding summers in New Mexico. Careful technical study of O'Keeffe's studio materials, color chips, and paintings may reveal whether and how O'Keeffe's careful study and experimentation with Doerner's material recommendations ultimately manifested themselves in her finished works after 1934.

These tangible manipulations in paint, many of which developed and evolved over the course of the artist's career, formed the "language" that Georgia O'Keeffe used to present her experiences in the world. Keck understood this language and did her best to preserve it—and O'Keeffe allowed it, even though it changed the look of her paintings to a certain degree.

Today, when we examine a painting by O'Keeffe and consider its appearance and preservation, we must realize that we are likely looking at a painting whose appearance falls somewhere on an interesting historical continuum. The painting is not necessarily just the work of O'Keeffe. First, it is possible that we may be looking at one of the few O'Keeffe paintings that, once it left the artist's studio, was properly glazed and backed by the new owner, given reasonable preventive care, and remained untouched, uncleaned, unvarnished, and unrestored. This is the closest we may get to the artist's idea of "right" at the moment she completed it.

Next along the continuum are paintings that Keck cleaned and varnished in collaboration with the artist. Though changed slightly, these paintings represent a visual state that the artist found acceptable, sometimes no more than a year after they were completed. More altered from their original "historic" condition are cracked and damaged paintings that Keck lined and mounted, first on Masonite-faced, hollow-core panels and later on softer Cellotex-faced, hollow-core panels, again with the artist's knowledge and approval. In these cases, the painting might properly be understood to be an O'Keeffe-Keck, with the final appearance of the work a compromise between what Keck could do to remedy cracks and planar distortions and what O'Keeffe felt were acceptable visual changes to her paints.

Further along the continuum are O'Keeffe paintings that conservation students and colleagues of Keck treated, with the artist's approval and with the knowledge of Keck's decades-long relationship with the artist. It is possible that some of these treatments altered the original state of the paintings less than Keck's early treatments by virtue of the less-intrusive methods practiced in more recent times. Way down the continuum we might find paintings treated by conservators who had no knowledge of either Keck's dialogue with O'Keeffe, the conventions for acceptable appearances approved by the artist, or the precise and extensive visual language that was the essence of O'Keeffe's studio practices.

The profession of conservation and those concerned with the preservation and understanding of the paintings of Georgia O'Keeffe owe an enormous debt of gratitude to Caroline Keck. Caroline and her husband, Sheldon Keck, were among the first conservators in the United States to insist that the practice of art conservation was a profession with a formal and scientifically based body of knowledge. They rejected the craft-guild secrecy of old-world restorers and their claims to rejuvenate and improve tired and damaged paintings. The Kecks insisted that the modern practice of conservation should, first and foremost, "do no harm." For the Kecks, conservation treatment measures should not alter, confuse, obscure, or damage any remaining undamaged characteristics of a work of art. They insisted that conservators avoid using materials or techniques that might become irreversible or that might endanger the preservation of the object when removal was attempted in the future. They also insisted that modern conservation practices should be as concerned with *preventing* damage to artworks as with *repairing* them. Caroline Keck helped develop and insisted upon scientifically based methods for backing, framing, handling, crating, and environmental control. She also maintained that a professional art conservator had an obligation to full and permanent disclosure and documentation of the materials and techniques used to treat artworks. In her profession of conservation, a work of art should not be treated in any way that might alter the original visual properties of the work.[19]

Contemporary professional conservation practices follow closely in the footsteps set by Caroline Keck. The principals of "first do no harm," prevention before correction, reversibility, documentation, and the improvement of a professional body of knowledge remain central guideposts to professional conservators everywhere. Perhaps now more contemporary artists know and work with conservators than at any previous time. But that ground was first explored by O'Keeffe and Keck.

NOTES

1 *In 1993 Keck gave the letters to the Georgia O'Keeffe Foundation, Abiquiu, New Mexico. The foundation provided a copy to the Georgia O'Keeffe Museum Research Center Santa Fe, New Mexico, where they are now available. Barbara Buhler Lynes, director of the Georgia O'Keeffe Museum Research Center and curator at the Georgia O'Keeffe Museum, where I have served as conservator since the opening of the museum, made these materials available to me. We have often discussed the information in them, O'Keeffe's art materials that were in her studio at the time of her death in 1986 and that are housed at the Research Center, and the character and quality of the numerous O'Keeffe works that are in the museum collection or that have been loaned to it for exhibitions. I would like to thank her for this, as well as for her help on this essay.*

2 *Barbara Buhler Lynes,* Georgia O'Keeffe: Catalogue Raisonné, *2 vols. (Washington, D.C.: National Gallery of Art; New Haven, Conn., and London, England: Yale University Press; Abiquiu, N.M.: The Georgia O'Keeffe Foundation, 1999).*

3 *Judith C. Walsh, "The Language of O'Keeffe's Materials: Charcoal, Watercolor, Pastel," in Ruth E. Fine, Barbara Buhler Lynes, Elizabeth Glassman, and Judith C. Walsh,* O'Keeffe on Paper *(Washington D.C.: National Gallery of Art, 2000), 78.*

4 *Felrath Hines Papers, 1913-1993, Archives of American Art, Smithsonian Institution, Washington, D.C.*

5 *Examples in the letters of both the conservator's and artist's willingness to destroy canvases that could not be properly conserved include Keck to O'Keeffe, May 22, 1955; O'Keeffe to Keck, May 19, 1958; Keck to O'Keeffe, October 3, 1959; O'Keeffe to Keck, December 7, 1959; and O'Keeffe to Keck, January 25, 1960.*

6 *Keck to O'Keeffe, May 25, 1955, "I know by now just about how much one of your surfaces can stand and when it can be expected to react properly."*

7 *Keck to O'Keeffe, November 3, 1960.*

8 *O'Keeffe to Keck, August 9, 1950.*

9 *Keck to O'Keeffe, June 29, 1960.*

10 *Walsh, "The Language of O'Keeffe's Materials," 57.*

11 *Georgia O'Keeffe,* Georgia O'Keeffe *(New York: Viking Press, 1976).*

12 *Perry Miller Adato,* Georgia O'Keeffe, *1977 (transcript, 1998).*

13 *As the principal conservator for the Georgia O'Keeffe Museum since 1997, I have had the extraordinary good fortune to closely examine over five hundred works by Georgia O'Keeffe, covering the span of her career. Most of these have been from the collections of the Georgia O'Keeffe Museum and the Georgia O'Keeffe Foundation, while the remainder has come from the many museums and private lenders who so generously loaned paintings to exhibitions about O'Keeffe and American modernism. The observations describing O'Keeffe's skillful studio techniques reflect the study and documentation of these works over the past eight years.*

14 *Keck to O'Keeffe, October 3, 1967.*

15 *Sarah Whitaker Peters,* Becoming O'Keeffe: The Early Years, *2nd ed. (New York: Abbeville Press, 2001), 8.*

16 *On May 31, 2005, the Georgia O'Keeffe Foundation and the Georgia O'Keeffe Museum announced the transfer of its assets to the museum, which includes art, archival materials, and the Abiquiu house. The transfer is expected to be completed by early 2006.*

17 *Georgia O'Keeffe to William Howard Schubart, March 27, 1951, in Jack Cowart, Juan Hamilton, and Sarah Greenough,* Georgia O'Keeffe: Art and Letters *(Washington, D.C.: National Gallery of Art, 1987), 258.*

18 *Personal communication, Barbara Buhler Lynes, director of the Georgia O'Keeffe Museum Research Center, Santa Fe, 2005.*

19 *Code of Ethics, International Institute for Conservation, American Group, May 27, 1967 (Washington, D.C.: IIC-AG, 1968).*

Pastel

GEORGIA O'KEEFFE AND CONSERVATION

Judith C. Walsh

Courtesy of Georgia O'Keeffe Museum Research Center, Santa Fe, New Mexico. Photograph: Matthew Marston.

In 1951 Georgia O'Keeffe queried her new dealer, Edith Halpert, "What would you think of a pastel show—It could cover all the years as it is something I have always returned to and could be very handsome—or even pretty . . . "[1] Halpert apparently agreed, as the next year she opened *O'Keeffe Paintings in Pastel: 1914-1952*.[2] The segregation of this medium was new for an O'Keeffe exhibition. The artist and her husband, Alfred Stieglitz, had often included pastels in her yearly shows, but hung them side by side her works in oil paint.

O'Keeffe's description of her pastels as "handsome" or "pretty" seems to differentiate them from the oil paintings and at the same time understates the case. In her pastels, O'Keeffe used a limited number of colors in calculated tonal harmonies to create the forms. Sometimes the colors are closely related, sometimes they are far apart on the color wheel, and at times they are even complementary. As it is the values or tones of the colors that are most carefully balanced, the lines can seem to merge into color, while colors shift from one to another—as Charles Demuth described it, "Colour as colour, not as volume, or light,—only as colour. The last mad throb of red just before it turns green, or the ultimate shriek of orange calling upon all the blues of heaven for relief or support."[3] Seemingly a modest use of color, the effect is sumptuous. But this she also does in oil paint.

So why are the pastels singled out and experienced as more subtle in effect than similar images in oil? Perhaps it is because pastels present a uniformly matte surface. Pastel painting removes from deep color any interference from the irregular gloss inherent in oil paint. The reflected light from the pastel hits the viewer's eye without the glare one gets from an oil medium or even the most subtle varnish layer, so an unequalled depth of color is perceived. Without the reflection of gloss, even the smallest variation in texture

Pastel painting removes from deep color any interference

from the irregular gloss inherent in oil paint.

is apparent. Viewers can see in some areas of O'Keeffe pastels the pattern left from the ridges of her fingertips when she pushed the powdery pigment into the paper support.

Different from oil painting technique, pastels are used pure. The artist cannot mix the dry colors on a palette, but rather each possible color must be sold already mixed. Pastel sticks are made by the addition of only a small amount of gum binder to white chalk and a pigment. The range of colors is manufactured by adding a constant increment of white to the pure pigment. High-quality pastels are sold nestled in paper cradles inside sturdy boxes, the ranks of sticks lined up by color from palest to most intense. Each color variation is immediately visible and available for use.

Weighed against these positive factors is the tremendous delicacy of the resulting image. Since the sticks are made with the minimal amount of medium, they require the pressure of the artist's hand to set the pigment in place. Pushing hard was O'Keeffe's only option to ensure her unfixed pastel would stay together. The pastel can powder and flake as it is applied, but it can also be dislodged by any later touch, shock, or vibration. If a pastel is badly damaged, the conservator is at a loss: there can be no miracles of in-painting or cleaning for these pictures. Alfred Stieglitz was particularly worried about the fragility of O'Keeffe's pastels. His handwriting can be found on frame backings warning against handling, turning the pastel upside down, dropping, jarring, or shaking. He demanded "Care," "Great Care," and even "Greatest Care!!" O'Keeffe herself was more confident. She said, "They're a lot sturdier than you think."[4]

O'Keeffe made pastels throughout her career, from 1915 to 1975, although pastels were relatively rare in her overall work. From the thirty-eight-year period covered by the Halpert show, more than ten times as many paintings as pastels survived. At first O'Keeffe's pastels seem to be early renditions of images that were later worked up in oil paint. Pastel replaced watercolor as her "sketch" medium when the solidity of opaque color became important to her, about 1919. It was during this time that she was in New York on Stieglitz's invitation, working to develop her painting style and aesthetic, which was, in large part, a replication of the surface texture she found in pastel.[5]

Pastel also seemed to suit certain of O'Keeffe's projects. From time to time, O'Keeffe used pastel for repetitions of images that did not appear in oil, such as the series *Yellow Sweet Peas* (1925), *White Sweet Peas* (1926), and *Pink Sweet Peas* (1927), or the two portraits of the American artist Beauford Delaney (1943). On a trip to Maine in 1922, O'Keeffe explored images of the sea in pastel. In this case, using pastel saved her from the burden of obvious comparisons with Winslow Homer, who had made iconic images of the sea in both watercolor and oil.

By 1930 the surface of her paintings—which she so carefully constructed and of which her conservator, Caroline Keck, so eloquently despaired—had changed to look very much like the surfaces of her pastel paintings. Color was used pure but completely blended shade into shade in thin applications that were teased into place by soft or bristle brushes, which imparted patterns that echoed the finger ridges left in her pastels. A ridge of paint often bordered the areas of clear color that did not blend into another, much like the simple build-up of color found in her thickly applied pastels. Apparently, O'Keeffe found pastel's inherent working properties of body, clean color, and uniform lack of gloss to be so seductive and right for her images that she chose to replicate those effects in oil paint. Even the boxes of color chips found in her studio could be part of this effort. (Perhaps they are notes on achieving in oil paint the scale of tones of color so easily found in pastels.)

It is interesting to note in the correspondence between O'Keeffe and Keck how often they discuss a protective glass or varnish on her pictures, necessitated by the artist's resistance to varnishing the paintings. It was, after all, Keck's ability to varnish the paintings that cemented their relationship. O'Keeffe's reluctance to use varnish can be seen as a parallel reaction to her reluctance to use fixative on the pastels.

Artists have used pastels, despite their fragility, ever since technology could provide clear glass that was big enough for a frame.

Some artists have sprayed pastel pictures with fixative, a resinous mixture that consolidates the surface of the pastel by binding the particles together in a matrix of the dried resin. Inevitably, any fixative alters the surface of a pastel. Some colors become more saturated, while other colors shift slightly. A modicum of gloss might be imparted. Today, so-called "workable" fixatives let the artist rework already sprayed areas, thereby allowing the piece to be fixed lightly several times as the color builds up. Usually, though, the last touches are left unfixed to preserve the matte surface. Interestingly, O'Keeffe did fix many of her charcoal drawings, but more than likely none of her pastels have fixative on them.[6]

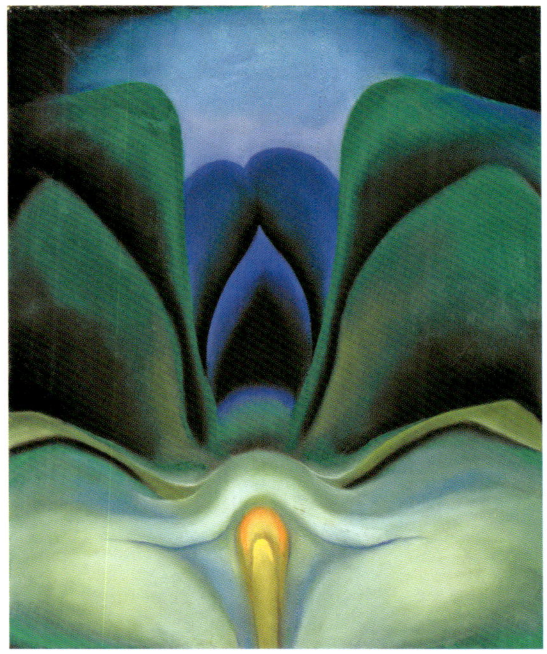

Blue Flower, 1918, pastel on paper mounted on cardboard, 20" x 16". Promised gift, The Burnett Foundation, Georgia O'Keeffe Museum, Santa Fe, New Mexico 1.1998.72. Photograph: Matthew Marston. © 1987 Private Collection.

Yet O'Keeffe's assertion that her pastels were "sturdy" is actually correct, despite their unfixed state. She evolved a system of construction for these works, a system that recent conservation research has determined is the best hope pastels have for long-term survival in today's hectic world of art travel and museum exhibition.[7]

As a schoolgirl, O'Keeffe used black construction paper for pastel. This paper has a marked surface texture that can catch and hold the powdery pigment. It is not durable, however, since it becomes brittle as it ages. By the time she turned to pastel again, as a maturing artist, O'Keeffe used moderately textured drawing papers that had been adhered overall to thick gray cardboard. These papers were too smooth to be used for unfixed pastel, and some have had flaking problems. For a few works in the mid-1920s she used cardboard alone that she covered with a sandy gesso ground. Finally, by 1929 O'Keeffe had sheets of tan, sand-covered paper or a highly textured golden-brown paper mounted to thick, stiff cardboard for her use in pastel. Solid mounting and deep texture in the sheet gave the pastel particles purchase and protection from vibration in travel. Indeed, O'Keeffe's pastels seem to have suffered relatively little in their travels back and forth, across the country from New York to New Mexico on trains or even across town "in the back seat of a taxi" as they were delivered to dealers and exhibitions.[8]

Among the pastels that were found in her collection at the time of her death was the dark-blue and brilliant-green *Blue Flower*, from 1918. Abstract and therefore perhaps open to misinterpretation, O'Keeffe withheld this image from the public.[9] It was never displayed during her lifetime. It was, however, apparently damaged during her lifetime, probably by broken glass. The work was restored carefully in two or three areas, most likely by O'Keeffe herself.

Blue Flower was created on a coarse paper—one that was perhaps brushed with a sandy ground before drawing. The paper was mounted at the edges to a very thick, grey cardboard of the same size. All of that was done before any drawing on the sheet. Once the paper was mounted, O'Keeffe could begin. Her method, as documented from other pastels, probably began with a pale pastel under-drawing to outline the forms. Then, O'Keeffe apparently set out a limited palette for each image, using perhaps six or seven colors in a series of tones. Long, thick strokes of color were laid on, side by side; sometimes she used the side of the stick to fill in large areas. She then blended the strokes of color on the sheet with her fingers. She complained to Stieglitz of the wear and tear on her hands when she used pastel, remarking that it took the skin right off the tips of her fingers.[10] Later, when she used pastels, O'Keeffe apparently wore rubber gloves to protect her hands.

Blue Flower is evenly "saturated" with the powdery medium and shows very little surface texture from the direction or force of the strokes of the pastel sticks, except in the flower's pistil. At the lower right, and at the center right-hand side of the painting, there are a few areas that show a completely different texture. These areas are located within surrounding smooth areas of the same green or blue colors. They are made up of many small, stippled strokes of one pastel color applied next to the other, with no blending or smoothing. The stippling represents repaired damage to the pastel, again most likely done by O'Keeffe.

The damage to the pastel might have come from poor handling as the picture was framed or from broken glass within the frame. Both sorts of damage can be seen in the picture. The surface of the pastel shows small scratches that are clearly from broken glass, and under magnification tiny shards of glass "glitter" can be seen on the surface. In addition, the faint impression of four fingers in the surface of the picture at one side betray a hand wrapped around the cardboard, touching the face, probably during framing.

She complained to Stieglitz of the wear and tear on her hands when she used pastel, remarking that it took the skin right off the tips of her fingers.

The repair of the pastel is unobtrusive, since it matches perfectly with the color of the surrounding area. No doubt, this restoration required access to the same pastel sticks the artist used to make the picture. This makes O'Keeffe the obvious one to have done these repairs. She alone would have had access to her own materials and the pastel itself. She also had the skill required: Georgia O'Keeffe used to "spot" Stieglitz photographs. That is, she would perfect the images by painting out any white spots that occurred on the finished print from dust in the negative, or she would scratch out any black mark that inadvertently occurred on the print with a sharp pen or needle. She used a series of water-based colors available from a photographic supply house to tone out the scratches she created or the small white spots that inevitably occurred on a photographic print. The materials she used for this purpose were found among her effects in the library at Abiquiu, still held together in a box marked "Photo Materials" in O'Keeffe's hand.[11]

Also in her library at Abiquiu were found two editions of the book *The Materials of the Artist and Their Use in Painting: With Notes on the Techniques of the Old Masters* by Max Doerner (1870–1939), a professor at the Academy of Fine Arts in Munich. On November 20, 1934, O'Keeffe received a copy of the 1934 English first edition, in which Stieglitz inscribed "For Georgia." A second edition of the volume was published in 1949; both were found in her library and both were annotated and marked by O'Keeffe.[12]

Of particular interest here is Doerner's chapter six, "Pastel Painting." The author gives the "natural history" of pastels—how they are made, which pigments are used, which are preferred as light-fast, the characteristic of high-quality pastels, and some methods for their use. He urges the reader to make his own pastels and to prepare a textured "ground" for pastel painting, both of which O'Keeffe did.[13] He discourages the use of fixative, listing all the difficulties inherent in its use. Finally, Doerner discusses "Restoration of the Pastel."[14] He instructs that "dark grooves of color caused by drops of water on a carelessly framed pastel" should be scraped carefully with a penknife, then lightly worked over with the crayon. Doerner advises that large areas of lost powder, such as what likely occurred in *Blue Flower* or what would occur if drips were scraped off, "can be restored somewhat to their original effect by carefully applying new color in a stippling manner." This is just what we see in the damaged areas of *Blue Flower*.

O'Keeffe lived a life that was dedicated to art and was remarkable for the variety of ways she served art and art making. She was at various times artist and model, protégée and mentor, exhibitor and exhibition designer, or installation technician. She was an avid art student and a dedicated teacher. At one point she worked in commercial art and design. She tried to manufacture her own paints and pastels. She played the role of registrar for the galleries that Stieglitz owned. She managed the estates of artists, and in forming the "key set" of Stieglitz's work after his death produced a de facto *catalogue raisonné* of his work. She collected art and gave it generously to public collections. It is clear now that based on her treatment of Stieglitz's photographs, the treatment of her own pastels, and her correspondence with Caroline Keck, she was also minutely interested in the details of the conservation of artwork. The publication of letters between O'Keeffe and Keck, her longtime friend and conservator, and the accompanying exhibition show another facet of her consuming interest in art as both an idea and an object.

NOTES

1 *Judith C. Walsh, "The Language of O'Keeffe's Materials: Charcoal, Watercolor, Pastel," in Ruth E. Fine, Barbara Buhler Lynes, Elizabeth Glassman, and Judith C. Walsh,* O'Keeffe on Paper *(Washington D.C.: National Gallery of Art, 2000), n. 34.*

2 *Barbara Buhler Lynes,* Georgia O'Keeffe: Catalogue Raisonné, 2 vols. *(Washington, D.C.: National Gallery of Art; New Haven, Conn., and London, England: Yale University Press; Abiquiu, N.M.: The Georgia O'Keeffe Foundation, 1999).*

3 *Charles Demuth, statement in* Georgia O'Keeffe: Paintings *(exhibition catalogue, 1926), as quoted in Barbara Buhler Lynes,* O'Keeffe, Stieglitz and the Critics, 1916 – 1929 *(Chicago: University of Chicago Press, 1991), Appendix A, 258.*

4 *Author's conversation with Doris Bry, 1999.*

5 *Walsh,* O'Keeffe on Paper, *2000, 70-71.*

6 *See Walsh,* O'Keeffe on Paper.

7 *Harriet Stratis, "Pastels in Traveling Exhibitions: Guidelines for Their Preparation, Transport and Installation," paper delivered at the American Institute for Conservation 26th Annual Meeting, Arlington, Va., 1998, unpublished. Stratis, a paper conservator at the Art Institute of Chicago, studied the transportation of pastels for the recent Odilon Redon and Degas exhibitions installed there. She found the most stable structure for pastel painting is well-fixed pastel pigment, or pastel pigment firmly adhered to the surface of rough paper. It is best if the coarse paper is mounted solidly to a rigid card or paperboard and framed under non-static glazing. This is exactly what O'Keeffe finally used.*

8 *Author's conversation with Doris Bry, 1999.*

9 *See Lynes,* O'Keeffe, Stieglitz and the Critics; *and Barbara Buhler Lynes, with Russell Bowman,* O'Keeffe's O'Keeffes, the artist's collection *(New York: Thames & Hudson, 2001).*

10 *I am grateful to Barbara Buhler Lynes, who told me of this in a conversation about these issues.*

11 *Confirmed by author's communication with Constance McCabe, photograph conservator, National Gallery of Art. For more information, see Constance McCabe, "Coatings on Photographs by Alfred Stieglitz," in* Coatings on Photographs: Materials, Techniques, and Conservation, *edited by Constance McCabe (Washington, D.C.: American Institute for Conservation of Historic and Artistic Works Photographic Materials Group (AIC/PMG), 2005).*

12 *Max Doerner,* The Materials of the Artist and Their Use in Painting: With Notes on the Techniques of the Old Masters, *trans. by Eugen Neuhaus (New York: Harcourt, Brace and Company, 1934; rev. ed., 1949).*

13 *Walsh,* O'Keeffe on Paper, *71.*

14 *Doerner,* The Materials of the Artist, *253-54.*

The Letters

The year 1946 was a difficult one for O'Keeffe personally and professionally. That February Alfred Stieglitz, O'Keeffe's husband and dealer, had shown fourteen of her new paintings at his gallery An American Place, as he did almost yearly. On July 13, however, the great photographer died. He was eighty-two.

O'Keeffe needed help to carry on her career, as well as to disperse Stieglitz's historic collection of nineteenth- and twentieth-century photographs, paintings, prints, and drawings to American museums. She soon got that help. By October she had chosen an assistant, Doris Bry; a new gallery, Edith Halpert's Downtown Gallery; and a conservator, Mrs. Sheldon Keck. O'Keeffe was then fifty-nine years old and Caroline Keck thirty-seven.

In addition to being a generation apart, Keck and O'Keeffe had very different lifestyles and personalities. Keck, for instance, had two young children and O'Keeffe none. Nevertheless, they appear to have bonded from their first meeting. It may just have been a chemical connection, but there are some evocative facts to consider. Both had husbands who were older and more powerful in the world than they. Both had known the gender bitterness of working under a glass ceiling in their chosen fields. Both had learned to be fierce about the territory of their respective crafts. And they liked to be in charge. (Sometimes Caroline would consult with Sheldon about a canvas treatment, but the final decisions about O'Keeffe's works were hers.) Both women also could be disagreeable—but they never were with each other.

At the time of their meeting O'Keeffe was already famous, but that didn't stop Keck from voicing her opinion when she saw fit. They seem to have accepted each other's foibles without difficulty, and they practiced a similar perfectionist work ethic. Their prime concern was for the condition of O'Keeffe's paintings. This is what fueled their unique friendship, and the letters that passed between them allow readers to see how their relationship grew.

O'Keeffe began to include spontaneous details about her simple, joyful, hardworking days in New Mexico and the making of her art there. Keck's letters start out briskly professional and then lighten up, becoming affectionate in tone. But these changes took a while. Not until 1956 were formal salutations dropped for "Dear Georgia" and "Dear Caroline." O'Keeffe's ingrained habit of signing her full name persisted long after they were on a first-name basis. Some of their communications aren't signed at all—presumably because they were in a hurry.

In the letters presented here, sentences and paragraphs have been omitted that are not germane to this publication. The deletions are marked with ellipses. O'Keeffe's carefree spelling and punctuation have been kept for their original flavor. The paintings referred to in the letters are often undated, with imprecise—and changeable—titles. (O'Keeffe and Stieglitz were casual about her titles until 1944, when Rosalind Irvine began to work with O'Keeffe on the laborious task of cataloguing her paintings.) Works have been identified, or deduced, whenever possible.

After reading the whole correspondence, perhaps what sticks most to the mind is that no words (not even theirs) can describe the enigmatic visual and psychological impact of paint color. The job of "mitigating" the artist's intentions with color requires intuition, expertise, and complete integrity. These Caroline Keck had. Painters know perfectly well that their works are continually made new by beholders, and O'Keeffe wanted her beholders to begin where she left off—not with the injuries of time and travel.

Let the artist and conservator speak now to each other.

Sarah Whitaker Peters

1947–1949

From the very beginning, Keck never hesitated to tell it like it was to O'Keeffe. Her eye was highly developed and her watchword as a conservator was "first do no harm." She was mindful that O'Keeffe intended her colors to balance and harmonize. The oil medium loses saturation with time, but colors can be stabilized. Toward this end, Keck sprayed O'Keeffe's paintings with a carefully controlled, light acrylic varnish. (For Keck's words on this painstaking method, see her letter of December 29, 1960.) There are two brief, undated notes from O'Keeffe to Keck from this period thanking her for the work done and granting the requested authorization for further work.

In 1949, with her chosen and keenly felt responsibilities of placing the Alfred Stieglitz Collection in museums finished, O'Keeffe moved permanently to New Mexico.

. . . In 1964 the New York State Histori

February 13, 1947

Dear Miss O'Keeffe;

The big canvas of THE WAVE, 1928,[*] *was sprayed to protect the surface. There isn't a thing you can do about the crackle on it. It is the same old business of the quick drying darks, veridian and mars violet again, I think. It may not go much further and then again it may crack so far it will flake off, but even lining wouldn't stop this. I just wouldn't worry about it, as there is nothing you can do.*

On the ABSTRACTION, 1930,[†] *one edge of the composition board had chipped up and was just about to drop off. I set this back when I cleaned the surface, which was VERY dirty, it was then sprayed.*

PEDERNAL, NEW MEXICO, 1936,[‡] *was clean, as it is very toothy we sprayed it twice, to keep dust out of the brushstrokes. You did some repainting on this and the surface will always be uneven.*

The delightful little KATCHINA, 1936,[§] *was full of dirty finger marks around the edges and is rubbed at the corners, it was cleaned and sprayed.*

On the tiny panel, there is a chip off to the wood 1 5/8" from the bottom on the right edge, and in the upper left corner a chip in the top paint layer. There was a slight bit of dirt on the edges from handling, but the panel is in wonderful condition, no warp, split or curvature. I enclose the bill [for thirty-five dollars].[∫]

Sincerely,

Mrs. Sheldon Keck

* Probably *Wave, Night* (1928), *catalogue raisonné*, 644.

† Because this work is on composition board, Dale Kronkright thinks it is probably *Abstraction* (1930), *catalogue raisonné*, 702.

‡ Probably *Pedernal, New Mexico* (1936), *catalogue raisonné*, 901.

§ Kronkright's guess is that this is *Kachina Doll* (1938), *catalogue raisonné*, 942. Keck misspelled Kachina.

∫ The last paragraph of this letter refers to another tiny painting, possibly *Red Pear with Fig* (1923), *catalogue raisonné*, 409.

June 17, 1947

Dear Miss O'Keeffe:

Thank you for the postcard authorizing us to experiment with SKUNK CABBAGE, we will let you know how it works out.*

I am glad to say that the painting ABSTRACTION VI,† 1928 now looks excellent. Some of that mould had been there quite a time. I took it off with repeated applications of benzine, applied with a tiny sable brush, following the lines of your brushstrokes, but it was a horribly ticklish job as the paint was extremely tender. Then we[1] sprayed it, diluting the spray way down the first time and following this with a second normal mixture. It certainly came to life beautifully, and I don't think the bloom [webs of tiny cracks caused by the penetration of water vapor into the varnish surface] will come back. As to the others, we removed a few fingermarks here and there but they did not present any problems. In every case, however, the glass is dirty on the INSIDE as well as the out, also I wish you could make some provision for keying the canvasses [sic] *properly, and having them held in place by screws and not nails. My favorite frames are those where you have had the man attach them with screws thru the side centers, these permit expansion of the canvas and hold the paintings firm without exposing them to the bad effect of nailing. I know we are awful on framing because we are always more concerned with the relation (physical) of the frame body to the painting and its support than we are interested in the appearance!*

Sincerely yours,

Mrs. Sheldon Keck

* *Skunk Cabbage* (1928), *catalogue raisonné*, 627.
† *Abstraction No. VI* (1928), *catalogue raisonné*, 615.

March 18, 1949

Dear Miss O'Keeffe:

I enclose an enlargement of our record photograph of RED CANNA. I have marked "A" all the surface damages which appeared to be the same substance; a sooty, grease black, and which was extremely tough to remove. I had trouble with the line that went thru the pure red part of the leaf. I am very sorry to admit that I did not succeed in competely eliminating the mark and I did loose [sic] *paint along the line . . . . As you know your pure color areas are almost impossible to clean . . . . I had to use a very mild solvent mixture of turpentine, benzine and a touch of diacetone alcohol—which was highly dangerous—but the only thing that would move that black. DON'T send me another to clean, I got so upset doing this one that I couldn't eat until it was done, and acted generally, according to Shel, like a restorer at her first job!*

Sincerely yours,

Mrs. Sheldon Keck

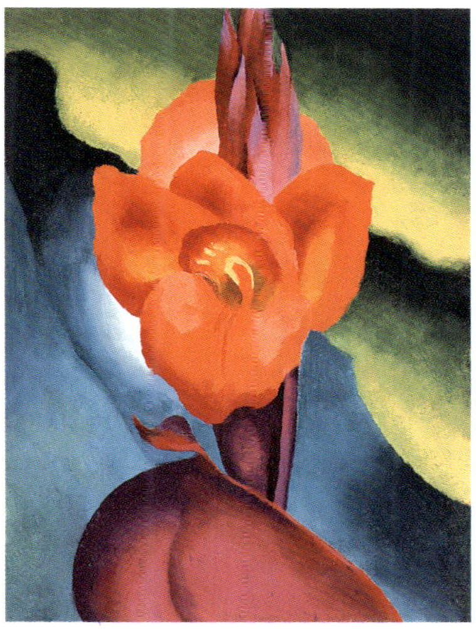

Red Canna, 1919. oil on board, 13" x 9 1/2". Collection of High Museum of Art, Atlanta, Georgia. Purchase with funds from the Fine Arts Collectors and the 20th Century Art Acquisition Fund and gift of the Pollitzer Family in honor of Anita Pollitzer, to whom the artist originally gave this work. 1996.18.

* A painting titled *Red Canna* (1928) is listed as destroyed in the *catalogue raisonné*, Appendix II, 129. But it is also possible that this is *Red Canna* (1919), *catalogue raisonné*, 296, because it is recorded as being sprayed with butyl methacrylate polymer by Keck in March 1948.

1950–1955

O'Keeffe's first dated letter, dashed off from Abiquiu on August 2, 1950, reveals her growing reliance on Keck's judgment. By 1955 Keck had become one of O'Keeffe's closest friends, one to whom she would offer help and encouragement whenever she could. That feeling was mutual. O'Keeffe even offered her secluded Ghost Ranch house to the entire Keck family for a month as her guests.

The artist took a pardonable pride in being able do *everything* about her paintings herself. She made it clear to Keck that she knew exactly what she was doing—whether the process was dangerous or not. If, in her judgment, she failed, the canvas was usually doomed. She is known to have destroyed thirty-five paintings in 1952 that did not measure up to her standards.

O'Keeffe's activities in the Abiquiu studio were her closely guarded secret. In 1951, however, she shared some unusual shop talk with William Howard Schubart, Stieglitz's nephew and her trusted financial advisor.

> The studio looks like an attic—it always does when I work—it would undoubtedly distress you—one ten foot table is full of canvas and stretchers and hammers and tacks—then there is a small table full of little pieces of canvas covered cards painted tones of all of the colors I have [these are her color chips]—every day—or should I say night—I stretch a little canvas. It hurts my hand so I do a little at a time—my palette is very clean—my brushes too—The palette is on a table I can wheel about—another one is on a window sill—the easle is over there by the window—another easle is on the window sill—This table—ten feet long and four feet wide has many little piles of papers—I always think they are not going to be there one day—that I will have attended to all of them—but it never is that way.[2]

O'Keeffe's pigments behaved differently in the atmosphere of New Mexico than they had in the greater humidity of New York, and she did not share this information with Schubart. Keck recorded that O'Keeffe kept

> a little black-covered notebook in which were listed weather conditions, and materials used for different paintings (at least during one summer at Lake George . . . I don't know the time period possibly covered because [she and I] only made search for materials on one group of ptgs). [They] had developed minor traction crackle (infuriating to Georgia), limited to green and purple areas. The little book stated the weather was damp; the canvas a certain preprimed purchase, and the colors both MARS. Hard to prove which if any of these factors caused the crackle, but fascinating to have the data to weigh.[3]

The whereabouts of this notebook are unknown. If she kept a similar one in New Mexico, it has not been found.

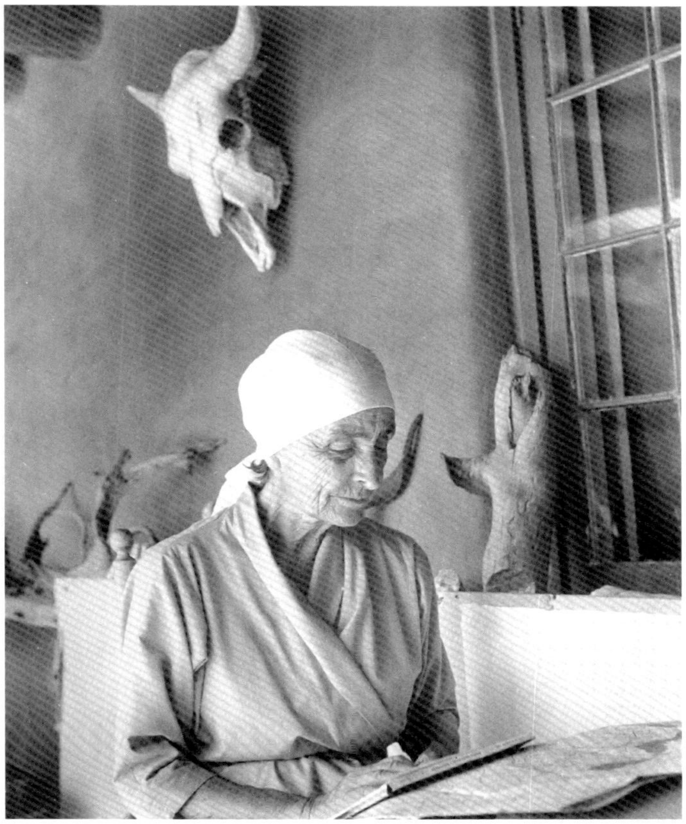

Todd Webb. *O'Keeffe on the Portal, Ghost Ranch, New Mexico*, 1964, silver gelatin print.
Courtesy of Evans Gallery, Portland, Maine.

August 2, 1950

Dear Mr. and Mrs. Keck:

I hope both of you and the little ones[4] are well and that you are having a good summer.

Mrs. Halpert writes me about that Rams Skull with Tan Leaves* having a mark down one side and that possibly it should be relined. Will you write me about it and tell me what you think should be done—also the price. They took the glass off at the Downtown [Gallery] before it was sold without asking me and got it so dirty you had to clean it before you sprayed it. I was always very annoyed about their taking the glass off that way. I suppose the canvas has been pressed by the stretcher —I wonder if the surface and paint is cracked. Will you let me know and if you can fix it.

I also have a painting here that fell off its stretcher and has a tear about an inch long. May I send it to you now to do what you can with it? I plan rather vaguely now to have a show in October. If I get this painting off to you immediately may I have it back by October 15th? That is could I have it to show in N.Y. by Oct. 15? If not I'll show it with the hole in it and have it fixed afterward. May I hear from you.

Sincerely,

Georgia O'Keeffe

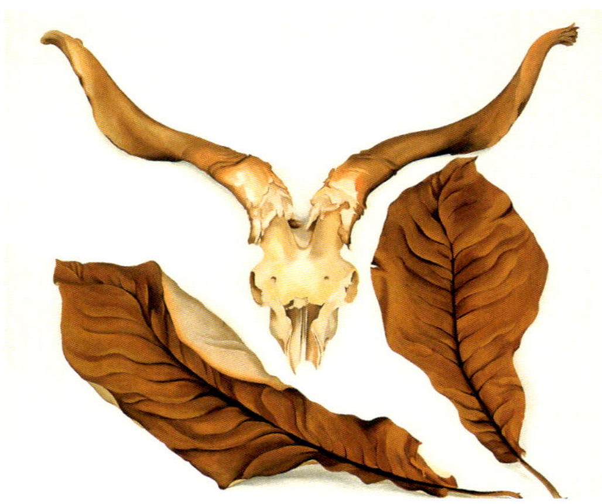

Ram's Skull with Brown Leaves, 1936. oil on linen, 30" x 36". Collection of Roswell Museum and Art Center, New Mexico. Gift of Mr. & Mrs. Donald Winston, Mr. & Mrs. Frederick Winston, and Mr. & Mrs. Samuel H. Marshall. RMAC 1957.018.0001. Photograph: Richard Faller.

* *Ram's Skull with Brown Leaves* (1936), *catalogue raisonné*, 881. This is one of many title shifts—formal and informal.

18 months ago, we were invited to draft a

August 7th, 1950

Dear Miss O'Keeffe:

. . . . Of course we can take care of the torn painting for you. I wouldn't think of having it in an exhibition torn, send it straight along and as soon as I get it I will report back to you and promise the work can be done in time. I am always delighted to be of service to you.

As to the RAM'S SKULL WITH BROWN LEAVES . . . . there is very little to be done. The paint film is definitely cracked along the inner edge of the stretcher, but the painting cannot be keyed out unless you reframe it and the cracking is not severe enough to warrant the expense of a lining; there does not appear to be any cleavage along the line of crackle, but there is always that possibility. If the owner wishes to have the painting lined, our charge would be $100. If it were lined it would probably not have to be reframed since the wax-resin adhesive prevents the canvas from being so responsive to changes in humidity.*

. . . . But you know how I feel about your frames, they make life hard for the painting. I don't think this painting has been abused; it is quite pristine. The damage to the RANCHO CHURCH† one would make you weep, it is so outrageous and cannot be repaired satisfactorily because the scratch is only a fraction deep into the paint film and any attempt to retouch it would make it even more noticeable, the finger marks and smudges we can clean off easily . . . . Let us know what your wishes are and we will do our best to fulfil them.

Sincerely,

* See asterisk in letter of August 2, 1950.
† Probably *Ranchos Church, Front* (1930), *catalogue raisonné*, 703.

Abiquiu, N.M.
8/9/50

Dear Caroline Keck:

Today I have packed a monstrous box that I am sending to you. It has 5 paintings in it. The torn one you will write me about. There is one similar to it that should be sprayed along with all the others.

There is one big painting 4 feet by 7 feet*—so you must expect a very large box, tho it is only about six and a quarter inches deep. I plan to have a show at the American Place.[5]

Forgive me that I send you such cumbersome things to bother with.

About the Ram's Skull with Tan Leaves†—I am afraid there will always be quite a bit of changes in the canvas with the weather and considering that maybe it should be lined.[6] It is painted on very thin canvas. I am willing to get another frame for it if you think that would fix it because I can always use that one. Will you remove the frame and key the painting out as you seem to think it should be keyed.[7] If it is alright when you get the canvas taut I will have my frame man make a new frame for it so will you let me know. If keying it out doesn't help as you seem to think it should then line it. The lining that would keep the painting frame contracting and expanding so much might be best. But try keying it out first and see what you think—and let me know.

It is a comfort to think of how careful you are. I want to do what ever you think best for that painting.

Sincerely,

Georgia O'Keeffe

* *Spring* (1948), *catalogue raisonné*, 1163.
† See asterisk in letter of August 2, 1950.

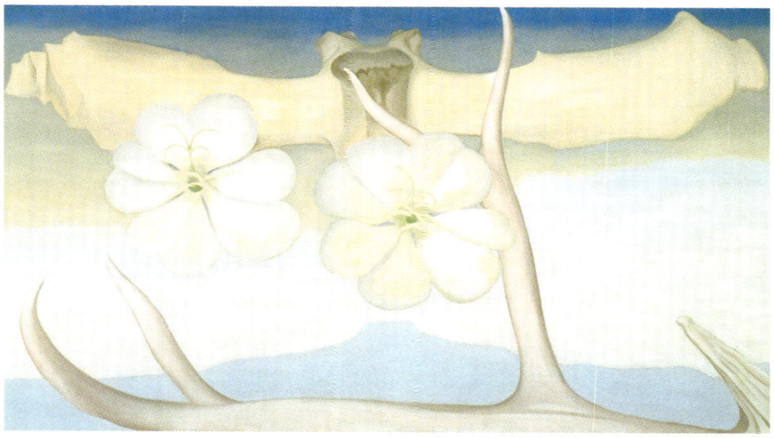

Spring, 1948. oil on canvas, 48 1/4" x 84 1/4". Collection of Georgia O'Keeffe Museum, Santa Fe, New Mexico. 1997.06.28. Photograph. Malcolm Varon. © The Georgia O'Keeffe Foundation.

August, 1950
87 State Street, Brooklyn, N.Y.

Dear Miss O'Keeffe:

The big painting with the bones came over about ten days ago and after due deliberation we decided it should be sprayed with the butyl methacrylate polymer, which we did and returned the painting two days ago.*

Couldn't say that the spray altered it at all. There isn't much tooth on the canvas but there is just enough to catch dust and there are so many pale areas which, if they became greyed would alter the entire color plan of the painting. Now that it is sprayed, tell the owners IF the surface should pick up dust in about five or ten years, it can be cleaned off with Benzine without in any way disturbing the surface of your paint film.

I am very glad it is to be hung without glass. It is a big painting and very light and would have been almost impossible to place in a room where it could be seen properly without reflections on the glass.

Very sincerely yours,

Mrs. Sheldon Keck

* *Spring* (1948), *catalogue raisonné*, 1163.

Abiquiu, N.M.
8/25/50

Dear Mrs. Keck:

.... I am flattered that you approve my packing. I always thought I could make my living that way when I can't make it painting.

I knew all those paintings would be loose on the stretchers in your climate as the canvas was stretched in this dry place. It makes a great difference. Where they get board backs that will help them a little. I think you had better line the torn painting. Also the skull with brown leaves. The latter painting is so delicate that is is always in danger as it is now. I know such things when I paint as I paint but I do it anyway.

I will bring the large blue painting back here after I show it as I know that no one will buy it. Here it will stay flat on the stretcher and be alright, and I enjoy it on the wall myself.

It is a comfort to be able to send paintings to you as I never expect anyone else to be careful ....

Sincerely,

Georgia O'Keeffe

Abiquiu, N.M.

11/27/53

Dear Mrs. Keck:

That Barn painting was left at the Down Town Gallery to be returned to you to keep till you have time to fix it. I am writing John Marin with this mail to send it to you if it hasn't already gone to you. I will be interested to see what you are able to do with it. In this climate where it is always dry it is [illegible] canvas stuck up on panel. When it is taken to the damper climate there is trouble — I'd not use it any more tho I like it.

I am looking forward to your book with great interest —

Sincerely,

Georgia O'Keeffe

Letter from Georgia O'Keeffe to Caroline Keck, November 27, 1953. Collection of The Georgia O'Keeffe Foundation, Abiquiu, New Mexico.

Abiquiu, N.M.
11/27/53

Dear Mrs. Keck:

That Barn painting* was left at the Downtown Gallery to be returned to you to keep till you have time to fix it. . . . I will be very interested to see what you can do with it. In this climate where it is always dry that canvas stands up very well. Where it is taken to the damper climate there is trouble—I'll not use it any more tho I like it.

I am looking forward to your book with great interest.[8]

Sincerely,

Georgia O'Keeffe

* We know that in 1953 Keck treated three barn paintings. Kronkright is quite sure that these were 575, 806, and 807 in the *catalogue raisonné* and that this one is the privately owned 806. The two others belonged to O'Keeffe.

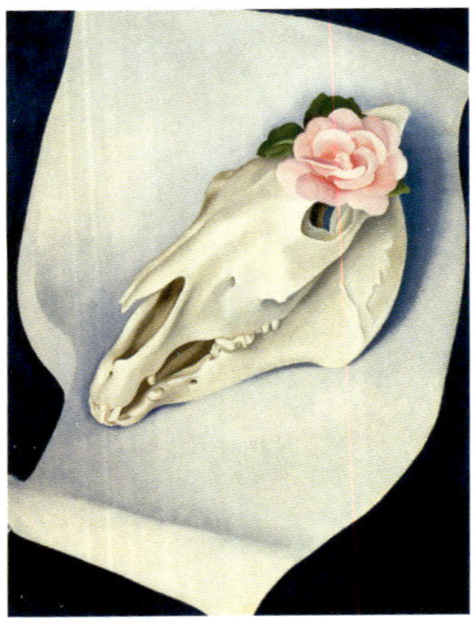

Horse's Skull with Pink Rose, 1931. oil on canvas, 40" x 30". Collection of Los Angeles County Museum of Art, California. Gift of The Georgia O'Keeffe Foundation. AC1994.159.1. Courtesy of Museum Associates/LACMA.

August 10th, 1954

Dear Miss O'Keeffe:

I have finally completed the work of mounting "HORSE'S SKULL AND PINK ROSE" on a prepared panel. . . .*

I had a perfectly foul time with it. All because of the ultramarine blue. It must have been applied straight from the tube because it wasn't bound at all; everything that touched it made it bleed off. I got in a real tizzy with it and finally decided that whether it came off or not the painting had to be penetrated with wax to stop the cracks and the cupping that was causing so much trouble, so I went right ahead and did the job and the loss be hanged. It wasn't so bad when the job got done, but I would have liked to have ironed once more around to even the slight bumps but decided that since the painting was now safe, the slight irregularities would have to stay rather than lose more blue. I touched it in and glazed over where it had thinned out, since that way your brushstrokes were in no manner effected and the color brought back to its correct intensity, but Lordy what a nuisance that blue was. Every other part of the painting was firm as a rock but the blue came away when I went over it with a dry cotton swab, just powdered off. I gave it a good solid spray over the blue so that it is set in place now and should not bleed off any more. There isn't any white with it at all, if you recall and the stuff just isn't stuck to the canvas properly.

You know how I hate to lose any of your color ever, so this upset me more than it should have since the rest of the task went so nicely. The painting looks very well, I must admit, but it wasn't fun. Aside from encountering that special blue again, I would say if we have any more cracking from the metal frames this method of mounting will attend to the trouble excellently. The panels are well constructed . . . and the use of CELOTEX as a base from the mount lets the canvas quality continue, which doesn't happen with a solid board mount so well; that seems to make the whole thing look wooden rather than fabric. You really wouldn't know it was a solid structure just looking at the surface. I like that part. . . . I cleaned that nice window painting of yours at the Modern Art† a few weeks ago and was delighted the way it came out, crisp and fresh as you painted it. It is in excellent condition too. I hope you had a good summer and did lots of paintings—none with straight ultramarine!

Sincerely,

* *Horse's Skull with Pink Rose* (1931), *catalogue raisonné*, 775. Note the slight name change.

† *Farmhouse Window and Door* (1929), *catalogue raisonné*, 653.

May 22nd, 1955

Dear Miss O'Keeffe:

. . . . I must say that painting "Antelope Head with Pedernal" upset me no little. I do hate so to see any of your canvcsses* [sic] *in that state. I think we should line it at once and then fill the tiny losses. I don't like that type of cleavage and wonder what the canvas was and whether or not you have any records on weather conditions? There are indications that it is cleaving in other areas as well as the two active spots. It will cost $100 to fix the painting and I can undertake it as soon as you authorize me to . . . . I thought all the other paintings of yours which I saw looked all right, of course you know how I feel about unframed paintings so there is no sense going into it again. But your work does not profit by dirty finger marks and it is impossible to expect people to have clean hands all the time or even to have persons who move paintings know where to place their hands and a frame does spare the painting from unnecessary damage. I am just as fanatic about the physical welfare of a painting as you are about the quality of what you produce, but we can't get together on this, I'm afraid.*

If life hadn't been quite so hectic for me I was going to write to you and suggest that you let me play with that wonderful and tragic Jonquils† *canvas. I have a theory that I might be able to save it and I will never forget it or the awful state it was in. I know by now just about how much one of your surfaces can stand and when it can be expected to react properly, but on that one I am uncertain because of the advanced stage of its decay. If I could fix it, I would charge you plenty but if I couldn't I would [not] charge you anything, which seems just and proper to me.*[9] *But I don't honestly know whether it could be done right. I hate the thought of your destroying the canvas, although I admit that should happen unless it could be repaired correctly . . . .*

Sincerely,

Mrs. Sheldon Keck

* *Antelope Head with Pedernal* (1953), *catalogue raisonné*, 1264.

† Kronkright is reasonably certain that the "tragic Jonquils" is *Jonquils I* (1936), *catalogue raisonné*, 887, because Keck was first given it to treat in 1947 but failed.

Abiquiu, N.M.
5/29/55

Dear Caroline Keck:

Enclosed find check.

Yes fix the "Antelope Head with Pedernal". I think there never was any paint on that spot in this. (I think it was upper right hand corner. I don't remember the canvas but if you can cut off a little piece I could tell . . . . I am afraid nothing can be done with the Jonquill canvas.

I am delighted to hear that you may come out here for a month.[10] You can look at the canvas here if you come. If you don't come I will send it to you but I don't think anything can be done with it. It is the only piece of that canvas I ever used . . . . You need bring nothing but your selves and the simplest country clothing. It will be fine if you can come. Can you tell me about when it would be. You understand that the house [Ghost Ranch] is in a very remote place but the surrounding country—a wide plain to a mountain in front—more plain to very colorful cliffs behind —is very handsome. The sort of thing that to me is always new.

There is electricity and all that goes with it—I can send a woman to clean up for you once or twice a week if you wish. Santa Fe is 68 miles —pretty good shopping for food about 4 miles, some 16 miles away. Distances seem shorter here than in the East.

I look forward to all of you with pleasure.

Sincerely—Georgia O'Keeffe

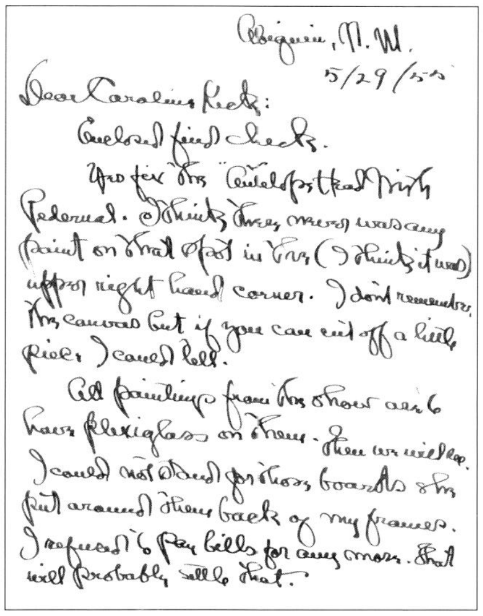
Abiquiu, N.M.
5/29/55

Dear Caroline Keck:

Enclosed find check.

As for the "[illegible] with Pedernal." I think there never was any paint on that spot in the (I think it was) upper right hand corner. I don't remember the canvas but if you can cut off a little piece I could tell.

All paintings from the show are to have plexiglass on them. Then we will see. I could not stand for those boards to be put around the back of my frames. I refused to pay bills for any more. That will probably settle that.

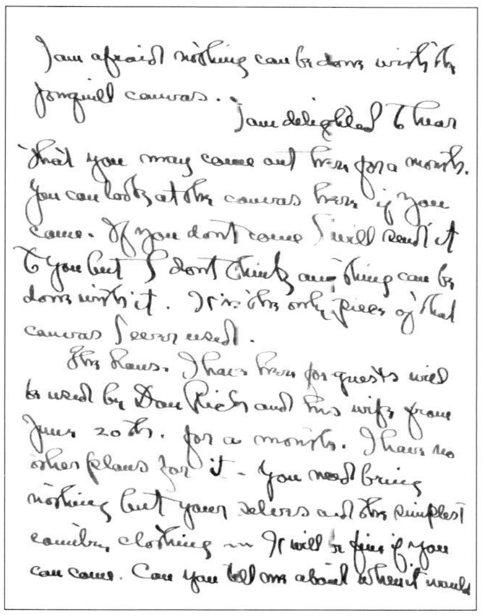
I am afraid nothing can be done with the jonquil canvas.

I am delighted to hear that you may come out here for a month. You can look at the canvas here if you come. If you don't come I will send it to you but I don't think anything can be done with it. It is the only piece of that canvas I ever used.

The house I have here for guests will be used by Dan Rich and his wife from June 20th. for a month. I have no other place for it. You need bring nothing but your colors and the simplest country clothing — It will be fine if you can come. Can you tell me about when it would

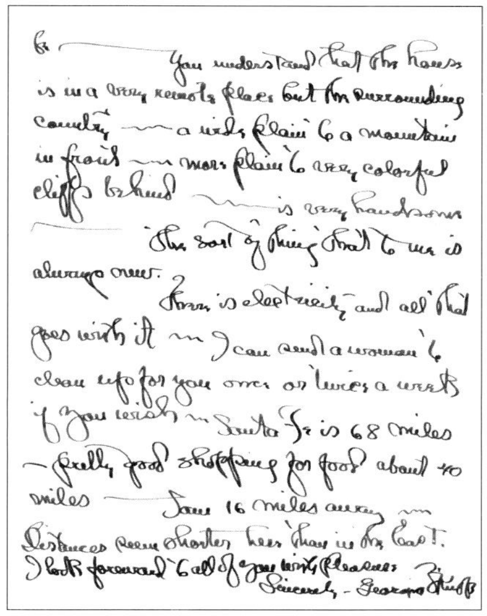
be —

You understand that the house is in a very remote place but the surrounding country — a wide plain to a mountain in front — more plain to very colorful cliffs behind — is very handsome — the sort of thing that to me is always new.

There is electricity and all that goes with it — I can send a woman to clean up for you once or twice a week if you wish — Santa Fe is 68 miles — pretty good shopping for food about 40 miles — I am 16 miles away — Distances seem shorter here than in the East.

I look forward to all of you with pleasure —

Sincerely — Georgia O'Keeffe

Letter from Georgia O'Keeffe to Caroline Keck, May 29, 1955. Collection of The Georgia O'Keeffe Foundation, Abiquiu, New Mexico.

September 12th, 1955

Dear Miss O'Keeffe:

I sent the "Skull with Pedernal" back to the Gallery last week, nicely wrapped too! I did much more than I planned on it but the painting bothered me. The frame pressed in too much. So, anyhow, I finally had another one of those solid structures made to order out of celotex and mounted the lined painting on it, and then put tiny washers inside the screw-holes of the metal frame and ended up fairly well pleased with the whole. It looked nice and no one would ever know it had the celotex mount, which fortunately, will keep the corners from drawing and buckling.

I'm feeling my age badly. Can't see without glasses, ache in the joints, etc. All probably because I never did get away for a break and none of us can keep on in the saltmines forever....

Sincerely,

Mrs. Sheldon Keck

Abiquiu, N.M.
9/18/55

Dear Caroline Keck:

. . . . I am sorry you are so tired. Why don't you fly out here for a week or two with me. If you don't do that call Ida P. Rolf MA 7-0713 and tell her you are a friend of mine and ask her if she will come to you and work on you.[11] I assure you she will make your life much easier. It is $15.00 an hour but it is worth it. Just take my word for it . . . . For your eyes call Clara Hackett . . . Now don't laugh at my suggestion—I am years ahead of you and I know. You just try.

G O'K

1956–1959

When her 1950 show ended at An American Place (barely noticed by the critics), O'Keeffe closed Stieglitz's gallery, leaving her past with him behind. In the hope of finding new ideas for her painting, she decided to travel. Interested for many years in the Hispanic culture, she went first to Mexico. She was sixty-six years old when she visited Europe—preferring Spain to France. A trip to Peru followed, where she fell in love with the "violent" colors there, making many sketches that she developed later. In the spring of 1959 she went on a three-and-a-half-month tour around the world. What she saw in China and Japan had a direct effect on her future abstraction, which became more severe—even calligraphic (as in *Winter Road I* of 1963).[12] During this period she also oversaw several exhibitions of her work, mainly at The Downtown Gallery.

The Keck family visited Ghost Ranch in the summer of 1956. Although no thank-you notes survive, it was apparently a very happy time for all concerned. O'Keeffe, who is too often—and wrongly—thought of as antisocial and austere, especially enjoyed the Kecks' two young sons. The boys responded warmly to her, as subsequent letters reveal. Still, she liked her own company. Solitude, however, was not easy to attain, as she sometimes complained to Keck.

Abiquiu, N.M.
3/9/56

Dear Caroline Keck:

Of course I want all of you to come but my plans have not really been definite till now.

June here is not quite as good as later. We have at that time a tiny little biting creature—black and very small while the sun is out, with the sunset it vanishes. It is with us till about July 10th. I don't mind it much but children might if their skins are not tough.

Also I am going to Peru on March 19 or 20th for three months if all goes well. So I would not be home till the middle of June. I think you will find middle August to middle September better anyway. About Aug. 20 the days begin to be cooler. It is a very fine time.

.... I would love to have the spray outfit if you would help me start with it but I wish to pay for it myself and to have no words about it.

.... The house is furnished for living as I live in it—comfortable, easy to keep. You might each bring a searchlight as we have snakes and I never go out at night without a searchlight even tho there is electricity—sweaters—and that is about all. I look forward to your coming very much.

Sincerely,

Georgia O'Keeffe

You will want to drive about and walk about to see the country, so don't plan to work on anything.

April 30th, 1957

Dear Georgia:

.... Your customer [name deleted] ... is a real louse. Thanks to your photograph, which I herewith return since the insurance company did as you suggested and purchased another somewhat darker print, we could prove beyond doubt that the "damage" he claimed was not any change whatsoever in the painting. It is that little brushstroke in the upper left hand corner, actually it runs along a slightly ridged canvas thread so that it becomes more noticeable in a raking light. There is no question at all but what it is your intent and has always existed.

.... I have a firm intention of asking insurance companies for $10,000 (if they give me $5,000 I will be happy) towards the expenses involved in our proposed seminar on "Conservation of Paintings" which we hope to hold at the Brooklyn Museum in the fall of 1958. For one week we want to give lectures and demonstrations on two levels, one for our colleagues and one for museum personnel and collectors, to show all that is known today of the very best methods for preserving and caring for paintings. We figure on inviting three top people from Europe and 5 from the States, with guest lectures on special subjects such as how to photograph condition, what kind of packing cases work best, etc. and also set up a travelling show to send around the country on why and how paintings deteriorate and the best way to preserve them. Believe it or not museum people need this terribly. All the millionaires we know will give money for purchases but preservation doesn't seem showy enough to interest their purses. But I die hard. Much meaner than Shel, as you noted!

Affectionately,

April 8th, 1958

Dear Georgia:

Herewith list regarding paintings we discussed for your reference:

Near Abiquiu, damage due to pressure from hand within hand hole; removed surface film and replaced with fresh varnish,* *no charge*

Skull with Pink Rose, protruberance due to screw-eye, fingermarks and surface dirt. Set down bump (NOT completely gone) removed varnish surface, will resurface, replace removed former inpainting and seal reverse with sheet foil *$60.00*

Horseshoe and Feather, acute cracking due to pressure against inner rim of stretcher strip. Line and then mount solid surface *$150.00*

Orange Plain (for Mr. Slick!) removed two drips of white paint, will fill and touch in tiny digs, will do best possible on nasty center inpainting, resurface (insurance job will report to Mrs. H., with estimate) *$75.00*

When the one with bloom comes over that will be no charge too so forget it.

. . . . I hate to have you pay for everything and it isn't just because I feel beholden to you—money couldn't ever represent our wonderful heaven in Abiquiu—but you are always so exact about responsibilities, and I love your paintings too and always want them in good condition.

. . . . Will do my damnest on the Orange, but HOW I dread retouching your surfaces, seems like a sacrilege.

Affectionately,

* Possibly *Purple Hills* (formerly titled *Purple Hills Near Abiquiu*, 1935), *catalogue raisonné*, 870.

Abiquiu, N.M.
5/19/58

Dear Caroline:

Where are you? . . . . I want also to say that I don't want you slipping by and not charging me for things that you ought to charge me for. I see some items not charged for in this letter.[13]

At the moment I have 3 pictures I would like to send you for doctoring if I may, a small one that water dripped on the back of. It isn't much of a painting and if it is very difficult I will just throw it away.*

The tree with the tear in it—that [is] Lake George.†

The "From the Plains"—4 ft. by 6 ft.—30 x 36.‡ It is rubbed but can be spotted and I would like to have it varnished.

May I send them to you now or shall we wait till fall.

Spring green is turning to summer green, and as usual I think it's all very fine.

Best thoughts to all of you.

Sincerely,

Georgia O'Keeffe

* Kronkright thinks this may be *Misti Again—A Memory* (1957), *catalogue raisonné*, 1321, because it is one of three paintings known to have been treated by Keck during the second half of 1958.

† Kronkright identifies this as *Winter Tree III* (1953), *catalogue raisonné*, 1267.

‡ *From the Plains* (1952/1954), *catalogue raisonné*, 1262.

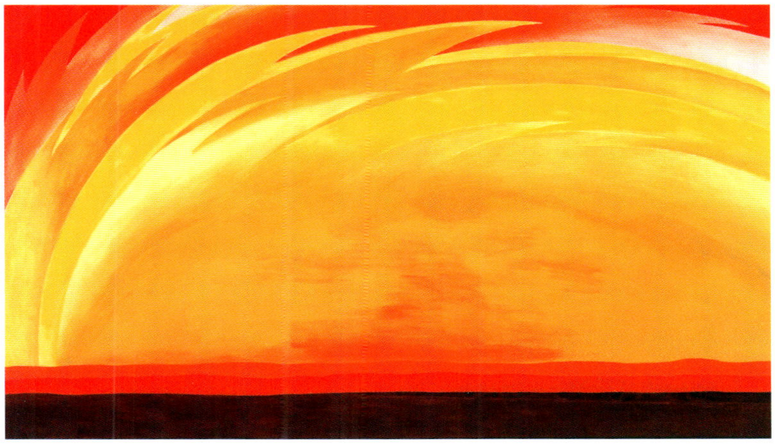

From the Plains, 1952/1954. oil on canvas, 47 11/16" x 83 5/8". Collection of The McNay Art Museum, San Antonio, Texas. Gift of the Estate of Tom Slick. 1973.22.

20% is understanding the theories behind this

May 23rd, 1958

Dear Georgia:

Sheldon is going fishing in Canada, but I am right here in the Salt Mine, send on whatever you want to. I will cherish it properly.

Have just finished working on "Small Black Iris" (its owner broke the glass, scratched and dented it—all repaired) and "Ram's head with white Hollyhock and Little Hills",† which was FILTHY. I am so pleased about it, a note on the reverse said it had been sprayed with PBM in 1948 by Keck, so I washed off the varnish neatly with straight petroleum benzine, and all the dirt and staining came away—the painting was just as fresh and crisp as when you finished it. Resprayed it and also replaced the cardboard as that was crumbling. Soaked off all the labels nicely and remounted them on the fresh cardboard.*

Said Larry Keck, when he saw that one "Oh, Georgia did that, there are the little hills . . . but that skeleton wasn't out at the Ranch?" I can't recall whether it was or not, but La is positive. He mooned over it for a bit and then wandered off up stairs to examine anew his own loot of skeletons and rocks from Abiquiu. What long and lovely ramifications that heavenly trip had for all of us.

. . . . There will be trouble with [name deleted] on the big Orange Plain‡ that was sold, he claims they never repainted anything. That is an impossible thing to argue about because we can't prove anything or where it happened. He was firm about it in a letter to me. Said they would pay charges for repair of digs and removal of white paint . . . so I will divide cost and not fret. I think it looked fair when it left here. I am finishing the little Horse Shoe with Feathers§ and will send it back Monday to Mrs. H[alpert]. I am really pleased the way the methacrylate varnish works, it catches all dirt and yellowing and comes off so simply your surface is uneffected [sic] *by it. I dislike to have your paintings get dirt into their surfaces, spoils them. This works nicely, thank God . . . . Love to you.*

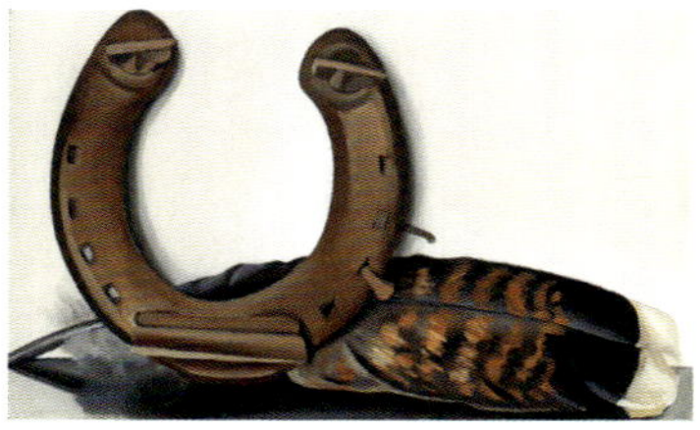

Horseshoe with Feather No. 1, 1935, oil on canvas, 8 1/2" x 13 1/2". Collection of The Georgia O'Keeffe Foundation, Abiquiu, New Mexico. Photograph: Malcolm Varon. © The Georgia O'Keeffe Foundation

* Kronkright says this is almost certainly *Black Iris* (1936), *catalogue raisonné*, 883.
† *Ram's Head, White Hollyhock—Hills* (1935), *catalogue raisonné*, 852. Note the slight title change.
‡ *From the Plains* (1952/1954), *catalogue raisonné*, 1262.
§ *Horseshoe with Feather No. 1* (1935), *catalogue raisonné*, 857.

Abiquiu, N.M.
7/1/58

Dear Caroline:

. . . . I would like to ask you a question. If I paint on pieces of this canvas that I have prepared myself—about 16 x 20 couldn't I have it mounted on some sort of board after I have the painting on the canvas? The canvas has a good tooth that I imagine could be mounted. It also is fairly stiff and flat when cut.

I would like your honorable opinion. I wanted to carry it in pieces so I could work on a trip.[14]

. . . . Best thoughts to all of you always.

Sincerely,

Georgia O'Keeffe

August 16th, 1958

Dear Georgia:

The crate with two paintings and the parcel post package arrived safe and sound. We are both mad about the "Cross", here we are broke as all hell with the costs of our new home and its recalcitrant plumbing to mention only one sad phase, and Shel said: "Gee, ask Georgia if that one is for sale and if we could ever try to buy it on time!" What a beauty, it is, and I don't think we ever saw it before.*

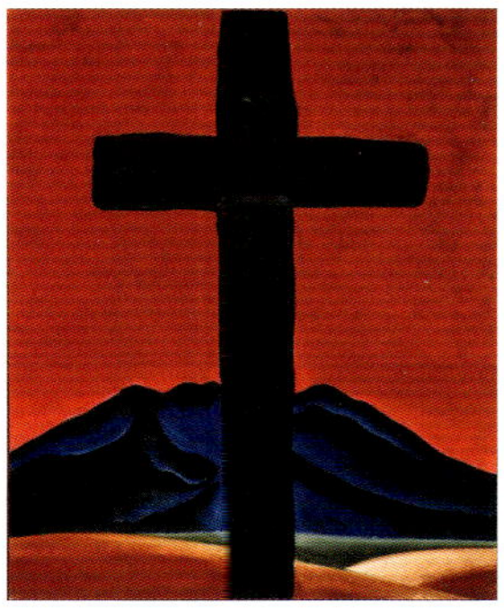

Cross with Red Sky, 1929. oil on canvas, 40" x 32". Collection of Gerald and Kathleen Peters, Santa Fe, New Mexico. Courtesy of Gerald Peters Gallery, Santa Fe, New Mexico.

This was a very unsatisfactory return, we have worked like blazes and gotten our part of the proposed Rockefeller Foundation conference on Conservation—what can be done to spread more understanding and better practices—done, but nobody else seems to have and we feel sort of down. We plan to go back to our vast shack next week, settle odds and ends there and bring everyone, including the cats and Larry home with us right after Labor Day. We will take careful condition photographs of the damages and forward them to you with complete reports for the insurance collection. Can you also collect on the tear to the "Tree"† and the water damage on the little one? The "Tree" should be lined, as I feel should the "Cross" too, but it depends on what the insurance people will pay on costs. The little one,‡ for best preservation should be lined and then mounted, I should say.

Boy, is that "Cross" ever handsome! I am looking at it right now and admiring. You did something fabulous with the black handling of the cross itself. What a relief you are after this modern crap we have around the studio, slop-slop paintings, you know, no craftsmanship and little feeling for what they slap together to make their "creation". . . .

I am so tired I ache. I do wish other people besides us would work at things and finish what they agree to do, but so many say "yes" and then never undertake a job because it involves too much effort. . . .

Our love to Betty and Flora and to the dogs and to the marvelous country-side, its stones and skies, just think[ing] about Abiquiu is restful. Don't stop painting, you are a joy.

Affectionately,

* *Cross with Red Sky* (1929), *catalogue raisonné*, 669.
† *Possibly Winter Tree III* (1953), *catalogue raisonné*, 1267.
‡ It is unclear what "the little one" is.

September 25th, 1958

Dear Georgia:

How wonderful to hear your voice, it brought New Mexico right into this room.[15]

. . . . [Sheldon] said I could at least have found out how much the "Red Sky with Cross" is, he hates to let it out of his grasp. I love it too, but as you once pointed out, I am so much meaner than he is. I look at our bills which come well up in the thousands at this time of year and I look at the receipts and agree there is a good bit owing—but I haven't got it and I still have to pay these gd bills. I do feel money is unimportant and only of use because it brings you things and experiences you enjoy but the stuff is so very necessary. Just for Shel's peace of mind, please, what is the price on the "Cross"? I would make it high myself, it is one of your bestest paintings.

The Winter Tree will cost $25.00 less since to my vast surprise it is on a special order stretcher now. How come? Absolutely nothing wrong with the stretcher and we used it again. Came out nicely . . . We are always trying for systems which make existence safer and easier for the painting. I have been upset about mounting ever since that nice job got damaged by some dope putting screw-eyes through the reverse. What upsets me is, that when such a stupid accident happens, it is so very hard to repair it unless you do the whole job over again—which is hard on the painting and also expensive. That it shouldn't happen has nothing to do with the fact that it CAN happen and must be foreseen.

What an excellent canvas the "Cross" is on. Much better than the one you used on the Tree, although as other paintings go, even that is very superior . . .

Affectionately,

Abiquiu, N.M.
10/16/58

Dear Caroline:

. . . . If you enjoy the Cross why don't you just keep it for a month or two—hang it up if you wish. I will just put it in my storage room if it is back here.

The fall days are wonderful here—I am at the ranch . . . I work hard I think but so little comes of it—I have been stretching canvas etc. Had a man to help me and he was pretty good but he has a bad cold so I said we would wait till he recovers—the colds they have here this year are very bad so I try not to get it.

On Monday I drove over the Santa de Christo Mountains almost to Las Vegas—the autumn color was wonderful—but it is a hard drive.

The summer has passed—I've been here most of the time and haven't had a single snake—maybe they don't like Presbyterians.[16]

My best to all of you,

G

October 3rd, 1959

Dear Georgia:

.... URGENT: –please check the tube of brown paint you used in RED 1958, 30x26, the one that had the "blotches". That tube is no good. Either it is badly ground or the medium is bad. The "blotches" I got rid of, they were due to uneven absorption of the paint—at first I thought it might be due to the canvas but under the microscope I could see the medium was gone from these areas, leaving them dry and causing the light to be diffusely broken. I replaced medium with poly butyl methacrylate and the tone returned to normal. After this had worked, I sprayed the surface. But what I cannot fix are the areas of drying crackle which have developed unevenly in the brown, not even related to your brush strokes especially, but obviously due to the amount of medium in the pigment. PLEASE do not use this color again. Maybe an other tube would be all right, but substitute something else for it if you can.*

.... Affectionately, in haste,

* *Red* (1958), *catalogue raisonné*, Appendix II, 95. This work is listed as having been destroyed.

Abiquiu, N.M.
12/7/59

Dear Caroline:

I have thought many letters to you but they don't seem to get written. I was at the [Ghost] ranch till a week ago. It was absurd the way I always hate to leave there, even if I only go up for the day[17] . . . As I look over the list of what you have done to paintings for me, I wonder if that painting "Red 1958" and no. 592641 is painted on a prepared canvas that I bought. I wish I could see it but I will wait till I go East or am having something else sent out here. It sounds in a very bad state.* I think I over painted it too and that is always bad . . . "Pedernal–From the Ranch" I had taken from the stretcher to throw it away but seem to have left it in the closet instead of burning it. When I found it I took it out and stretched it again. My sheepherder stretched it for me. I probably should have thrown it away.†

. . . . I would like to ask you about the large painting that hung over the fireplace in the large room at the ranch—mostly light blue and a little grey.‡ It is painted on absorbed coarse canvas.

. . . . I will be having a show at Worchester next fall and will probably want to send that painting, but aside from that I enjoy having it on the wall here and I don't usually enjoy keeping myself on the wall for very long. I rather think it should be relined. It has one of those circular cracked places that came from a good bump also. The canvas must have had the bump before I painted it. I don't remember.

. . . . With your experiences, will you tell me do you find that cobalt blue almost always cracks? It is such a beautiful color but I have such bad luck with it. Enough of this miserable business.

I hope that you and your family are all well and enjoying life.

My very best to all of you.

Sincerely,

Georgia O'Keeffe

* This work was later destroyed.

† Kronkright says this is either *Pedernal—From the Ranch I* (1956), *catalogue raisonné*, 1294, or *Pedernal—From the Ranch II* (1958), *catalogue raisonné*, 1334.

‡ The "large painting" is *Spring* (1948), *catalogue raisonné*, 1163.

1960–1965

O'Keeffe was given to writing Keck when the spirit moved her—mostly when she needed advice about her homemade primings and repairs, or when she saw that a painting suddenly needed professional attention. She professed not to care much about what she called "the approbation of the Art world," but in 1960 she helped Daniel Catton Rich organize a retrospective at the Worchester Art Museum, *Georgia O'Keeffe: Forty Years of Her Art*. Rich liked to say that it was easy to work with Georgia as long as you did things her way. And all museums, even the Metropolitan Museum of Art, had to learn never to mess with Georgia O'Keeffe (see O'Keeffe to Keck, January 22, 1964).

The artist continued to pack her own canvases for travel. She tried her best to prevent the frequent treacheries of cobalt blue, ultramarine, and Mars green. She also experimented with the spray gun after receiving apprehensive directions from Keck. In 1963 Doris Bry became O'Keeffe's official agent, taking over business arrangements for exhibitions and sales and, later, the technical communications with Keck about conservation.

Abiquiu, N.M.
1/25/60

Dear Caroline:

Those two paintings are in the box and will go to you tomorrow. I will get into the truck with these and go as far as Santa Fe. From there on they go alone. I will not remark on their defects, but am very curious to see if the green one comes out even where it has dried in. If it doesn't we might as well throw it away.

My best to you always and my greetings to your family.

Sincerely,

Georgia O'Keeffe

April 11th, 1960

Dear Georgia:

You haven't been as neglected as it seems! Both the paintings present serious problems. On the green one, we are now waiting to discuss what has happened with Bob Feller, of the Mellon Institute, who is due to visit us in about ten days. Did you use zinc white in it? The damage exists BENEATH your paint film, it is in the under layer or in the priming layer. Tests show that it can be lessened optically and may MAY possibly disappear with a lining, until we are more sure as to what the cause is we decline to state anything definitely.*

On the big one,† you know that there are two strong marks in the canvas due to thread irregularities! These will always be there. Also it will still react to changes in humidity even after it is lined, although to a much smaller degree. I hate to encourage you to line this, so expensive. It would cost $800 to do the job correctly and put the lined painting on a new expansion bolt stretcher. Do you want to spend that much? I worry about this because I cannot feel it is fully justified since it will leave the painting with the same thread marks it now has, less waves, but still some under damp conditions and be a great deal heavier and firmer . . . Will do the work if you want it done, naturally, but am hesitant to urge it.

May we make further tests with the green one? If you can work out a system of returning the original appearance it will cost you $350. On all of these I now prefer to use the expansion bolt, no key stretcher, saves wear and tear and is worth the expense in my eyes.

. . . . Every now and again I think of the "White Place" and other lovely wonders of your world. How marvelous that we had the opportunity to have known them.

Affectionately,

* *Ladder to the Moon* (1958), *catalogue raisonné*, 1335.

† The "big one" again is *Spring* (1948), *catalogue raisonné*, 1163.

June 29th, 1960

Dear Georgia:

. . . There is no charge for the work on "The Ladder". First painting of yours I was ever unable to preserve, made me ill. The trouble is definitely in the priming layer. The spotty situation is still very very faintly visible if you hunt for it, but the real headache is that the paint surface tends to flake off at the drop of a hat, and I can neither rebond it nor even infuse the fabric properly. Worked over it until I gave up in despair.

. . . . The big one was a tough job but should be fine, it may expand with extreme changes in humidity but you can enlarge the frame by inserting the end of a nailset into the bolt holes and turning them as indicated. If you dislike the metal stripping take it off, I put it on for safety in shipment to protect the edges. Had a special lining stretcher built for the lining fabric and the lined painting is on our latest love of a stretcher with no keys just the expansion bolt corners.

. . . . I think you are impossible to inpaint, but then I always have thought so, it never looks like your work, the surface shows the difference between your personal use of a brush and color and someone elses.[18] *That is one of the reasons I find it criminal to damage the surface of your paintings. There are artist's* [sic] *where this is not serious since others can compensate for their work with ease, but on your paintings everything not by you shows like a sore thumb. I dislike having your paintings travel but realize you must let them do so occasionally . . . .*

Affectionately,

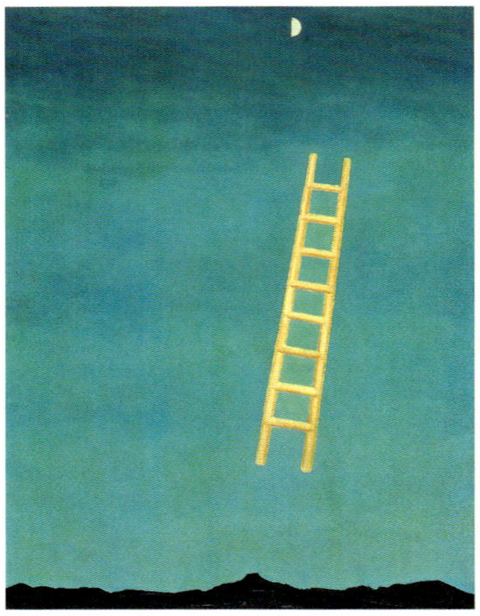

Ladder to the Moon, 1958. oil on canvas, 40" x 30". Collection of Emily Fisher Landau, New York (Amart Investments LLC). FL 197. Photograph: Malcolm Varon.

Abiquiu, N.M.
8/10/60

Dear Caroline Keck:

I have thought of you and wished for you many times.

.... Dan Rich and wife and daughter were here for two weeks about a show I will have in Worcester Oct. 3rd opening. After they left I had to pack the paintings with the help of my sheepherder. I can't spell as you have probably noticed. When it came to packing I took three canvases off stretchers. Under two I put cardboard as I was sure there would be dents if I didn't.

.... Painting seems to get harder and harder. I hope you will see my show in Worcester. I do not intend to have another restrospective show.[19] It is too hard .... I am enclosing check for that Ladder to the Moon that you sent a bill for and I understand almost died over. This at least will pay for the stretcher.

.... My best thoughts to your family, and you too.

Sincerely,

Georgia O'Keeffe

Abiquiu, N.M.
8/19/60

Dear Caroline Keck:

I have been taking a slight stretcher mark out of a canvas today as we experiment. I am doing it according to your little book[20] and I am pleased to say I think it is going to be alright. I have a big canvas with a dent in it and thought I would try the small one first. I am very pleased with it at the moment. If it isn't good in the morning I'll tell you.

.... I have one other canvas that is a song of horror that I want to send to Halpert because of that Friedman "Precesionist" show.[21] It is good and slopy and painted over a line or two. Some of it was painted last fall, some of it now.* For the color to be as it was painted it must be varnished. How old must it be before you spray that varnish, or whatever you call it on it? It is a funny painting for me maybe.[22]

Best to you always.

Sincerely,

Georgia O'Keeffe

I've been having a miserable time with crooked stretchers.

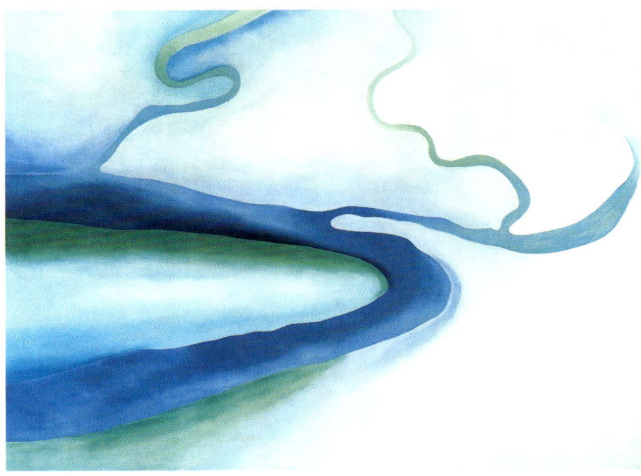

It was Blue and Green, 1960. oil on canvas mounted to board, 30" x 40". Collection of Whitney Museum of American Art, New York. Bequest of Lawrence H. Bloedel. 77.1.37. Photograph: Steven Sloman.

* *It was Blue and Green* (1960), *catalogue raisonné*, 1444.

for the Fellowships to support the students

September 5th, 1960

Dear Georgia:

. . . . Send me anything you want to and I will do my best. Cannot guarantee in advance, but unless there is something untoward I can usually spray a thin film of protection over your paintings even before they are a year old, although it is always best to wait.

I myself do not care for that Stretcher man in Kansas although several people use him. Sloppy craftsman. Quite expensive but excellent are the stretchers I more or less invented with the brilliant and craftsmanlike skill of our Jim Lebron.[23] *These are expansion type stretchers . . . These are exact, neat and beautifully finished. If you want to try him ask for a price first and see if you feel like risking the cost . . . . Work that I can recommend. BUT costly.*

. . . . luf in haste,

November 3rd, 1960

Dear Georgia:

I spent yesterday at Worcester Museum and have examined the paintings which Doris [Bry] listed in her note, together with Edmond de Beaumont, in fact we examined everything in your show . . . .

He is a very careful conservator and utterly trustworthy. He says he would rather die than have to line one of your paintings! So would I, sometimes. Only death isn't that easy . . . . Georgia, what happened in the lower left blue area of ["It was Blue and Green"]? Did you go back to this after an interval and add tone? Don't like the change at all, and very earnestly hope it will lessen considerably with the spray. Blue sometimes does this, separates from white admixture with either one winning the surface.

Edmond will send you list of all he sprays. Both he and I want as little handling of your paintings as humanly possible. He will ship to me all those paintings so indicated by you . . . DON'T pay for these, damn it.

Affectionately,

December 29th, 1960

Dear Georgia:

.... On your spray gun. One problem is that you need either an exhaust fan to draw out fumes when you spray, or you will have to do it out of doors, fumes are both toxic and flammable. If you get an exhaust fan you need one with an explosion proof motor, this is a special type which has the spark part concealed or like the one we have, the motor part is in a separate chamber from where you spray. I wish you had seen ours so it would be clearer to you. I can have Fisher Scientific send you the solvents and the resin (synthetic) for you to make your own mixture. You dissolve the resin in the solvent to make a thick viscous, honey like substance, which you then dissolve further only as you use it. It is colorless naturally, and when you use it in the spray gun you take a very small amount of the thick mixture and dilute it with benzine and Xylene, the more benzine the duller it dries, the more Xylene, the shinier it dries. According to the amount of air you use as you spray it goes on almost dry or quite wet. It is simple enough after you get the knack, but you must experiment a bit until you catch on. I hesitate to send you the mixture until you have either had a spray booth put up or made arrangements to spray out of doors, the excess spray settles otherwise like very fine dry snow, coating whatever is nearby as it mounts up. The art of spraying a painted surface is quite like the art of spraying paint, just a matter of learning how to manipulate the gun mechanism. But remembering how hard it is to get work done in Abiquiu I am leary of making it sound too simple. Let me know if you want us to send you a drawing of a spray booth, we can easily. Or if you just want me to order the materials for the spray mixture itself....[24]

Best love to you and to Abiquiu

Abiquiu, N.M.
1/2/61

Dear Caroline:

.... I have had so many things to write you about, it is awful that I don't get to it. In answer to your letter this morning about spraying, I am going to spray outdoors. To get anything built would be only a dream. Our winter days are often warm and still when the sun shines and it shines most of the time. The sun is really warm.

The man who makes my frames here is very ingenious. He sprays frames for me so I count on his assistance. The spray gun and compressor are here, also the long cord. If you will send me the materials [to spray on], with directions about mixing them I will begin to try.

The man who helps me stretch canvas etc. has been drunk for 10 days, in jail for part of it. He does many little things for me if he ever gets back. The simple country life is about as complicated as any thing I know of. I had a cat with a hernia, the vet fixed it up. New Year my male chow killed it. It was a very violent performance, at the foot of our outdoor Xmas tree. The cat bit me in excitement. I finally ended it all by throwing one of the kitchen rugs over the battle. The dog, covered with the rug, dropped the almost dead cat. I ran with the cat and put it in the car, visitors were arriving—spoiled the evening. When I looked at the cat a few minutes later it was dead. It was awful, but in some odd way I think that dog thought that cat just had to be killed.

.... Please send the spray materials soon. I want to spray before frames are put on, and get the whole mess out from under my feet.

.... I haven't a big envelope to send this in and I'm not going to have till I go to town on Thursday. Part of the country life.

My best to you all, for 61 and always.

Georgia

Abiquiu, N.M.
4/27/61

Dear Caroline:

There is a man who saw the Black Cross with Red Sky* in Worcester and thinks he wants to buy it. Would you be willing to write him a note and let him see it at your convenience. If you don't want to just don't. I don't care much about selling it, but he says he wants that and the White Rose I have here,† and that he is coming out here to see the White Rose . . . .

* *Cross With Red Sky* (1929), *catalogue raisonné*, 669.

† Kronkright is reasonably certain that the "White Rose" referred to here is *Abstraction White Rose* (1927), *catalogue raisonné*, 599.

Abiquiu, N.M.
5/ /61

Dear Caroline:

.... **I hope that young man will at least amuse me a little. I am very bored with the idea of his coming. I like my own company and it is hard to find and harder to keep.**

.... **Greetings to Sheldon.**

Sincerely,

Georgia

Abiquiu, N.M.
6/4/62

Dear Caroline:

.... I want to ask you about that masonite Jim LeBrun has rigged up for me. I wonder if you know if it is pressed wood. Its surface is very dark and smooth. Could I prepare it with lead and a little zinc white. I think if I do that I must sand it a little ...

However, I am at the Ranch and I find it very pleasant. It is always home to me in a way that the Abiquiu house is not.

.... It has been summer here and now is cold like fall. I have had on my woolens and woolen trousers for a week. I would rather be hot than cold.

Every morning I am up early and out in the hills with the dogs before breakfast. It is one of my special pleasures here. Then in the late afternoon I go again. They are waiting at the door for me now.

Give my greetings to your family, and just don't get buried in the salt mines.

My best thoughts to you.

Sincerely,

Georgia O'Keeffe

May 30th, 1963

Very dear Georgia:

I enclose a copy of my letter to Mrs. Prosser.[25] I am deeply depressed by our failure with this painting.* It is a lovely lovely one and Mrs. Prosser is devoted to it, beyond question she cares and cherishes it—I have had at least 3 long distance calls about the painting and endless letters of concern. I am so sorry it had to happen to this painting and to her. We are sure the trouble is related to the white, my dear, not that the priming isn't slippery, it is but wherever you had pure pigment there was bond, wherever admixture with white, no bond, flaked at any pressure. Priming was not cracked, we couldn't penetrate from the reverse—not by any method and we tried all—had to set down superficially with gelatin which is a very pure solution and never one we consider lasting. Painting looked lovely but made both of us ill.

Shel did tests for you on the enclosed panel and I have typed up his suggestions, the white is not the right one but all we had to test with—we never had oil colors around since we use dry ones in various mediums and make them up ourselves.

.... Shel asks if by any chance you could be using a tube of white which is old?

I have left the Brooklyn Museum, yesterday was my last official day there. We leave for Byberry Cottage today to ready the house for the move... We can take care of paintings no bigger than 36"x40" at Byberry—size of our storage vault is planned to accommodate this dimension but not larger; we will have all our lab equipment beautifully located in real nice working space...

.... Best love to you—and our apologies for failure. The boys would amuse you, each "creates". Larry in black and white and Keckie, oddly enough, sculpture. Keckie's little daughter is a delightful child, happy, relaxed and independent as a hog on ice; she is also beautiful—even to others besides her Grandmother.

We plan to buy a big poodle!

Affectionately,

. . . . Suggestions: SK [Sheldon to O'Keeffe]

You could wash the masonite on honeycomb panels with (1) Ammonia–household, diluted 1-2 parts water, rinse off if you use the so-called "sudsy" kind. Normally, ammonia evaporates off. Do not use it to dilute, if you think you put on too much you can always wipe it off.

(2) If use sandpaper to break surface, suggest #0 or #1.

(3) Gelatin size made 1 part gelatine to 30 parts water, is best applied in one thin coat.

(4) White oil paint. If you use white lead it will turn yellowish in time. If you use white titanium or Zinc white, dilute with mineral thinner or turpentine. Equal parts white lead and titanium might work well, thinned with turpentine. If you apply more than one coat, keep them both thin.
Georgia: [Caroline Keck]

On Jim Lebrons Honeycomb panels, when you finish, could you apply lip over metal stripping screwed into the wooden collar of the honeycomb? This would tend to prevent chipping at edges and damage from handling. You can paint the metal if you wish but it does give excellent cushioning protection at a very delicate point of the paint. Be sure you get aluminum not steel and be sure it is straight not curved on the inner face of the lipover (the curved kind cuts into the panel and damages it). We usually put it over with a thin piece of cardboard of white blotter on the face of the painting to keep lipover a fraction away from the surface. CKK

* *Two Austrian Copper Roses I.I* (1957), *catalogue raisonné*, 1314.

Abiquiu, N.M.
6/6/63

Dear Caroline:

I have just written Mrs. Prosser. I have offered that she exchange the painting for something . . . of equal value, or that she keep the painting till a year from now. By then the flower will have bloomed again and I may paint something else of it that she would want in exchange, or I offer to refund her money and have her return the painting to me here now. I can't do more. However it seems that you should be paid for your headache. You should send me a bill, please.

. . . . I wonder what it is like to be a person who is not busy every minnet.

Dont kill yourself moving. I know it is a hard chore. These fitting things into new places is always so difficult.

Best to both of you.

Sincerely,

Georgia O'Keeffe

I[t] seems I ought to offer to go and help you move but it is far to go and I know I would only be in the way. It is odd to think of you as a grandmother!

Abiquiu, N.M.
7/30/63

Dear Caroline:

I guess I have done something bad. I have painted two paintings that I like on some canvas not my own. They are too large for glass—36x48* and 48x84.† Awful sizes I admit but they are things I have seen when flying and the world up there looks very big so my paintings got big.

It will be so easy to put holes in them must do something about it. All I can think of is to stretch another canvas under them or have them relined before I let them go anywhere. Will you please tell me if you have any other idea.

. . . . At the moment I enjoy them tho I suppose they are a bit odd. I'm starting on another later this week.

. . . . My best to both of you, all of you.

Sincerely, Georgia

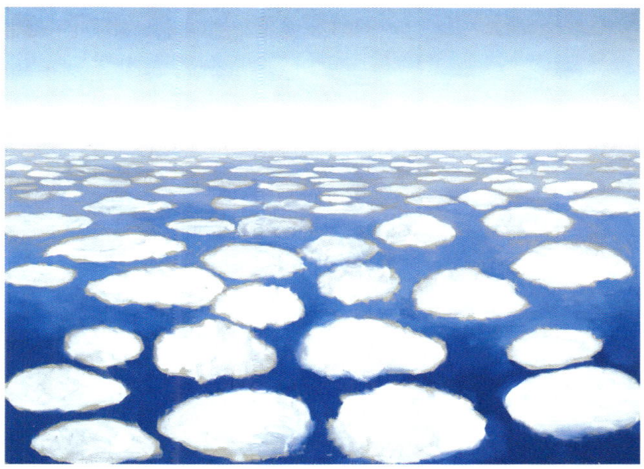

Above the Clouds I, 1962-63, oil on canvas, 36 1/8" x 48 1/4". Collection of Georgia O'Keeffe Museum, Santa Fe, New Mexico. Gift of The Burnett Foundation and The Georgia O'Keeffe Foundation. 1997.05.14. Photograph: Malcolm Varon.

* *Above the Clouds I* (formerly titled *Above Clouds I*) (1962-63), *catalogue raisonné*, 1474.

† *Sky Above Clouds II* (1963), *catalogue raisonné*, 1478.

Abiquiu, N.M.
12/6/63

Dear Caroline:

I am desperate with four little paintings—all under 12 inches—painted on a very delicate canvas prepared with only a glue size, about 1920 I think. I can hear you gasp for breath or maybe scream. But the canvas was lovely to paint on and I painted, I think, five paintings on it.

May I send one* to you because I think it should be fastened to a firm support—relined—and if doing one isn't too awful for you maybe you will do them all. I hope very much that they will fit into their frames when finished because I can not get frames as good now.[26]

.... I hope you enjoy your new place to live and work. Where I am is always wonderful to me.

.... My best to you and your husband. Does he still have his beard. I hope he has.[27]

Sincerely, Georgia O'Keeffe

* Kronkright points out that from Keck's notes we know that O'Keeffe sent *Apple Family—2* (1920), *catalogue raisonné*, 315. It is now at the Georgia O'Keeffe Museum, and it has been lined and installed.

Abiquiu, N.M.
1/14/64

Dear Caroline:

I was in N.Y. for three days last week and while there saw the Black painting of mine with the small white dot.* It is not flat. It is wrinkled in the corner, upper left. Could you line it and make it come out flat?[28]

.... My best to you always.

Sincerely,

Georgia

* *Black Abstraction* (1927), *catalogue raisonné*, 574.

Abiquiu, N.M.
1/22/64

Dear Caroline:

I have your letter of Jan. 18th. That Black Abstraction still belongs to me. It is only on loan till I give it to them [the Metropolitan Museum]. Next time I go to N.Y. I will go and look at it again. If I think something must be done for it I will just borrow it and carry it out of the museum myself and do as I please with it. If I do that could you line it. I think that is what must be done.

Abiquiu, N.M.
9/25/65

Dear Caroline:

A few days ago I came across your last years Xmas card with a note on it about that Red Flower painting.* Will you send me the painting here to Abiquiu so that I can see it. Then I can write that woman who had it and send it to her, tho I assume she is getting on very well without it. She took another in place of it.

How are you?

. . . . Greetings to Sheldon.

Sincerely,

Georgia O'Keeffe

* *Two Austrian Copper Roses III* (1957), *catalogue raisonné*, 1314.

October 16th, 1965

Dear Georgia:

I shipped your "COPPER ROSES" to you.

.... I am glad that in the time since I wrote you last Christmas and the receipt of your letter asking for the painting my discomfort over the painting proved justified. There is a TINY chip loss in the center, in a red area, the white priming shows as you will note. No explanation for this, it is in an untreated area and exactly the same kind of minute flaking we had peppered over the surface when it came to us. There appears to be no true bond between the priming and the paint layer. Since the priming is complete we cannot seal the paint by a penetrating adhesive and surface reattachment can only be made after an area lifts—so ... This is the only loss since I treated it three years ago, it is lined, and then the lined fabric mounted on a solid support. Damned situation, but we have had this once or twice before with slippery primings. I was fascinated to discover the minute missing flake of red. And I still don't know how to prevent this.

.... I understand you are painting bigger and bigger canvasses [sic]. *PFUI, you know how those upset me. So hard to protect ... Your "Skunk Cabbages"* which we inpainted half sections on, hangs at the end of the upper hall—very handsome—and has moved but just a hairs breadth in 20 years, 19 to be exact since Shel inpainted. We can see the separation with lenses but to the eye it is still solid color where he retouched the white cracks. No cleavage, no lifting, just slow and slight continued movement of those Mars greens and violets. Otherwise, my dear, as always you remain the top quality technician among artists. Also my pride.*

.... We are fine, getting older but still full of beans. I have a book coming out in December telling people in small museums and historic houses how to take care of paintings, practical advice. They need it.

.... The Museum of Modern Art is the only New York institution I still work for officially—10 to 15 days a year, their headache jobs and problems. All our pupils are doing excellently and busy as bees. Nice group of devoted and skillful people, we are happy about them. Only wish there were three times as many

.... luf and kisses, and throw a wink to the WHITE PLACE ...

* *Skunk Cabbage* (1928), *catalogue raisonné*, 627. First mention of this painting was in Keck's letter of June 17, 1947. The canvas had developed traction crackle in the Mars green and Mars purple areas. O'Keeffe intended to destroy it, but at Keck's request she gave the painting to her for experimental purposes.

1966–1981

During the late sixties O'Keeffe continued to paint, exhibit, and travel. In 1966 she prepared for and attended another retrospective, *Georgia O'Keeffe: An Exhibition of the Work of the Artist from 1915-1966*, at the Amon Carter Museum in Fort Worth, Texas. She also traveled to England, Vienna (to see the Spanish Riding School horses perform), Mexico, Lake Powell, and New York. In 1970 she oversaw the installation of yet another retrospective of her work at the Whitney Museum of American Art.

Early in 1971 she was diagnosed with macular degeneration and her central eyesight vanished, although she retained peripheral vision for some years. (She was eighty-four.) Color became more dulled and lines increasingly blurred. She made her last unassisted oil painting in 1972—*The Beyond* (*catalogue raisonné*, 1581).[29]

She continued to travel, she received awards and honorary degrees, and she worked to compile three books with commentary: *Some Memories of Drawings*, with Doris Bry (1974); *Georgia O'Keeffe* (1976); and *Georgia O'Keeffe: A Portrait by Alfred Stieglitz* (1978). Her final letter to Keck, after a gap of seven years, is dated July 28, 1981. Agapita Judy Lopez (who became director of the Georgia O'Keeffe Foundation) typed the letter, but O'Keeffe signed it herself.

Abiquiu, N.M.
1/22/66

Dear Caroline:

Your last letter was so full of travel I wondered if you would ever be home again. I am at home by myself and like it.

. . . . I have a painting that is all white with one very good line of raw umber on it.* I think it must be varnished to keep the white clean . . . May I send it to you to varnish, spray, call it what you will? The white may need a little cleaning.

. . . . You would laugh to see this big thing I painted last summer and you would have shuddered to see it being rolled up on the garage floor with a snow storm raging outside and the door open.†

. . . . Thanks for sending me the Red Austrian Copper Rose painting. It isn't really very good you know. I thought I would not disturb the lady who has settled down to live with another painting in place of it. It is on my rocks in the storeroom. You should have billed me for the box . . . .

Sincerely,

Georgia O'Keeffe

* *Winter Road I* (1963), *catalogue raisonné*, 1477.
† *Sky Above Clouds IV* (1965), *catalogue raisonné*, 1498.

October 3rd, 1967

Dear Georgia:

. . . . In 1964, the New York State Historical Association in conjunction with the State University began a graduate program in practical Museum training, administration and curatorial education. We have lectured briefly to the students each year. About 18 months ago, we were invited to draft a proposal for a special program in art conservation training, the way we believe it should be undertaken. By a fascinating fluke the idea for this was combined with a proposal for research work in ecology, and the biologists involved in this idea found that they and we shared many mutual concerns: basically both of us deal with behavior of the same materials, ours is inanimate and theirs animate states. It now promises to produce a remarkable joint program; the funds for buildings, equipment, staff and maintenance (and these are expensive!) are available from the Clark interest and the State, and plan is moving ahead.

We will be allowed to teach as we wish to, 80% of our program involves learning to perform the work of care, the other 20% is understanding the theories behind this. We will accept ten pupils a year. Teach them for two full years (no summer break) and then require an additional year of internship under a professional before we give them a certificate of competence. With the number of new museums mushrooming up all over, our graduates should fill a very urgent need. They will know how to use their hands and not just talk about what should be done, damn it.

As far as we have been informed funds are available for establishing the set-up but money will be needed for the Fellowships to support the students. The present figure is $6,000, a pupil, $3,000 annually for each. Are you completely tied-up with Fisk and your other endowments or would you be interested in a tax-deduction gift for a Conservation Fellowship for a student from the Southwestern USA? I have no idea whether you have tax problems or not but do recall the Fisk situation and so take the liberty of asking. Must admit that the idea of an O'Keeffe Fellowship for this program appeals to me strongly because it is so meaningful. Your paintings are altered, more than those of many other artists, when they are not maintained in their original state, and to keep them carefully requires respect and understanding on the part of people who presume to treat their damages. All forms of art will be exposed to hazards of travel and exhibition more and more—this is inevitable in our society—proper care must be taught.

You know me well enough to recognize that asking for funds is not to my liking. But I care so deeply and want so much to train while I still can, that I am willing to make this request. It may not appeal to you at all. If it should, I am told that the gifts should be made directly to the New York State Historical Association since as a teaching non-profit organization it is accorded full exemption by the Government revenue regulations.

This is an overlong letter and do forgive me if the notion does not fit your convenience. We have spent our whole lives taking care of paintings, trying to show why this is necessary and how it is best done. There are moments when I feel we have lived in vain, and then I get these glimmerings of hope. I can't help being excited.

Affectionately,

be exposed to hazards of travel and exhibition

Abiquiu, N.M.
4/12/68

Dear Caroline:

.... I had your letter last fall and should have answered it. You know Abiquiu is very poor and has so little place for any kind of entertainment for the young. They have to go about a mile up the road to find a large enough level spot to play baseball. Well, we are building a gymnasium and all my tax gift money went for that.[30] It is to be done through the church as we happen to have a very lively priest at the moment. He flies an airplane and rides a motorcycle. The liveliest thing we have had. Has the church—that means the whole village in a stir—and they like it.

.... Sincerely, best greetings to Sheldon. Does he still have his beard?

Georgia

Abiquiu, N.M.
7/1/68

Dear Caroline:

The first of July. Where do the days go to?

. . . . I have just had an odd experience—a girl came to see me who has come twice before.[31] This time she brought her work—creations—not paintings, not sculpture, but half painting half sculpture, that hangs on the wall as a thing. I thought quite beautiful. She brought seeds and beans, and very strong, wooden like seeds, butterflies, rocks, crystals, even a swallows bird nest. She has shown nothing, but when she does it seems to me it will be an event. Maybe I am getting odd living out here far away from what is being done but this seems to me something true. We will see. I write this because of your despondent feeling. She was a surprise to me. More of a surprise than any one who has asked me to look at what they do.

. . . . Our gymnasium is going up into the air. I shudder a bit at the thought of what it may look like but it is going up and I hope they will enjoy it.

. . . . I think of you and your bearded man with pleasure.

Sincerely,

Georgia O'K.

Abiquiu, N.M.
9/18/68

Dear Caroline:

. . . . I understand how you feel about the idea of living longer but I think we must jump along and see what it is all about.[32] I am feeling so well that I doubt it will be easy for me to quit.

All the best to you.

Fondly,

Georgia

Greetings to Sheldon

Abiquiu, N.M.
9/25/68

Dear Caroline:

I have here a painting—about 12x10 inches that I must have painted when I was about 16. It is a portrait of my youngest sister.* It is varnished, probably with mastic varnish, is not very clean. May I send it to you to remove the varnish and give it a very thin new varnish? Can you do it now or would you rather do it later? While you have it could you have it photographed and send me the prints with the negative.

. . . . Do not give photographs of the painting to anyone but me if you can have them made.[33]

Hastily,

Georgia

* *Untitled (Claudia O'Keeffe)* (1907-8), *catalogue raisonné*, 32.

October 28th, 1968

Dear Georgia:

It just occurred to me that my theory on what you want done with that little portrait of your sister could be wrong. I figured you did NOT want it lined or altered physically aside from being cleaned, consolidated and repaired?*

Those spots appear to be material which has extruded from the paint; in some places they are spatters of gummy resin but most of the dark spots are places where some nasty crap has completely eaten away the paint and left a dark translucent residue. I have cleaned the surface as much as possible, removed the deposits, filled the little black voids and coated the entire surface with a synthetic stabilizer, poly vinyl acetate. I would like to infuse the fabric with wax resin—without adding any lining fabric, but the paint is so crumbly in spots, it needs all the help it can get. I would merely take the painting off the stretcher infuse and replace it on the same stretcher, signature (!) would still be exactly as visible as it is now, fabric would be saturated with wax.

Anyhow, then I thought we had better retouch the little fillings and revarnish, and that would be it.

Perfectly simple to line and place the lined portrait on a new little support—but I didn't think that you wanted it so physically altered?

Shel took one photo of state before treatment, will take others as necessary, have all negatives in an envelop for you. Fret not at all.

Love, in haste,

* *Untitled (Claudia O'Keeffe)* (1907-8), *catalogue raisonné*, 32. See letter of September 25, 1968.

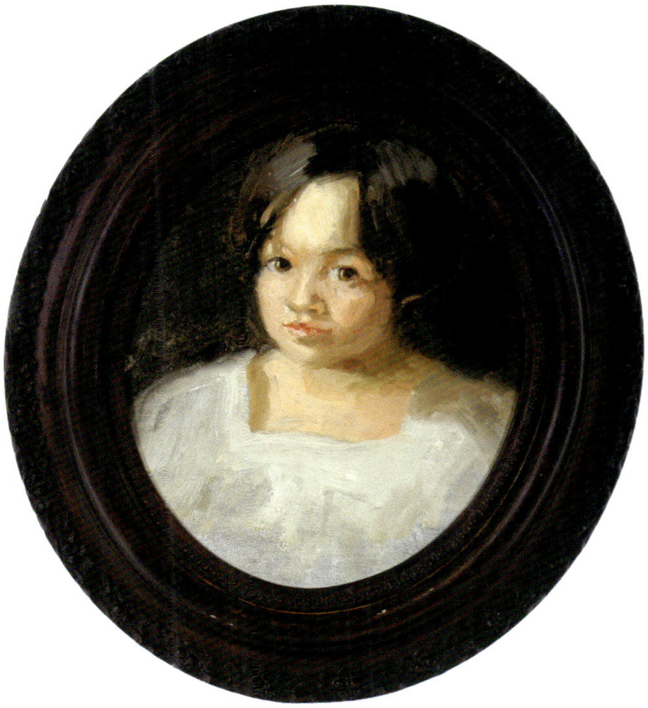

Untitled (Claudia O'Keeffe), 1907–8, oil on canvas, 12" x 10". Collection of Museum of Fine Arts, Museum of New Mexico, Santa Fe, Department of Cultural Affairs. Bequest of Claudia O'Keeffe, Museum of New Mexico Foundation, 1988. Photograph: Blair Clark

February 20th, 1969

Dear Georgia:

Your "Flagpole, Little House and Moonring" went back to you, as directed at Abiquiu, via REA collect, insured value $550, receipt # 43-12-11 Oneonta New York February 18th, 1969.

.... The surface is more glossy than usual. Unavoidable if we are to prevent the recurrence of dust load (which I removed and was considerable) since the canvas used has a non-absorbent type ground. All brushstrokes are clear, the protective film is kept at a minimum and the present reflectance will diminish within a few months in the atmosphere. The ultramarine had chalked, it is ok now. Frame held with four small screws into old nail holes for easy removal. I found this an interesting painting, shows directions which you expanded in later concepts sort of gathered here.

Affectionately,

quest. It may not appeal to you at all.

Abiquiu, N.M.
2/21/69

Dear Caroline:

I sent that painting off to you today.* It is an old one I was about to throw away but Dan Rich paid to keep it. I was tempted to use the vacuum cleaner on it but didn't. I know it is very dusty but it is also very rough. Kindly varnish it. I left frame barely attached to make packing easier.

All thats best to the two of you.

Sincerely, Georgia

Return it to me here. I could give some student a scholarship this year if you wish.[34]

* *Flagpole* (formerly titled *Flagpole—Little House & Moonring Lake George*) (1925), *catalogue raisonné*, 481.

March second, 1969

Dear Georgia:

. . . . You are kind to mention the Fellowship. I hesitate to ask you since by now we know more concerning amounts required and they are sizeable. Course is two full years. Estimates now figure $2,400 per year for a single student; $5,000 per year for a married student with offspring, making a total of $4,800 or $10,000 for the course respectively. That is a lot of money but it is also a hard study period. Please do not consider this unless it fits your financial picture. We are considering Foundation assistance for our students who cannot pay their way. There is no question but that I hope to have a student from the southwest part of the States, desperately needed for that section.

The general need is acute. Hardly a week goes by but what we are appealed to regarding some butchering of artifacts by a "well intended" ignoramous. Unfortunately so many of the paintings so dealt with are no longer returnable to their original state. I know we are old fashioned in our concepts but hope we never change. Small chance. People who presume to treat the creations of their betters require knowledge, ability and humility, and too few of them possess these qualities. Not every structure is preservable but, damn it, not every artist gives a hoot what happens to his painting once he has been paid for it. I realize I have a strong emotional reaction to your paintings, partly based on my appreciation of them and partly based on my respect for your integrity as an artist; when any painting created by you suffers a damage, the repair can never be fluffed off without negating the exactness of your concept. Of course this is not true for the vast majority of contemporary productions, but it should be. We still decline to treat a painting we feel incapable of preserving, and far too often neither owner, artist or museum for that matter, understand our viewpoint. A means for preservation may be discovered but right now we are unable to correct physical faults we cannot understand. We cannot claim knowledge we lack.

I feel my age and my inabilities more than you do but that is because you are creative and I only repair. If we can swing it, I want this school to get underway imbued with our beliefs and teaching what we know must be taught. Perhaps it can, at this point I truly do not know.[35]

Affectionately,

Abiquiu, N.M.
3/9/69

Dear Caroline:

.... Will you work on a 40x30?* I seem to have stretched the canvas too near the edge of the roll and it has cracked down the whole side. It looks to me as if lining it would be the best that can be done. I regret it because it is a pretty good painting and I have so few flower paintings left.

.... Also tell me if the money given for Fellowships to students for your work is tax deductible?

* Judging from later correspondence, this may be *The White Flower* (1932), *catalogue raisonné*, 816.

March 13th, 1969

Dear Georgia:

.... The money given for Fellowships is definitely tax exempt. I quote: "The Master of Arts program, Conservation of Historic and Artistic Objects, is part of the Cooperstown Graduate Programs of The State University of New York. The fellowship programs for the various parts of the Cooperstown Graduate Programs are administered under contract with the State University by the New York State Historical Association. The New York Historical Association was chartered in 1899 by the Board of Regents of the University of the State of New York as a non-profit educational institution. It has been declared a tax exempt organization under Section 501(c)(3) of the US Internal Revenue Code of 1954. Fellowship grants should be made to the New York State Historical Association for use in the Cooperstown Graduate Programs."[36]

.... Are you sending the frame with this painting? Remember, they are always a fraction larger after lining—the two canvas thicknesses plus expansion makes about 1/8" difference all around. If I have to keep it exactly the same size, it means I have to bend over a fraction of the painted surface which is not sound. The metal frames are tight, we have had rough times refitting them after a lining unless they have a bit of leeway. Some did, but not all.

Affectionately,

Abiquiu, N.M.
3/17/69

Dear Caroline:

.... Do what you think best. If I have to get a new frame it will probably be metal.[37] Just go ahead with treatment as you think best. I will make scholarship gift when I return late in April or early May. At the moment I haven't much more money in the bank ....

Sincerely,

Georgia

May 14, 1969

Dear Georgia:

.... I did my best with the WHITE FLOWER but the cracks are still visible. I think that canvas is rather odd, you didn't by any chance ADD a layer of priming to it on your own? Anyhow, all that travel is what did our painting in rather than any faults in your stretching, which I found absolutely sound when I removed painting from original stretcher. Frame offered no protection, every handling by idiots banged painting end over end against corners, naturally this produced the marked diagonal cracking. As for your handholds cut into the backing, the pressure of curled fingers inside these openings directly corresponded to the isolated crackle patterns on the face. Well, it is at least consolidated, but if you travel it again to any extent as often as in the past, the crackle will return to cupped form, plastic memory. I wish this painting could be given a nice home and allowed to rest easy.*

.... Affectionately,

* See O'Keeffe's letter of March 9, 1969.

Abiquiu, New Mexico
August 1, 1972

Dear Caroline:

. . . . It seems to me you are having a worse time than you did when you were in the other Salt Mines. You had better move back to Brooklyn. You must have had a fine smashing of glass after the flood. I wonder if anything came out of the boxes whole.

I'm at the Ranch. I wish you were here to tell me more about these dreadful things that have happened to you. You would appreciate the dreadful things I would say to you. But I'm not saying them.[38] You have troubles enough.

With all my best thoughts, Georgia

GO'K/vr

Abiquiu, New Mexico
December 27, 1972

Dear Caroline:

. . . . I would like to ask you a question. I have a large piece of dark masonite that I have the idea I would like to paint on to fit into a particular place.* It's about 10' long and 2' high. Will you tell me what you think best to prepare it with? I think you told me once a long time ago, but I can't find your letter. Of course, I could stretch a canvas but it's a hard shape to stretch and I would have to have Lebrun make the stretchers. Don't bother to write me a lot. Just tell me what you think best to prepare it with if I use the plastic—or must I stretch a canvas?

Best thoughts for the coming year as always.

Sincerely, Georgia O'Keeffe

GO'K:vfr

* Unknown. Nothing by this description is recorded in the *catalogue raisonné*.

December 29th, 1972

Dear Georgia:

On your 10' x 2' masonite panel, wash the surface with household ammonia and water thoroughly and wipe dry with a cloth. Then allow it another day or two to dry completely.

Are you planning to paint with plastics? Acrylic colors in water emulsion? If so then you should prime it with one or two coats of acrylic gesso (permanent pigments sells this) and allow at least a week or two before starting to paint on it.

If you plan to use oil paint, then brush on one or two coats of Titanium White in oil, or white Lead in oil and let it dry the one or two weeks before going ahead.

Keep the priming fairly thin and well brushed out naturally. The ammonia wash is vital to remove the excess oil from the masonite surface and get a firm bond for the priming.

The only catch with the use of masonite, well prepared, is the danger afterward of shock in clumsy handling. A careless dropping and the surface can shear off. After you finish your painting if you could plan to frame the masonite with a cushion of rubber inside the rabbet of the frame this provides a safety bumper, absorbs any shock except ghastly ones. OK?

Have been meaning to tell you for ages now and always forget, because it has become so much a part of our lives I suppose, the Skunk Cabbage of yours we inpainted for rip crackle in the Mars Green and Mars Violet back in 1946 has barely expanded crackle at all in almost 30 years now and we should complete the inpainting and return the painting to you. We did it to a half-way mark, you may remember, to test the activity of that cracking. It still has a postcard in your handwriting attached to its reverse saying it was sent to us for experimental treatment. I am sure any of your dealers would welcome the painting after we filled in the uninpainted areas of those two colors. Nothing else in the painting cracked at all. Let me know what you want done.*

We both came down with flu and had to cancel our tour inspecting internships—will do this in a month or so when we are fully recovered and breathing quietly!

Best love,

* This was *Skunk Cabbage* (1928), *catalogue raisonné*, 627. See letter of October 16, 1965. O'Keeffe decided to donate the painting to the Kecks "for experimental purposes."

October 9, 1974

Caroline Keck
Byberry Cottage
Cooperstown, New York 13326

Dear Caroline,

Your letter is always a pleasure even if you tell of all your troubles. I must tell a little of mine. I fell and dislocated my left shoulder. I went to the hospital screaming in an ambulance. The young man who took me down said the noise shattered all the lower windows of the hospital. I'm just telling you all this so you know the summer has been rather gay.[39]

. . . . Sitting up here at the Ghost Ranch is very pleasant. This young man who does my letters is a potter and as my eyes are not very good, I have been trying to learn to make a pot. The day I made the first pot that wasn't embarrassing to show was the day I fell down. I want to tell you I've made one pot I wouldn't be embarrassed to show you. I still have someone to help me bathe and dress; also as I don't sleep I'm a lot of trouble in the night.

Life does become more difficult as you become an ancient. I always enjoy your letters even when the salt mines are deep. I'm not in the mine at the present. But I call this sitting around more difficult than the mines. Let me as a real ancient suggest that you stop getting so tired . . . .

Sincerely,

Georgia

Abiquiu, New Mexico
July 28, 1981[40]

Mrs. Caroline Keck
Conservation of Historic and Artistic Works
Cooperstown Graduate Programs
Cooperstown, NY 13326

Dear Caroline:

. . . . You have my permission to do whatever you think best for the painting, The Skunk Cabbage, 1924, and to publish the system if it works.

Also, I am willing to donate the painting for sale to the Foundation of the American Institute for Conservation [FAIC] to establish the fellowships in preservation research, but I do not care to have them named after myself and Stieglitz. Please let me know the results so we can prepare the proper papers, etc., and if you think this Peter Davidson can handle the sale well, it is fine with me.[41]

Sincerely,

Georgia O'Keeffe

GO'K/jl

NOTES

1 *"We" refers to her husband and fellow conservator, Sheldon Keck.*

2 *Georgia O'Keeffe to William Howard Schubart, March 27, 1951, in Jack Cowart, Juan Hamilton, and Sarah Greenough,* Georgia O'Keeffe: Art and Letters *(Washington, D.C.: National Gallery of Art, 1987), 258.*

3 *Letter to the author, February 13, 2003.*

4 *Caroline and Sheldon's sons, Larry and Keckie.*

5 *Stieglitz ran An American Place from 1929 until his death in 1946. During that time O'Keeffe took a powerful aesthetic hand in the seventy-five exhibitions held there. She chose the color of the walls (grayish white), she arranged the space, and she installed the shows.*

6 *"Lining" a picture to diminish raised cracks and creases means essentially to attach a new, secondary fabric or canvas with adhesive to the original one in order to reinforce and protect the whole.*

7 *A "key" is a small wedge of wood fitted into the joinings of wooden stretchers. Keys regulate the outer dimensions of the stretcher frame. To "key out" a painting is to hammer the wedge further into its slot. This forces the joint apart, spreading the wooden strips and enlarging the outer rim of the stretcher, which draws the canvas tight again.*

8 *Caroline Keck's "primer" of practical advice was* How to Take Care of Your Pictures *(New York: The Museum of Modern Art and The Brooklyn Museum, 1954). Always interested in how to do things for herself, O'Keeffe would sometimes consult it. But her bible from the mid-1930s on was Max Doerner's* The Materials of the Artist and Their Use in Painting: With Notes on the Techniques of the Old Masters, *trans. Eugen Neuhaus (New York: Harcourt, Brace and Company, 1934).*

9 *In a letter to the author dated February 13, 2003, Keck wrote, "As to our charges, we were never interested in fleecing clients and did the work because we loved doing it."*

10 *O'Keeffe bought the Ghost Ranch house and property in 1940, and it became her favorite place in the world. "Sometimes I think I'm half mad with love for this place." Quoted in Laurie Lisle,* Portrait of an Artist *(Albuquerque, N.M.: University of New Mexico Press, 1986), 362.*

11 *Rolf practiced a technique of muscle manipulation that she called "Structural Integration," more popularly known in New York as "Rolfing." It combined chiropractic, homeopathy, and osteopathy with Tantric yoga. O'Keeffe swore by it for many years.*

12 *For the most recent research on O'Keeffe's far-flung travels during the 1950s and 1960s, and their influence on her paintings of this period, see Hunter Drohojowska-Philp,* Full Bloom: The Art and Life of Georgia O'Keeffe *(New York: W. W. Norton & Company, 2004), 445-515.*

13 *O'Keeffe was always punctilious about paying her bills.*

14 *This planned painting "in pieces" for her trip around the world is not further referred to in the correspondence, and Keck's answer to the question is missing. It is doubtful that she succeeded in carrying out the idea.*

15 *O'Keeffe had recently installed a phone at Abiquiu.*

16 *A sly dig at the owners of a conference center on the Ghost Ranch, not far from O'Keeffe's house and property.*

17 *Ghost Ranch was sixteen miles from Abiquiu.*

18 *Inpainting is the retouching of losses to the paint surface, and it is difficult to do well. The new paint has to harmonize with the original for the longest possible period.*

19 *She would have several more.*

20 *Keck,* How To Take Care of Your Pictures.

21 The Precisionist View in American Art, *Walker Art Center, Minneapolis, 1960, curated by Martin Friedman.*

22 *Perhaps O'Keeffe "painted over a line or two" just to challenge being labeled a precisionist, which she hated.*

23 *James Lebron (1929-2005) was a master handler, framer, and installer of late-twentieth-century paintings. He worked for artists, prominent collectors, and the Metropolitan Museum of Art.*

24 *This clearly nervous letter cites how tricky it is to spray varnish on a painting. But Keck knew O'Keeffe too well to argue her out of trying it.*

25 *Mrs. John A. Prosser of Lake Forest, Illinois.*

26 *Keck's answer to this letter was not kept, but she doubtless did as O'Keeffe requested about the four little paintings.*

27 *Keck liked to say that O'Keeffe was responsible for his trademark beard. "He grew it while we were in Abiquiu, and Georgia's comment was, "Keep it Sheldon, an opinion on a Rembrandt is twice as likely to be respected with that beard.' He kept it." Letter to the author, February 13, 2003.*

28 *Keeping her paintings flat was all-consuming to O'Keeffe's sense of craft.*

29 *Keck's letters regarding the conservation of O'Keeffe's paintings were henceforth directed to Doris Bry, the artist's agent in New York from 1963 to 1977. Keck respected Bry's diligent efforts on O'Keeffe's behalf, as their frequent communications show. (Some of their letters are on file at the Georgia O'Keeffe Foundation.)*

30 *She made a contribution to Keck's project in 1969.*

31 *The girl's name is unknown. This is but one example of the little-known generosities to young people that O'Keeffe practiced.*

32 *Perhaps this is as close as O'Keeffe ever came to sharing her reverence for life with her old friend. Her sign-off, "Fondly," is a first. The letter from Keck on this topic is missing.*

33 *This request is typical of her lifelong need for privacy and secrecy.*

34 *She did give the scholarship.*

35 *This letter sums up Caroline Keck's personal and professional value system, as well as her admiration for O'Keeffe as a creative artist.*

36 *Keck's subsequent letter of acknowledgement and appreciation for O'Keeffe's gift is missing.*

37 *Despite Keck's often-expressed disapproval, O'Keeffe stuck obstinately to the sheet brass frames, plated and lacquered with nickel and copper, that she had designed herself.*

38 *A typically oblique reference to her increasingly problematic vision.*

39 *The "young man" is Juan Hamilton (born 1945), who became O'Keeffe's sole agent and companion for the rest of her life.*

40 *This was Georgia O'Keeffe's last letter to Caroline Keck.*

41 *It was sold for the benefit of the FAIC for three hundred thousand dollars.*

Color and Conservation

WORKS IN THE EXHIBITION

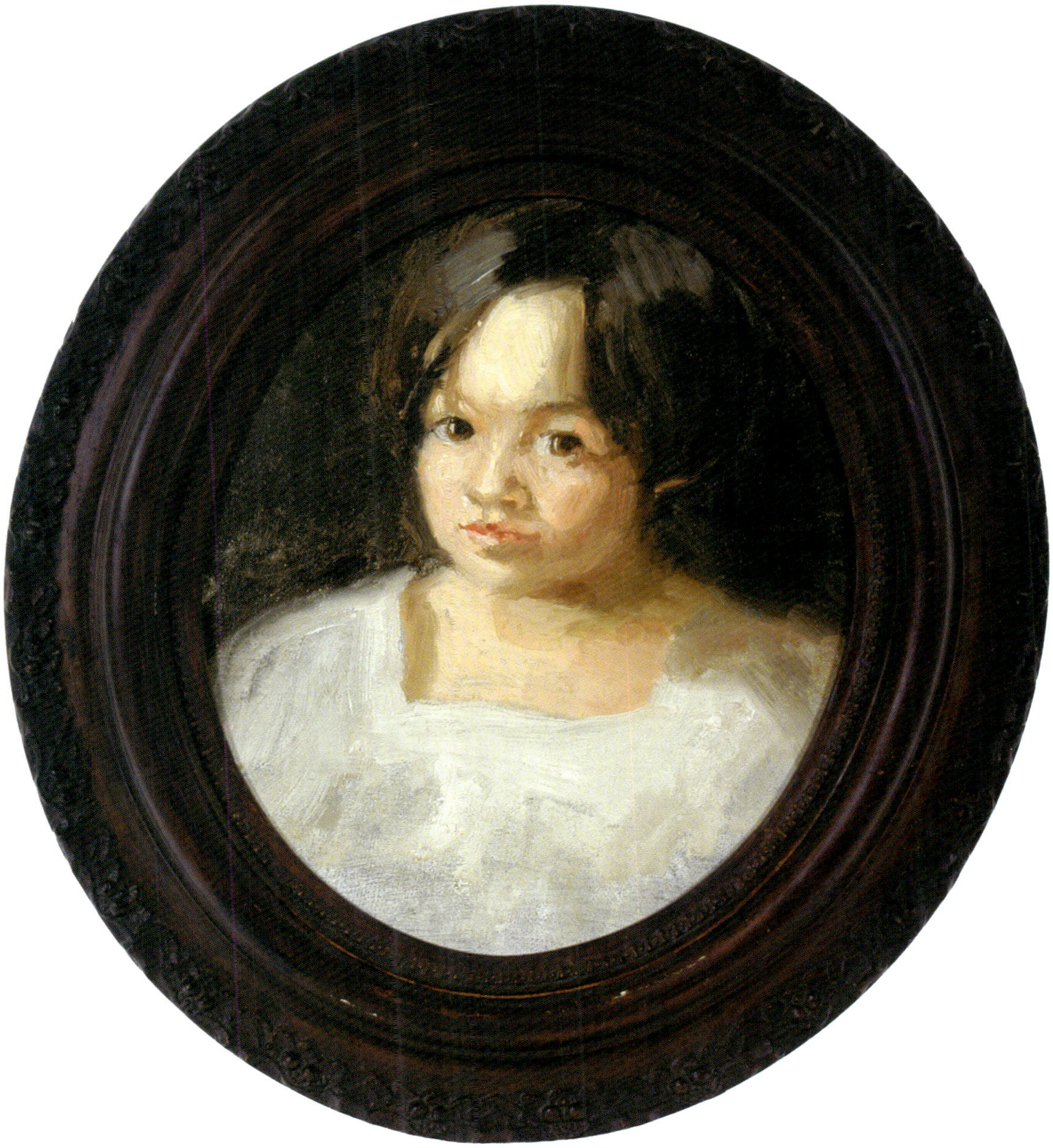

UNTITLED (CLAUDIA O'KEEFFE)
1907-8
oil on canvas, 12" x 10"
Collection of Museum of Fine Arts, Museum of New Mexico, Santa Fe, Department of Cultural Affairs
Bequest of Claudia O'Keeffe, Museum of New Mexico Foundation, 1988
Photograph: Blair Clark

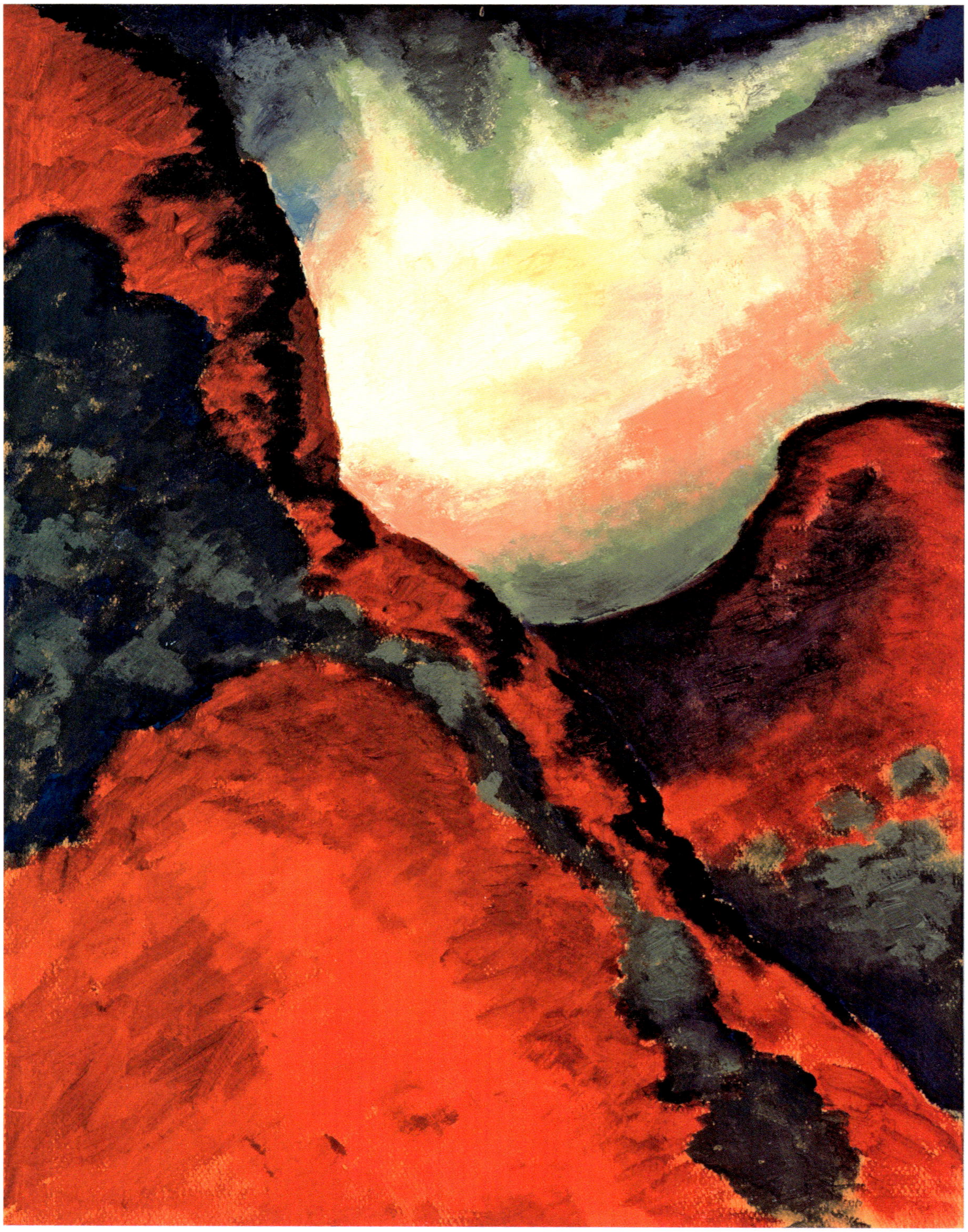

RED LANDSCAPE
1916-17
oil on board, 24 1/2" x 18 1/2"
Collection of Panhandle-Plains Historical Museum, Canyon, Texas
Gift of The Georgia O'Keeffe Foundation
1995.86.1

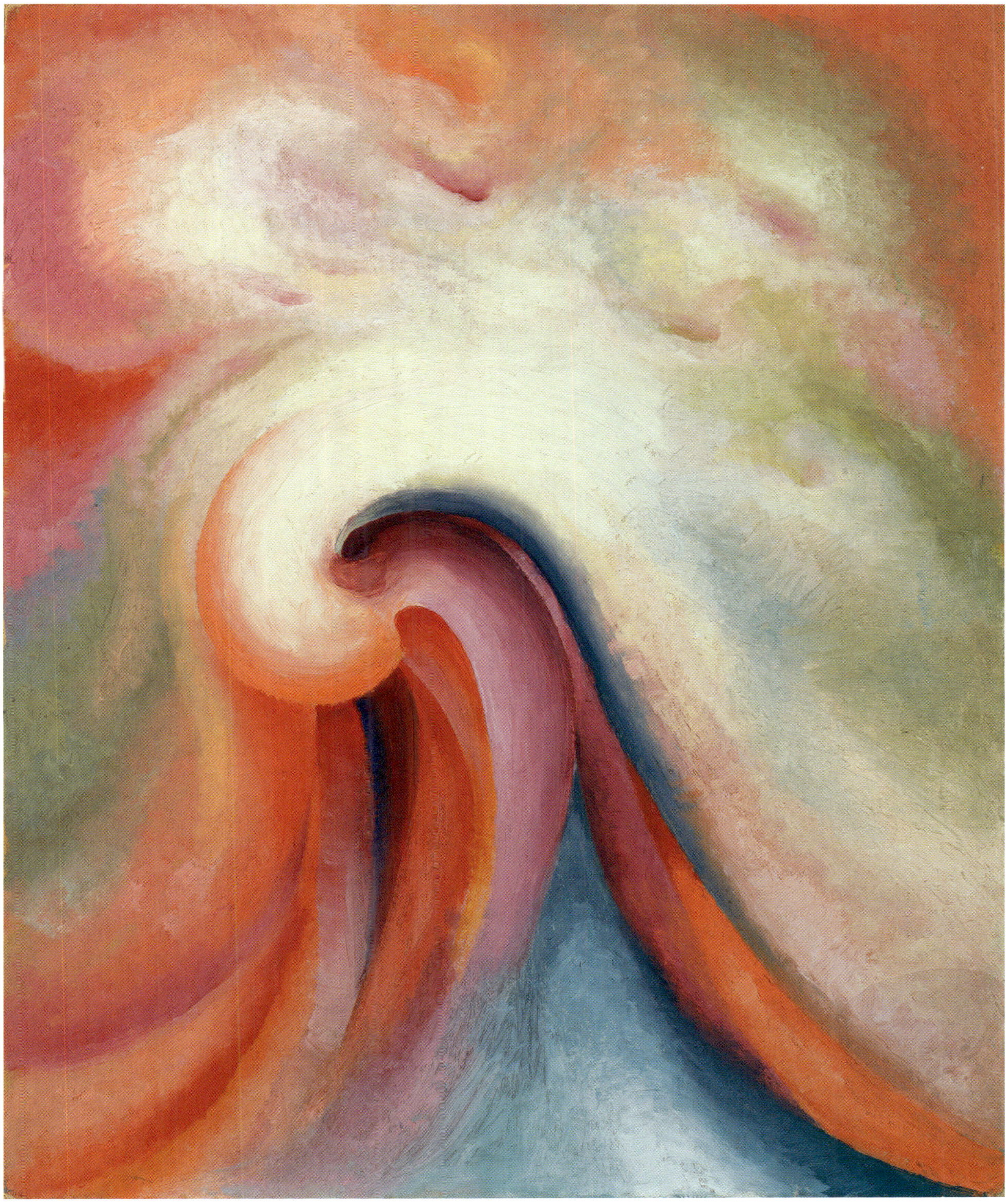

SERIES 1 — NO. 1

1918

oil on board, 19 3/4" x 16"

Collection of Amon Carter Museum, Fort Worth, Texas

Purchase with assistance from the Anne Burnett Tandy Accessions Fund

1995.8

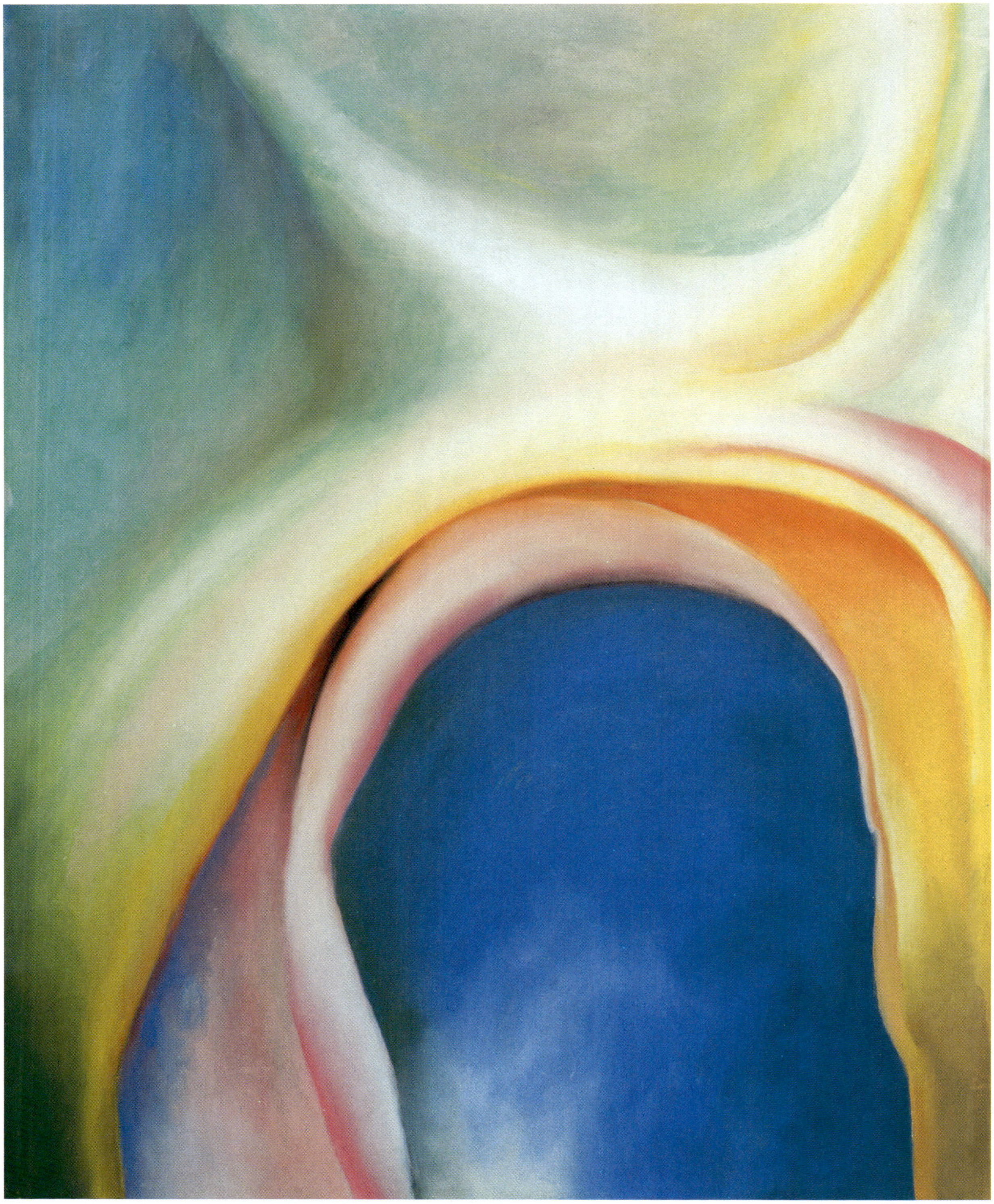

OVER BLUE

1918

pastel on paper, 27 1/2" x 21 1/2"

Private Collection

Courtesy of Memorial Art Gallery of the University of Rochester, New York

Photograph: James M. Via

Memorial Art Gallery of the University of Rochester, New York, only

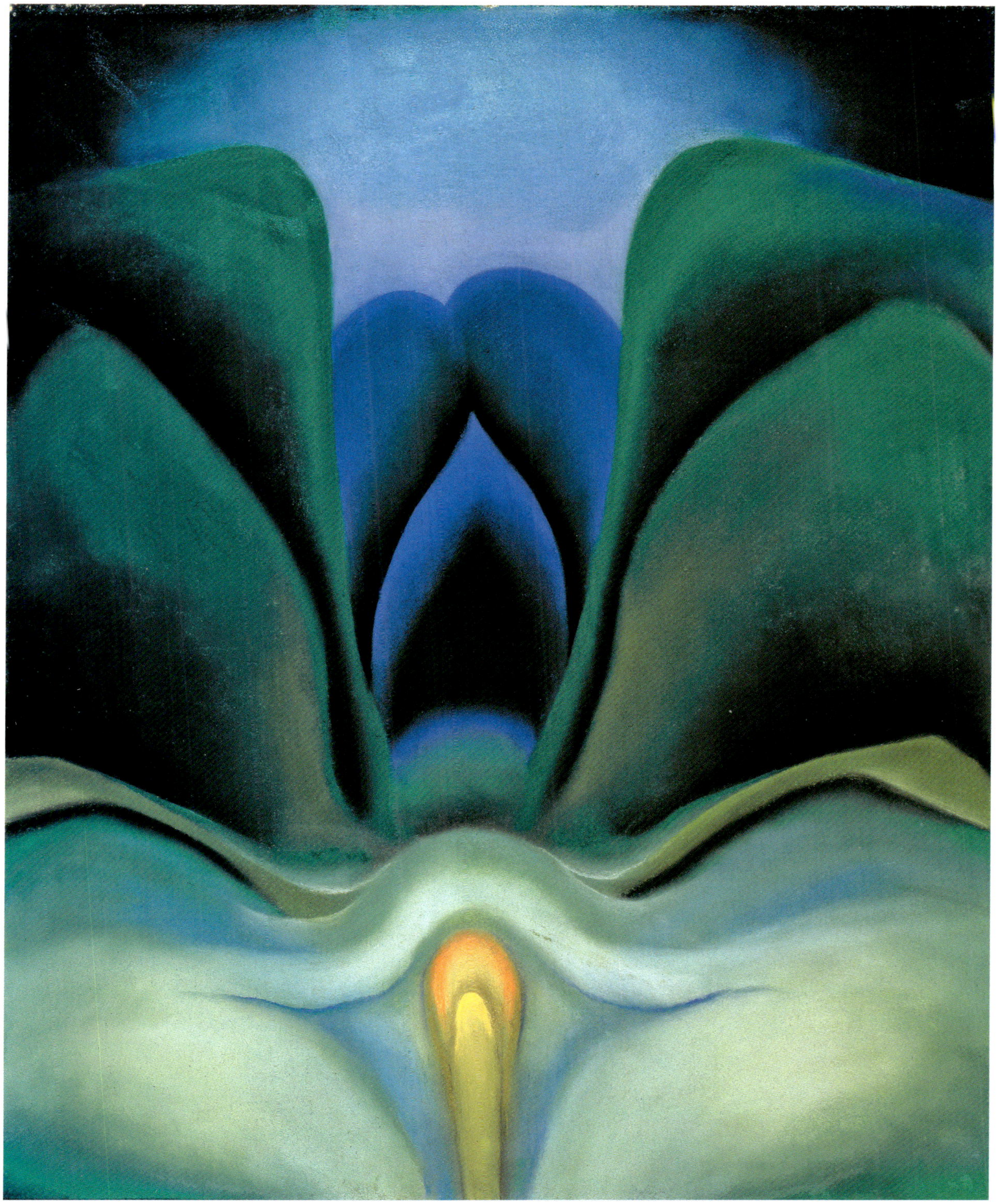

BLUE FLOWER

1918

pastel on paper mounted on cardboard, 20" x 16"

Promised gift, The Burnett Foundation, Georgia O'Keeffe Museum, Santa Fe, New Mexico

L.1993.7.2

Photograph: Matthew Marston

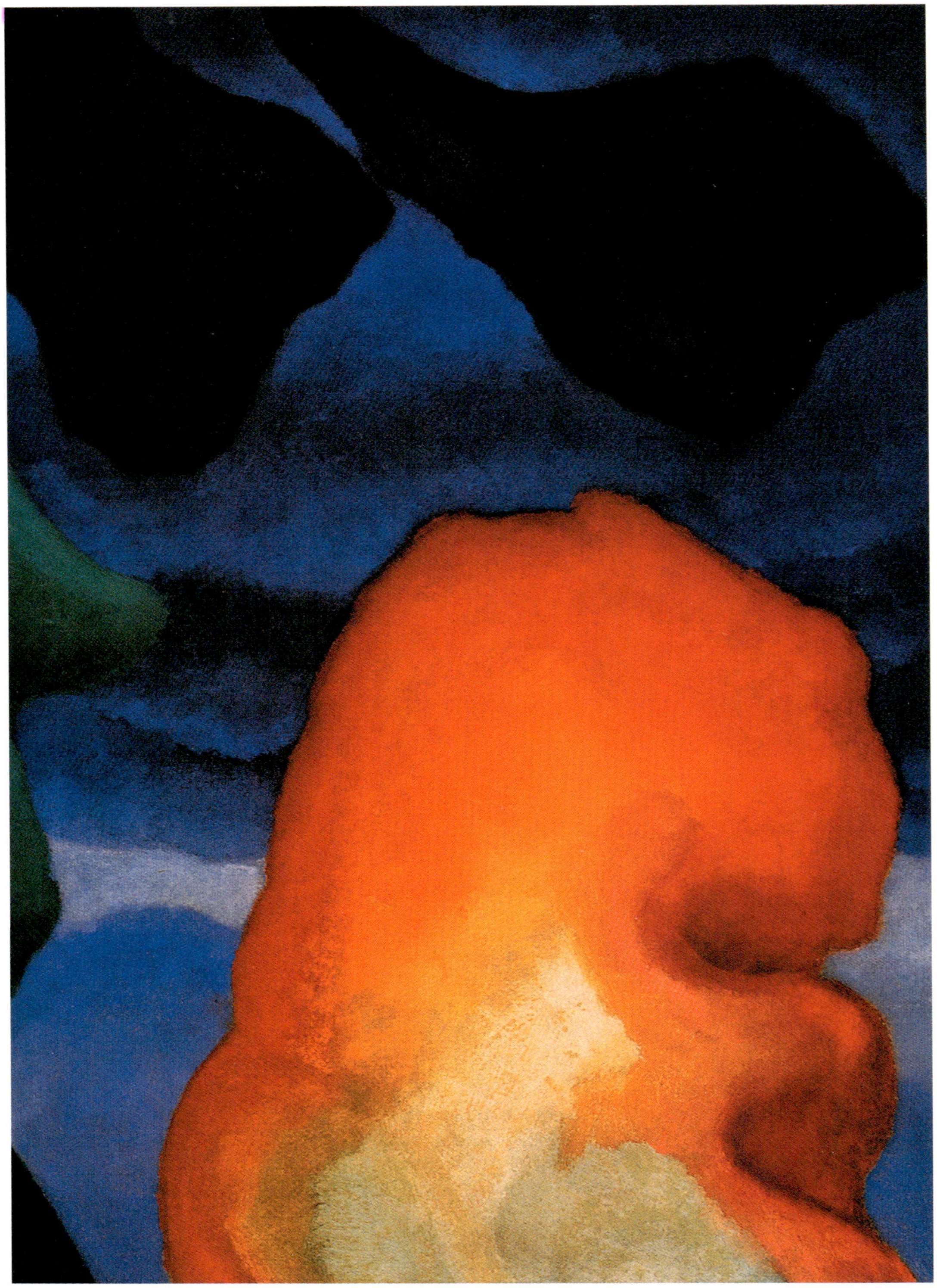

UNTITLED (ABSTRACTION)
1918
oil on canvas board, 19 1/4" x 14"
Collection of The University of Mississippi, University
Gift of Seymour Lawrence

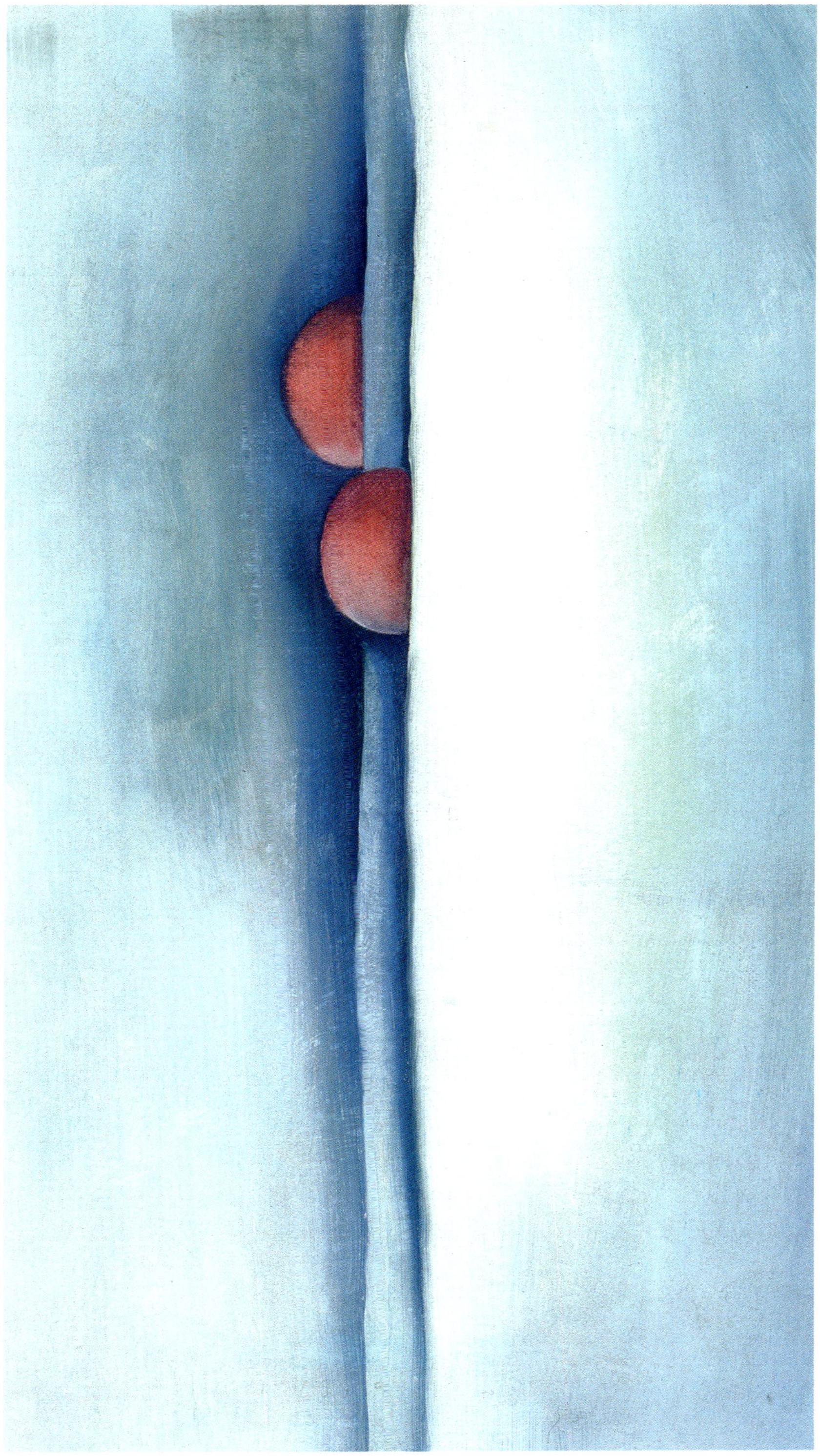

GREEN LINES AND PINK
1919
oil on canvas, 18" x 10"
Collection of Georgia O'Keeffe Museum, Santa Fe, New Mexico
Gift of The Burnett Foundation and The Georgia O'Keeffe Foundation
1997.05.07
Photograph: Malcolm Varon

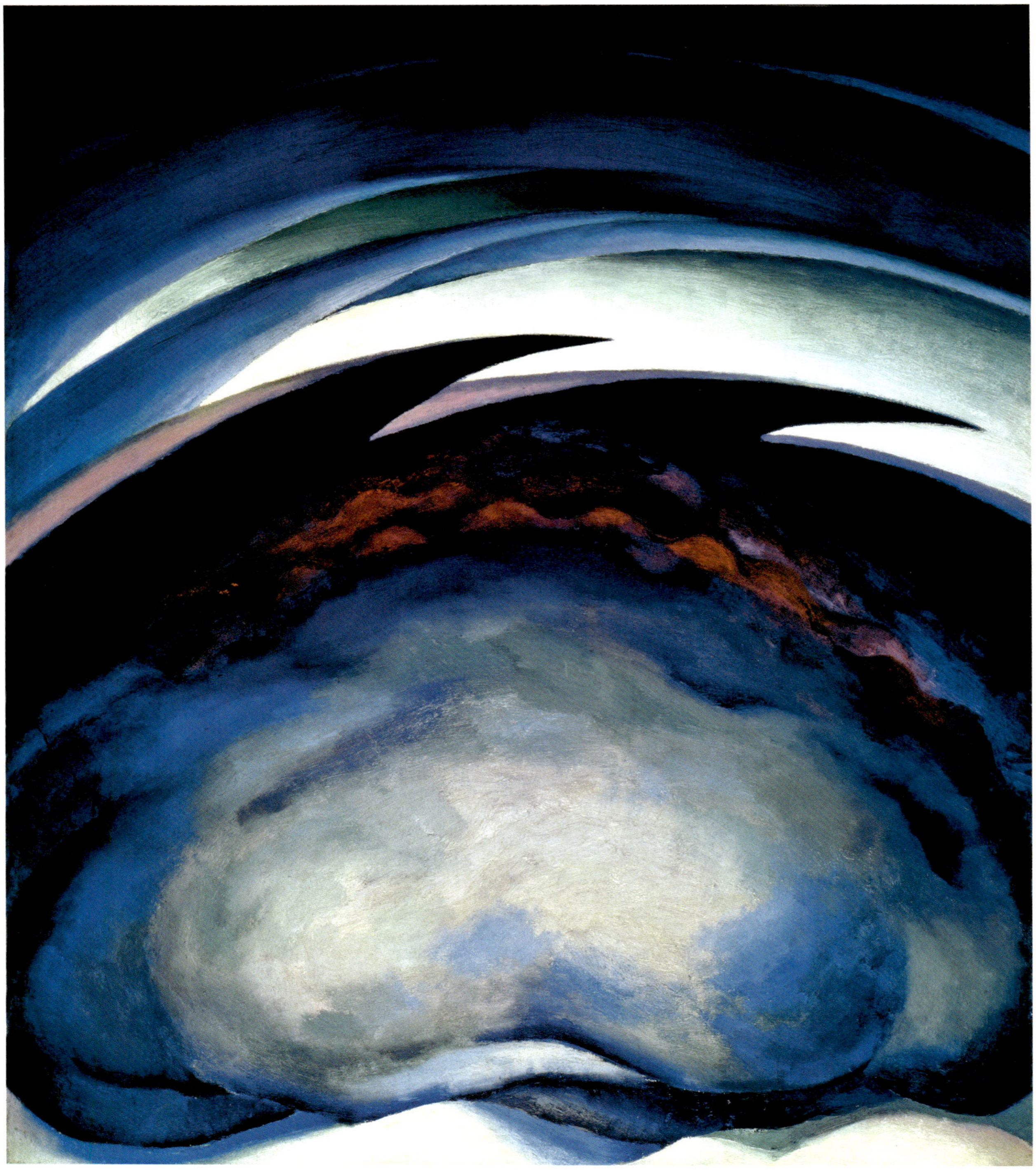

SERIES I – FROM THE PLAINS

1919

oil on canvas, 27" x 23"

Promised gift, The Burnett Foundation, Georgia O'Keeffe Museum, Santa Fe, New Mexico

L.1998.2.2

Georgia O'Keeffe Museum, Santa Fe, New Mexico, only

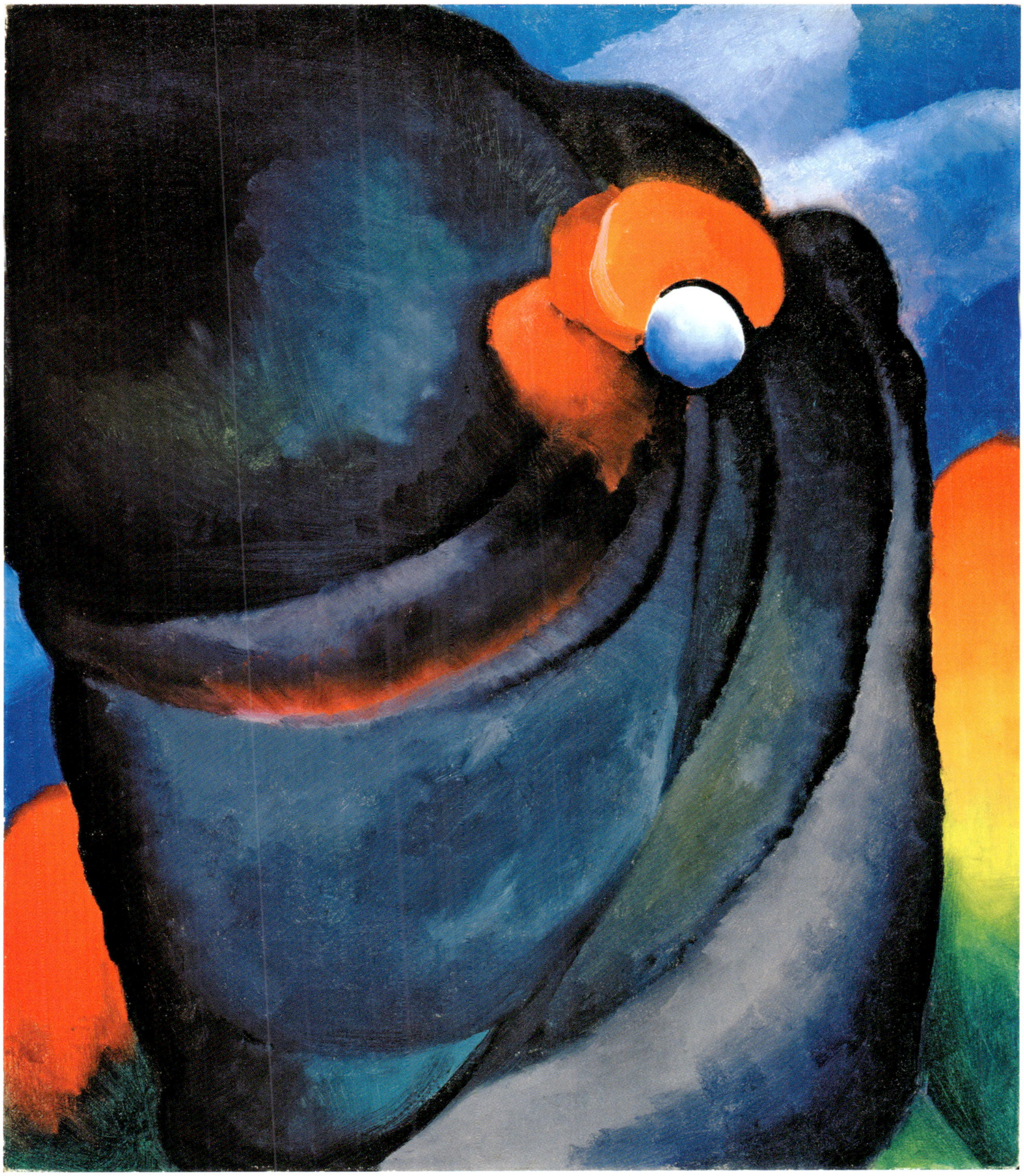

LAKE GEORGE, COAT AND RED

1919

oil on canvas, 27 3/8" x 23 1/4"

Collection of The Museum of Modern Art, New York, New York

Gift of The Georgia O'Keeffe Foundation

65.1995

Courtesy of The Museum of Modern Art/Licensed by SCALA/Art Resource, NY

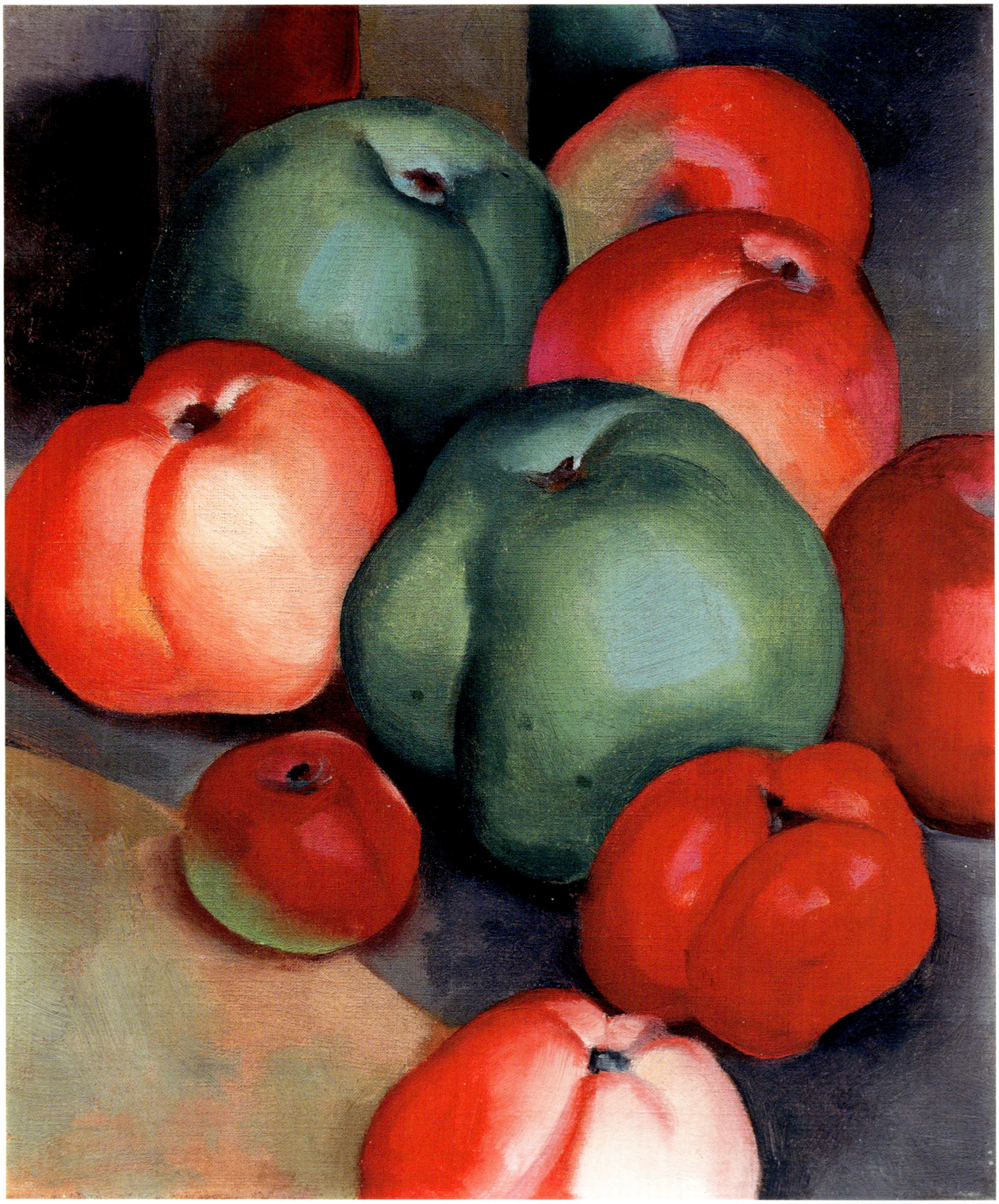

APPLE FAMILY A

1920

oil on canvas, 10" x 8"

Collection of Gerald and Kathleen Peters, Santa Fe, New Mexico

Courtesy of Gerald Peters Gallery, Santa Fe, New Mexico

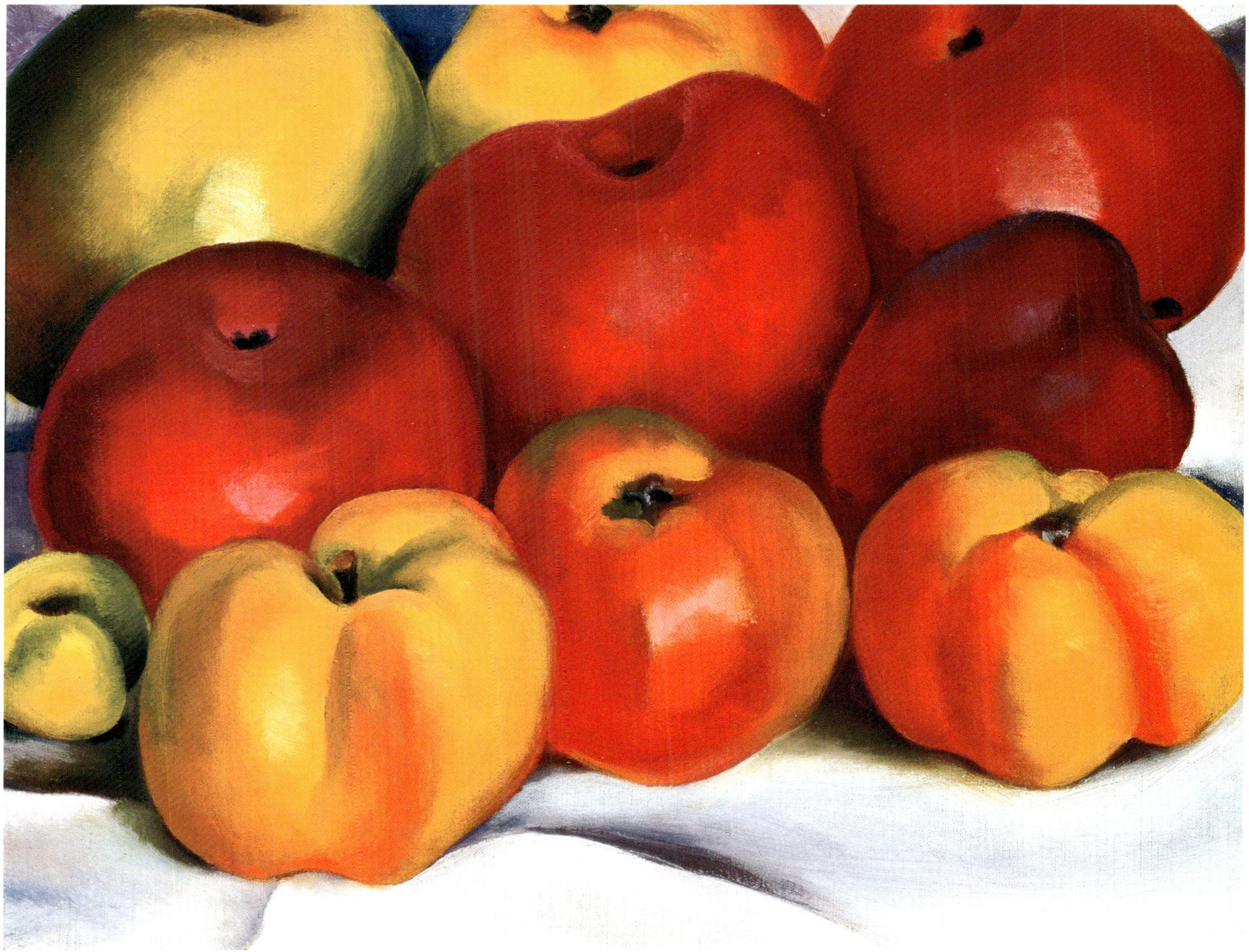

APPLE FAMILY – 2

1920

oil on canvas, 8 1/8" x 10 1/8"

Collection of Georgia O'Keeffe Museum, Santa Fe, New Mexico

Gift of The Burnett Foundation and The Georgia O'Keeffe Foundation

1997.04.03

Photograph: Malcolm Varon

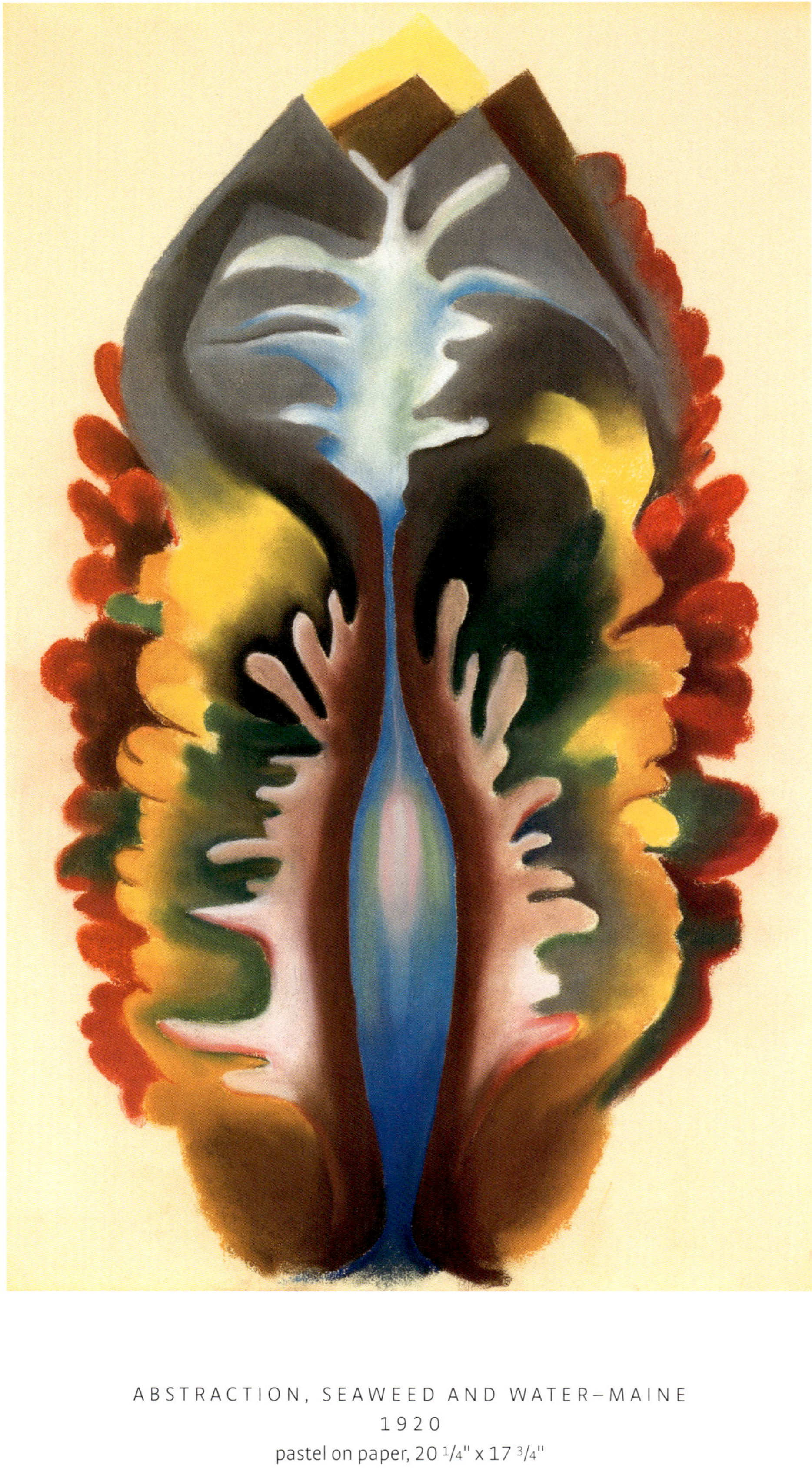

ABSTRACTION, SEAWEED AND WATER—MAINE
1920
pastel on paper, 20 1/4" x 17 3/4"
Collection of The Georgia O'Keeffe Foundation, Abiquiu, New Mexico

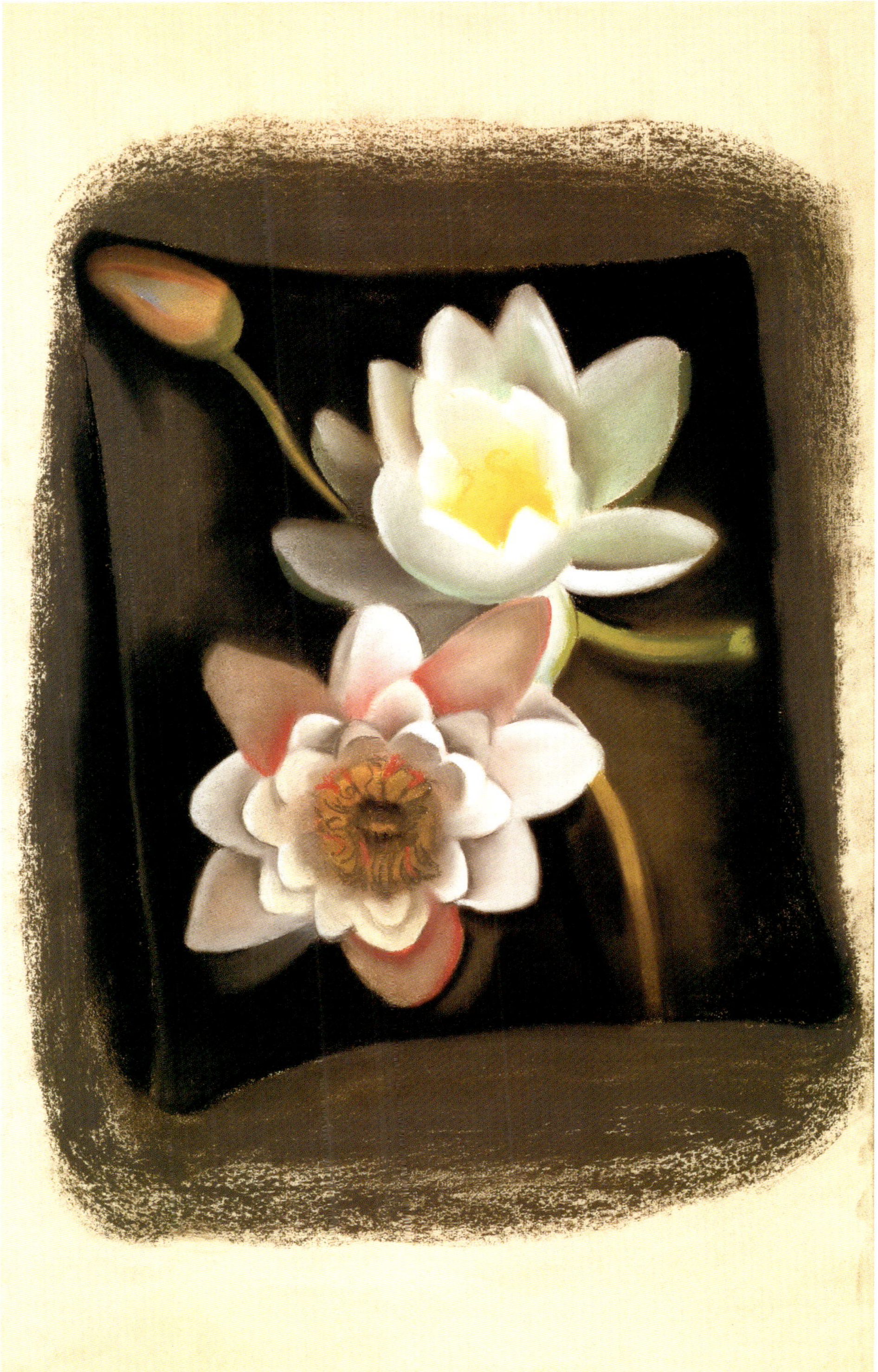

WATER LILY

1921

pastel on paper 28 1/4" x 17 1/2"

Collection of The Georgia O'Keeffe Foundation, Abiquiu, New Mexico

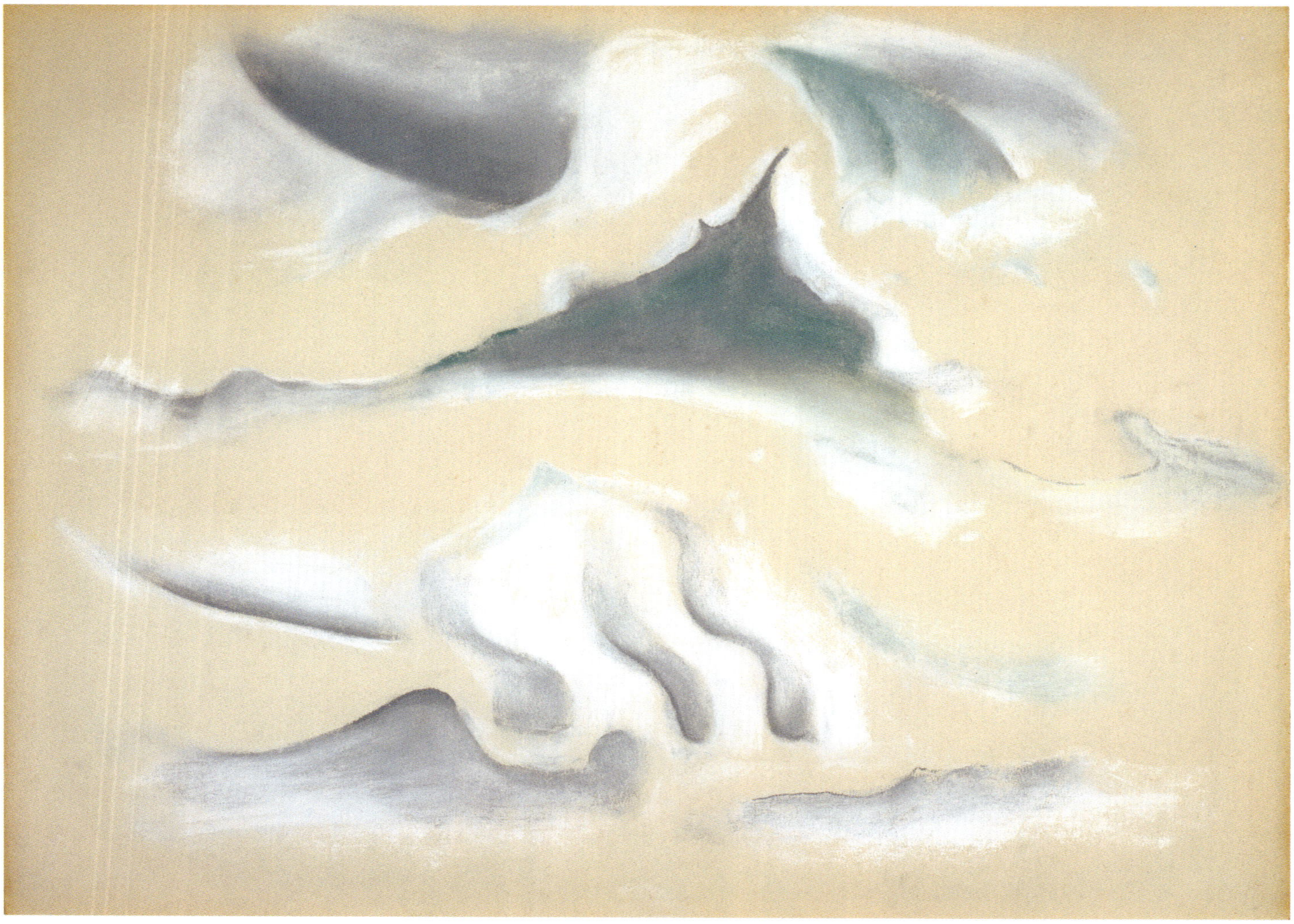

THE WHITE WAVE

1922

pastel on paper, 19" x 25"

Extended loan, private collection, Georgia O'Keeffe Museum, Santa Fe, New Mexico

L.1998.03.01

Photograph: Malcolm Varon

Georgia O'Keeffe Museum, Santa Fe, New Mexico, only

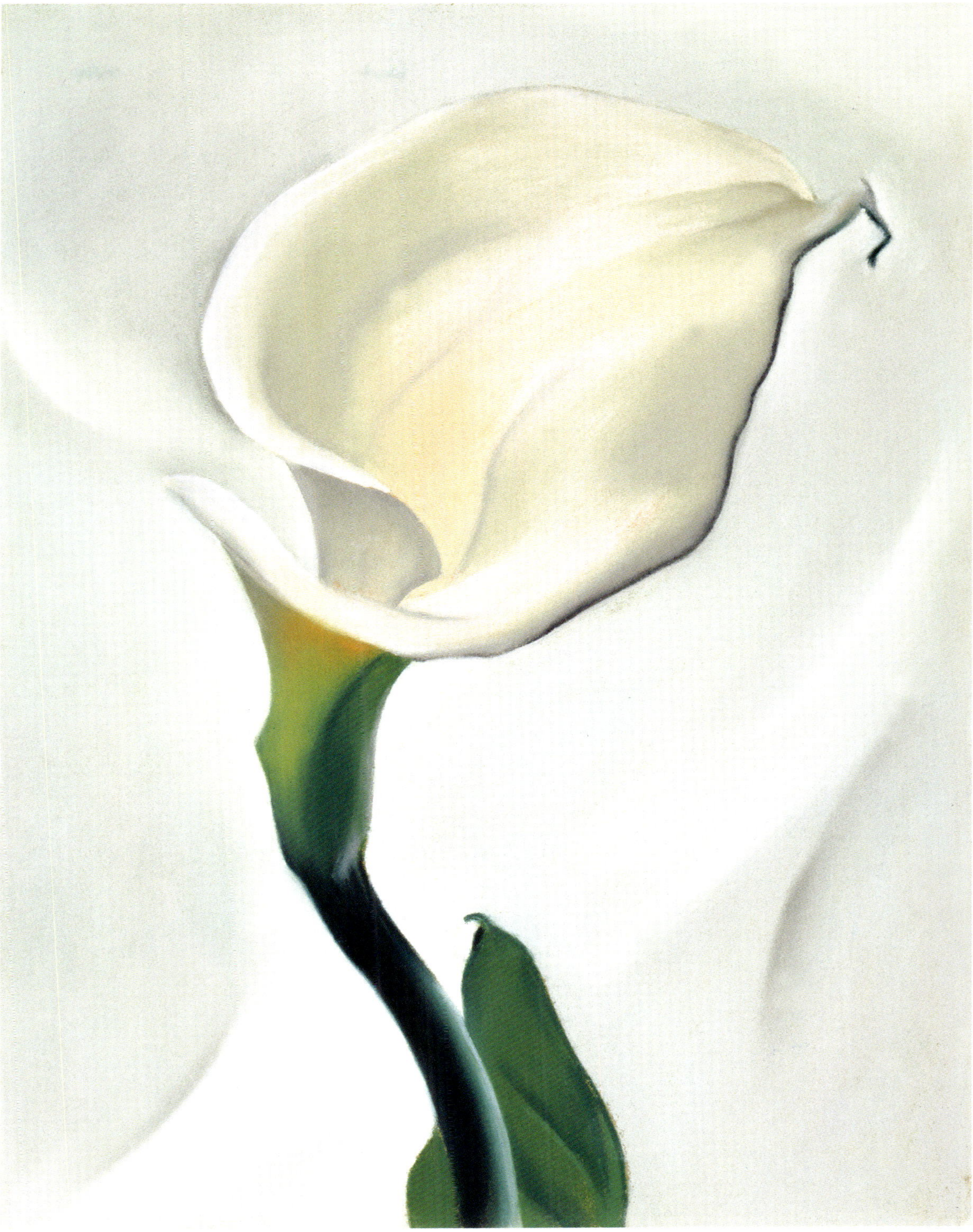

CALLA LILY TURNED AWAY

1923

pastel on cardboard, 14" x 10 7/8"

Collection of Georgia O'Keeffe Museum, Santa Fe, New Mexico

Gift of The Burnett Foundation

1997.18.2

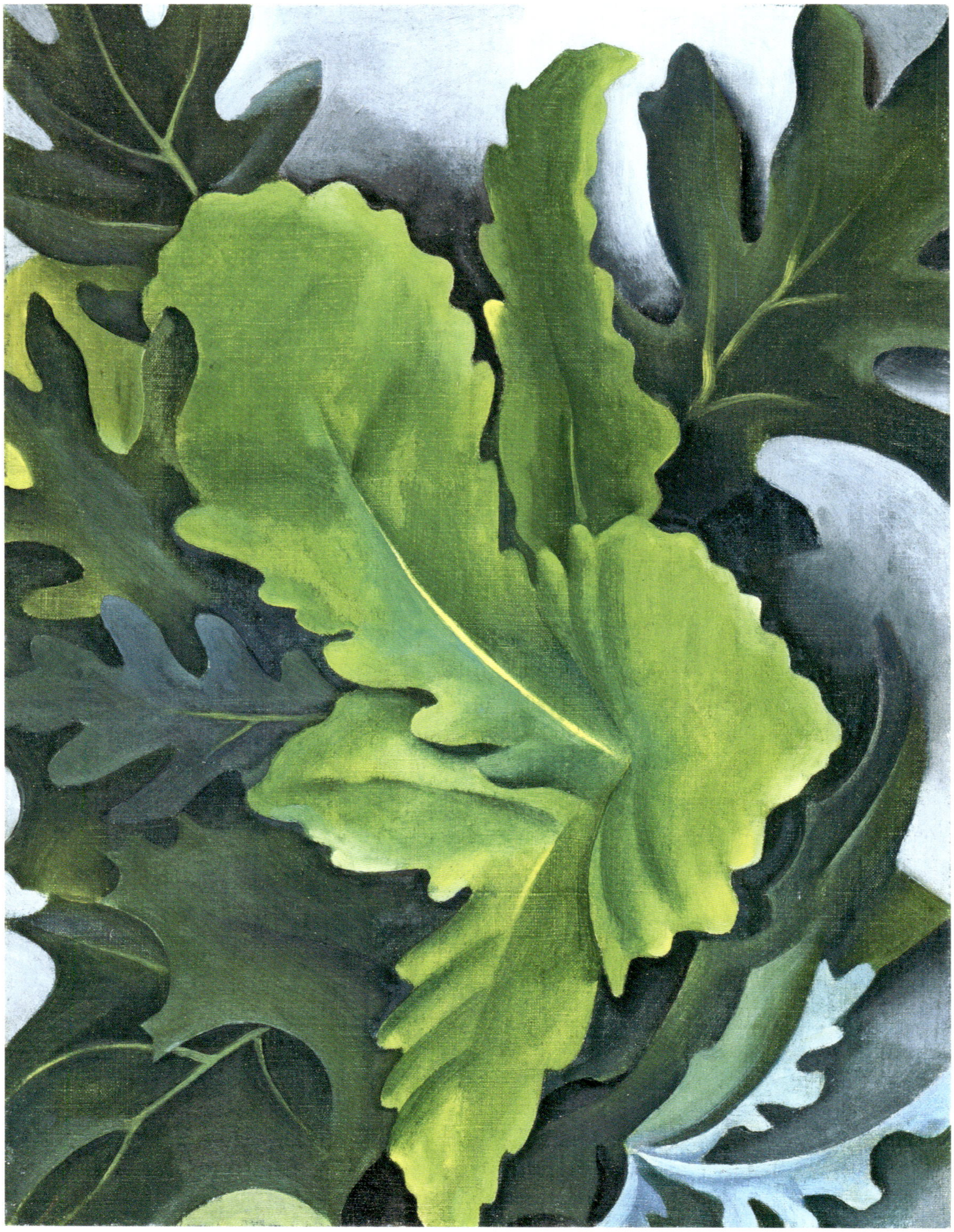

LEAVES

1923

oil on canvas mounted on board, 12" x 9"

Collection of The Newark Museum, New Jersey

Bequest of Cora Louise Hartshorn

58.168

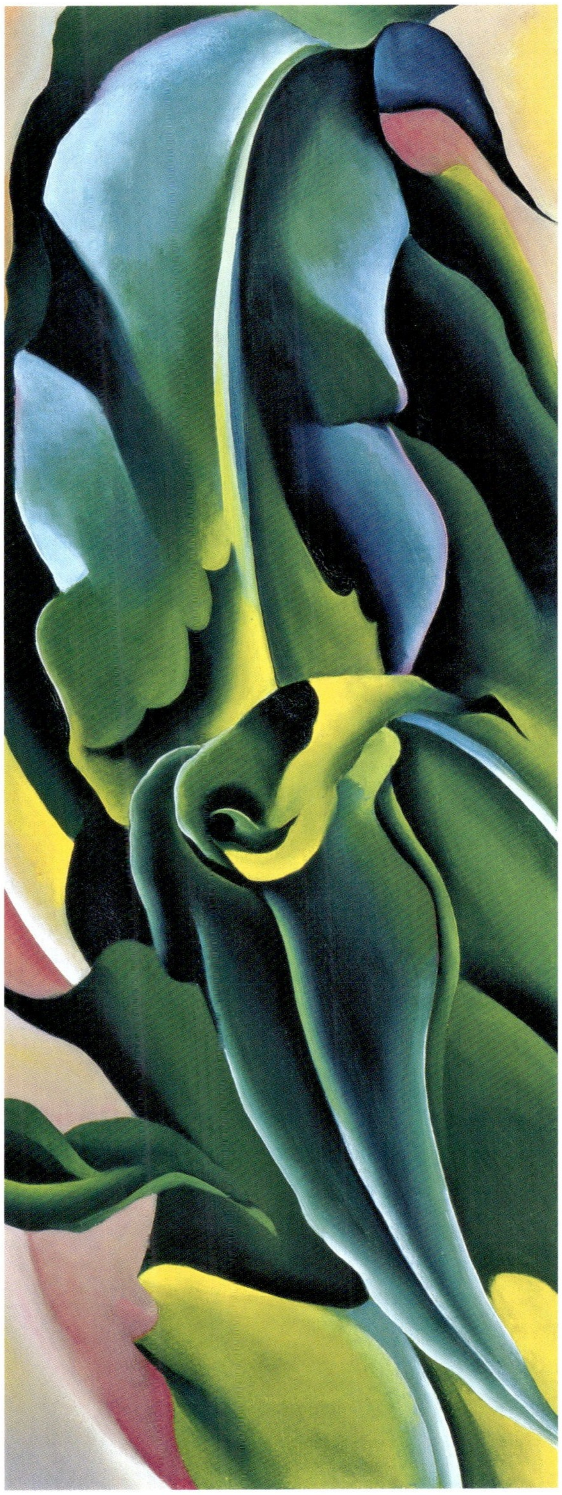

CORN, NO. 2

1924

oil on canvas, 27 1/4" x 10"

Collection of Georgia O'Keeffe Museum, Santa Fe, New Mexico

Gift of The Burnett Foundation and The Georgia O'Keeffe Foundation

1997.04.06

Photograph: Malcolm Varon

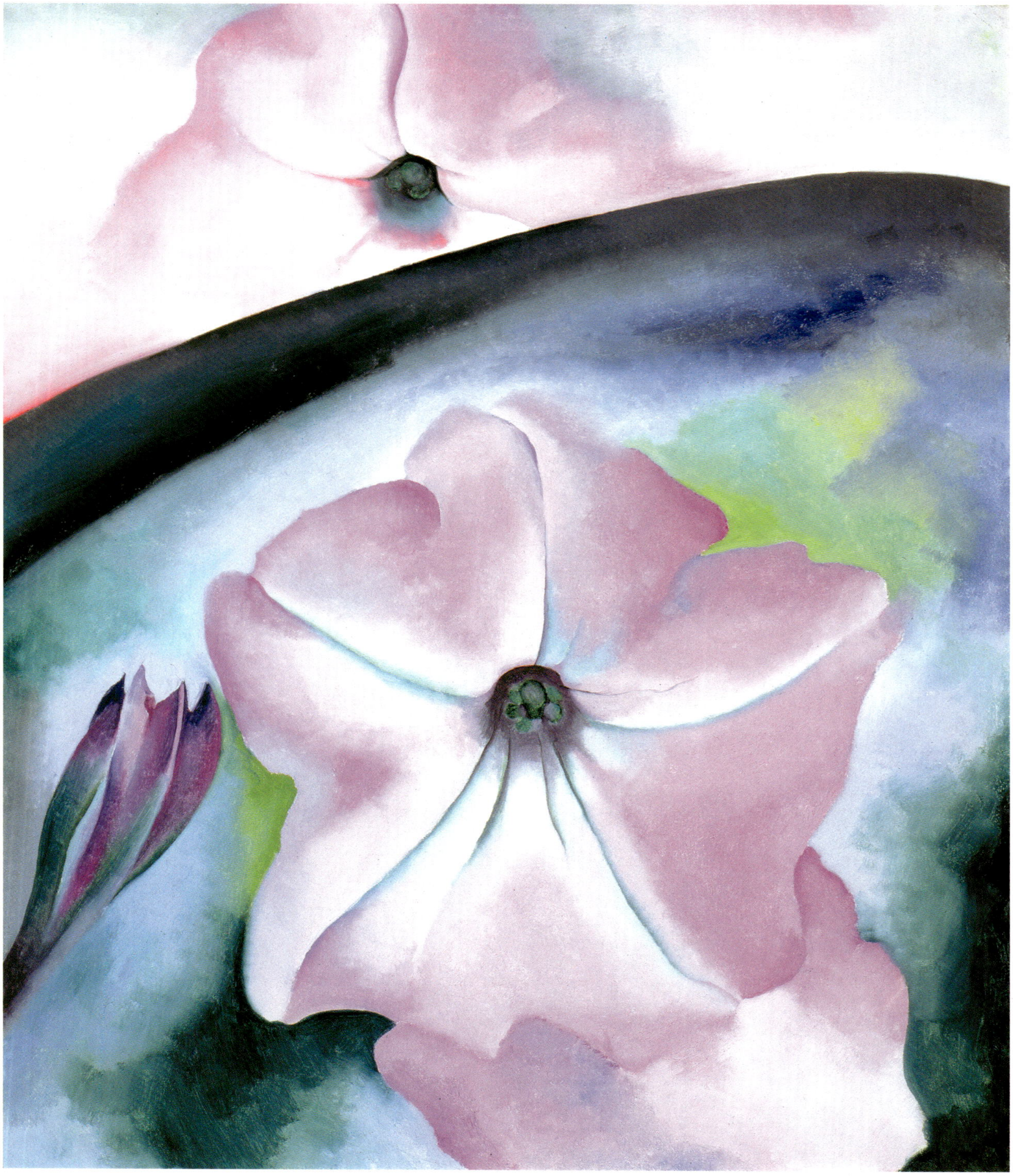

PETUNIA, NO. 2

1924

oil on canvas, 36" x 30"

Collection of Georgia O'Keeffe Museum, Santa Fe, New Mexico

Gift of The Burnett Foundation and Kathleen Peters

1996.3.2

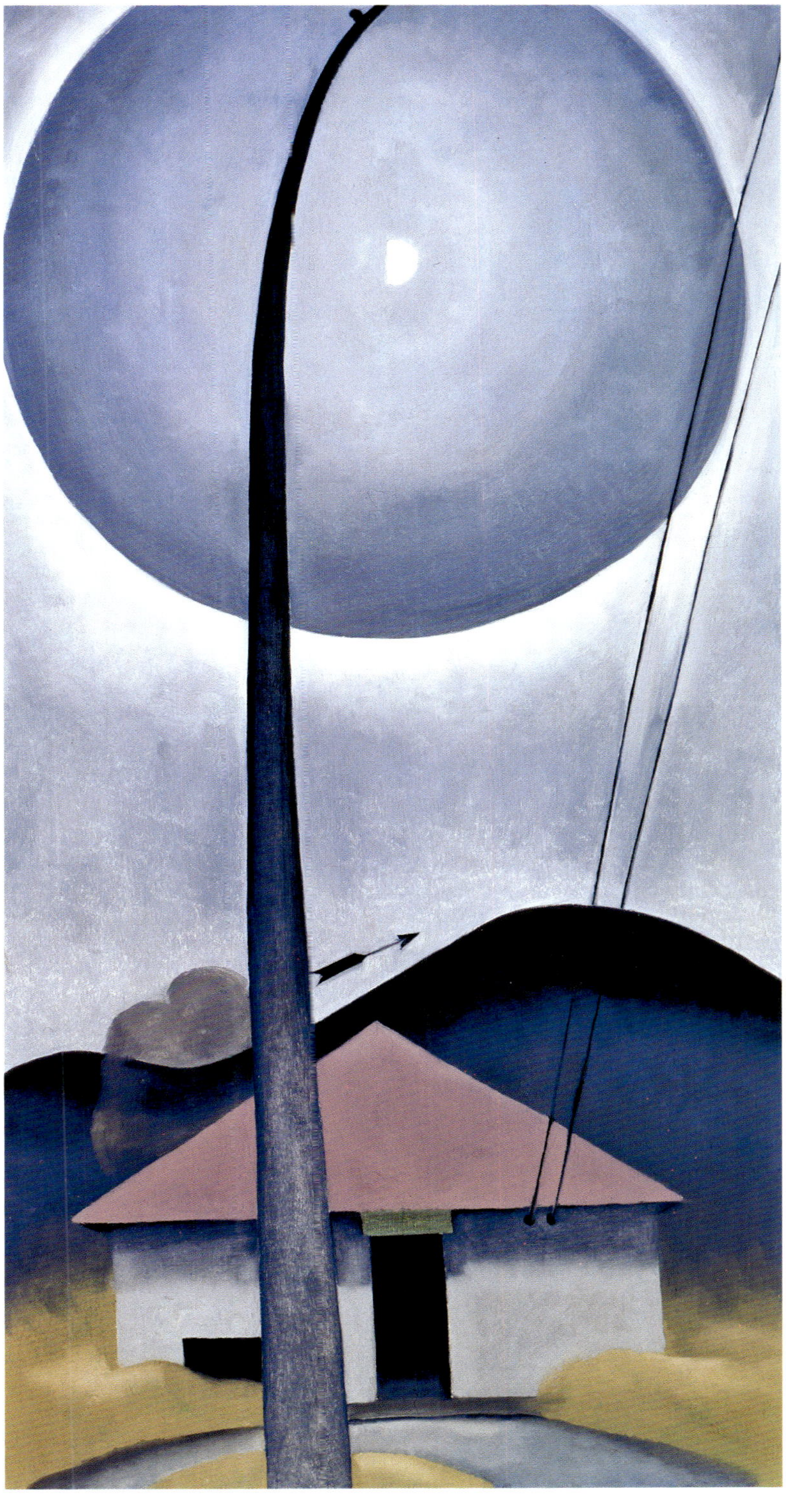

FLAGPOLE

1925

oil on canvas, 35" x 18 1/8"

Collection of Georgia O'Keeffe Museum, Santa Fe, New Mexico

Gift of The Burnett Foundation and an anonymous donor

1997.02.01

Photograph: Malcolm Varon

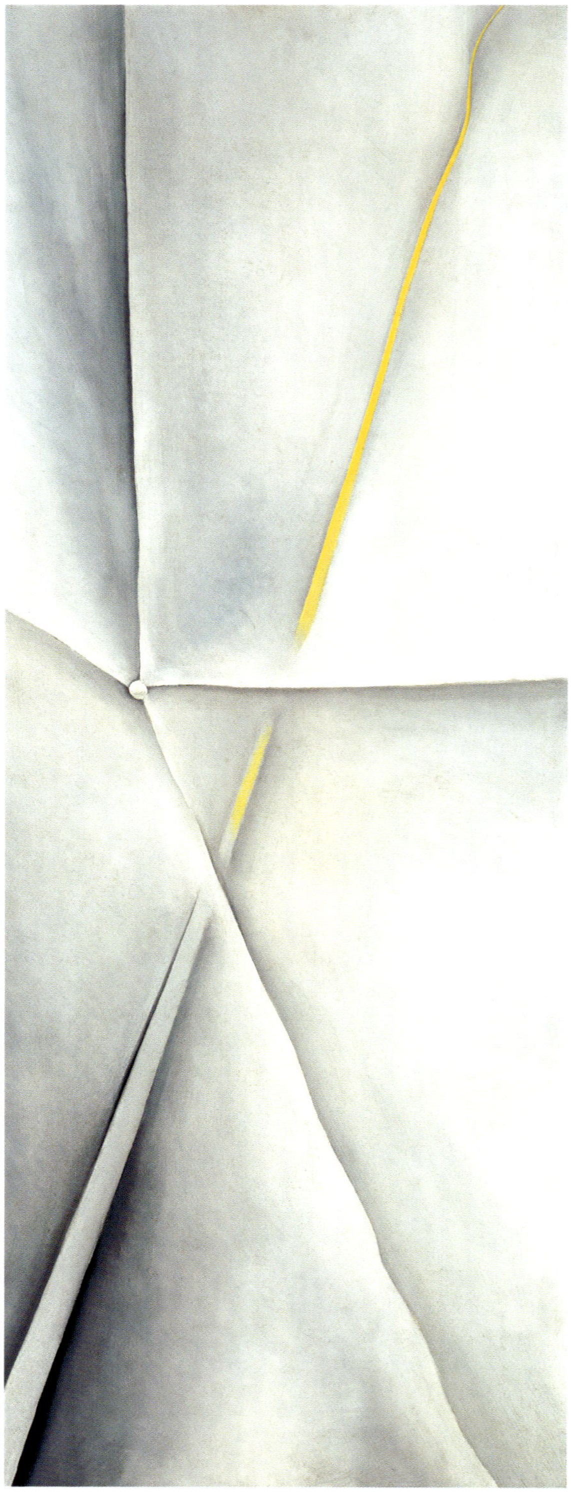

NEW YORK – NIGHT
1926
oil on canvas, 32" x 12"
Collection of Museum of Fine Arts, St. Petersburg, Florida
Gift of Charles and Margaret Stevenson Henderson, in memory of Hunt Henderson
1971.31

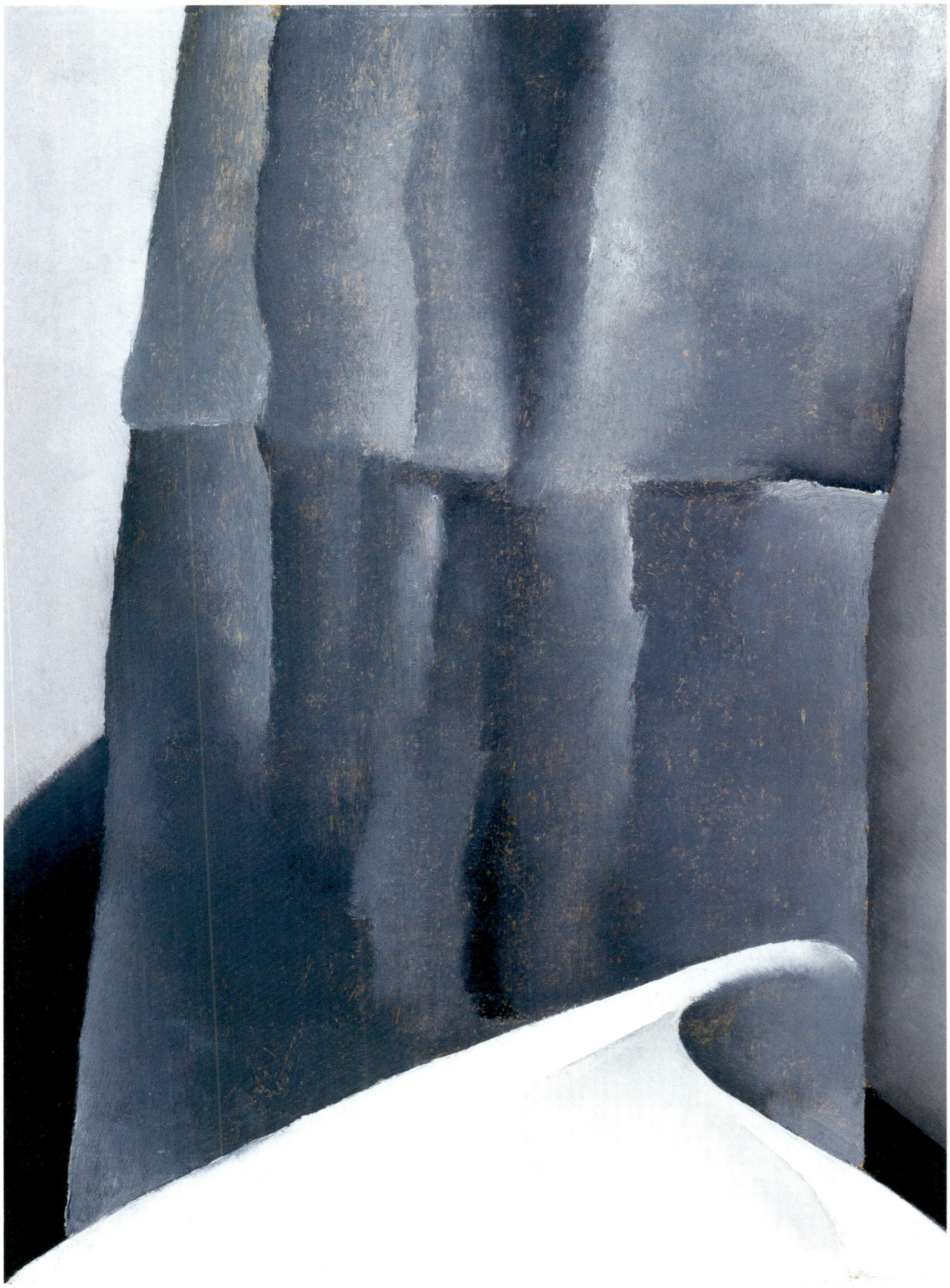

SHELL AND OLD SHINGLE IV
1926
oil on board, 9 3/4" x 7"
Collection of Museum of Fine Arts, Boston, Massachusetts
Alfred Stieglitz Collection, Bequest of Georgia O'Keeffe
1937.538a

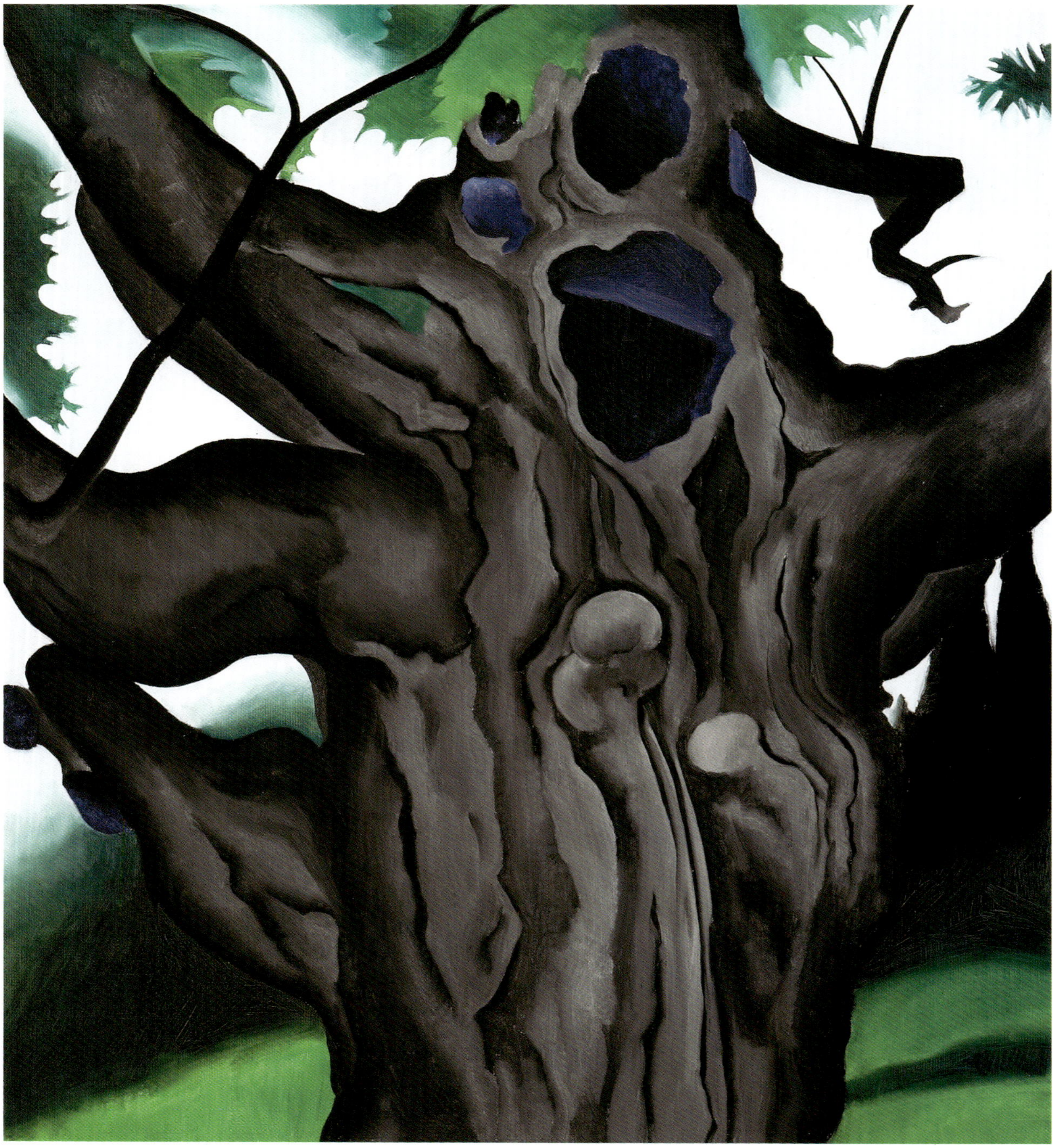

THE OLD MAPLE, LAKE GEORGE
1926
oil on canvas, 36" x 32"
Collection of Mississippi Museum of Art, Jackson
Purchase with funds from the Mississippi Arts Commission and Operation Snowball
1972.009
Photograph: Gil Ford Photography, Inc.

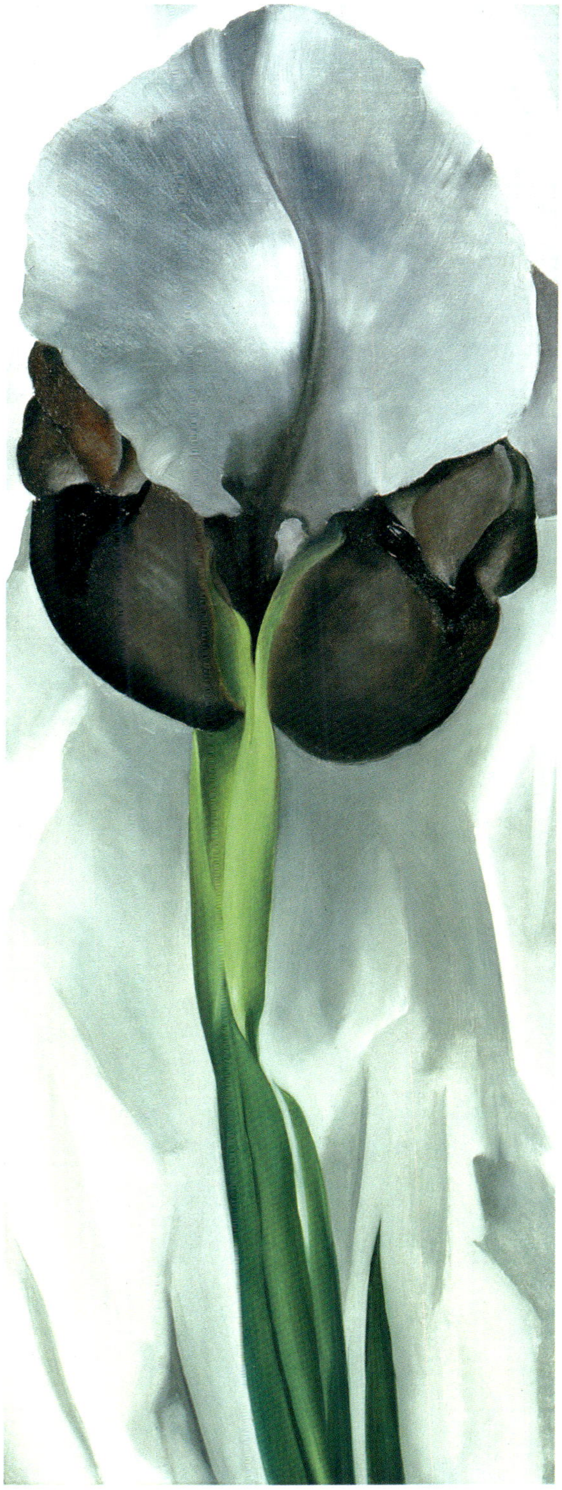

DARK IRIS

1927

oil on canvas, 32" x 12"

Collection of Colorado Springs Fine Arts Center, Taylor Museum, Colorado

Anonymous gift

FA 1954.4

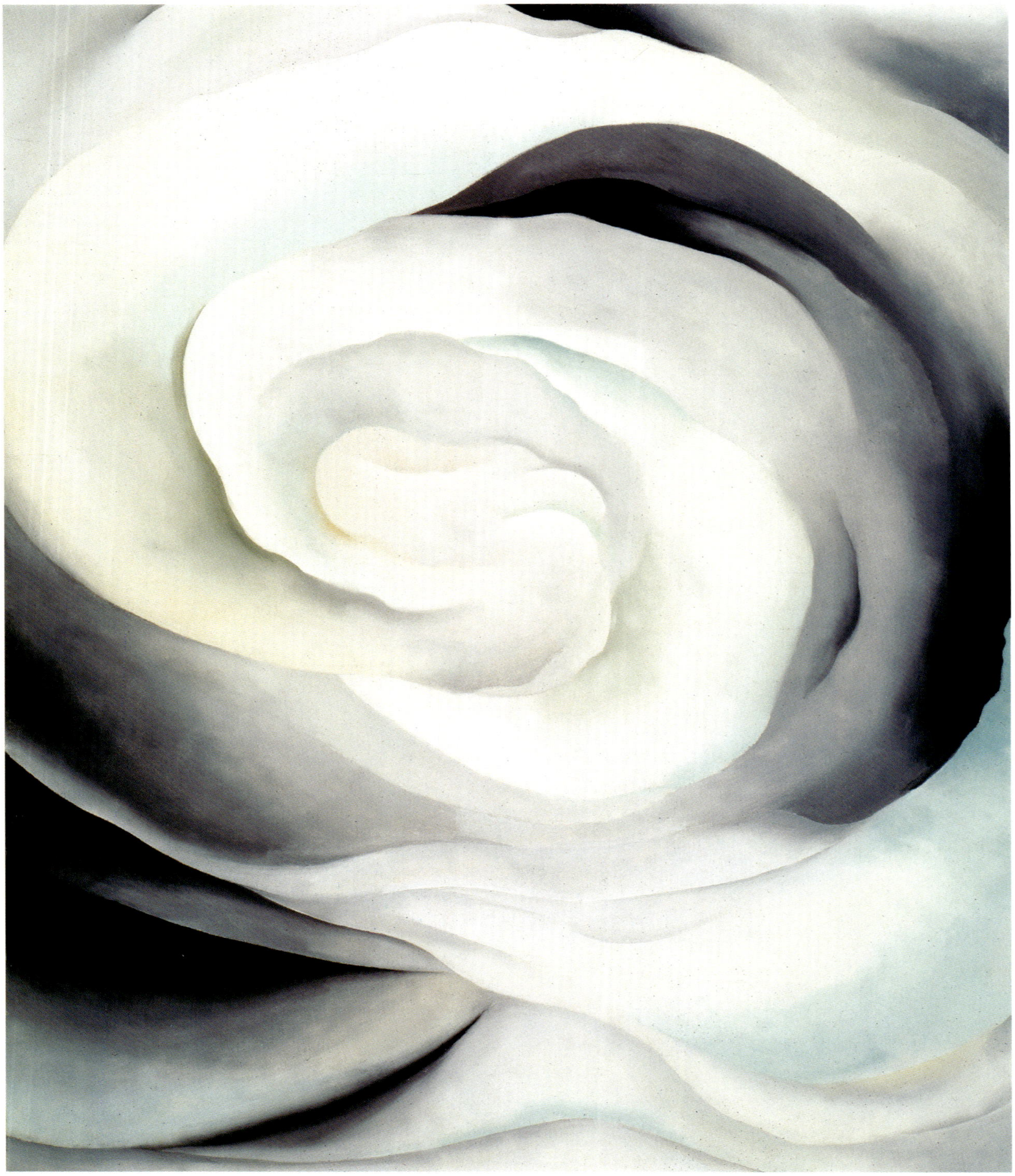

ABSTRACTION WHITE ROSE
1927
oil on canvas, 36" x 30"
Collection of Georgia O'Keeffe Museum, Santa Fe, New Mexico
Gift of The Burnett Foundation and The Georgia O'Keeffe Foundation
1997.4.2

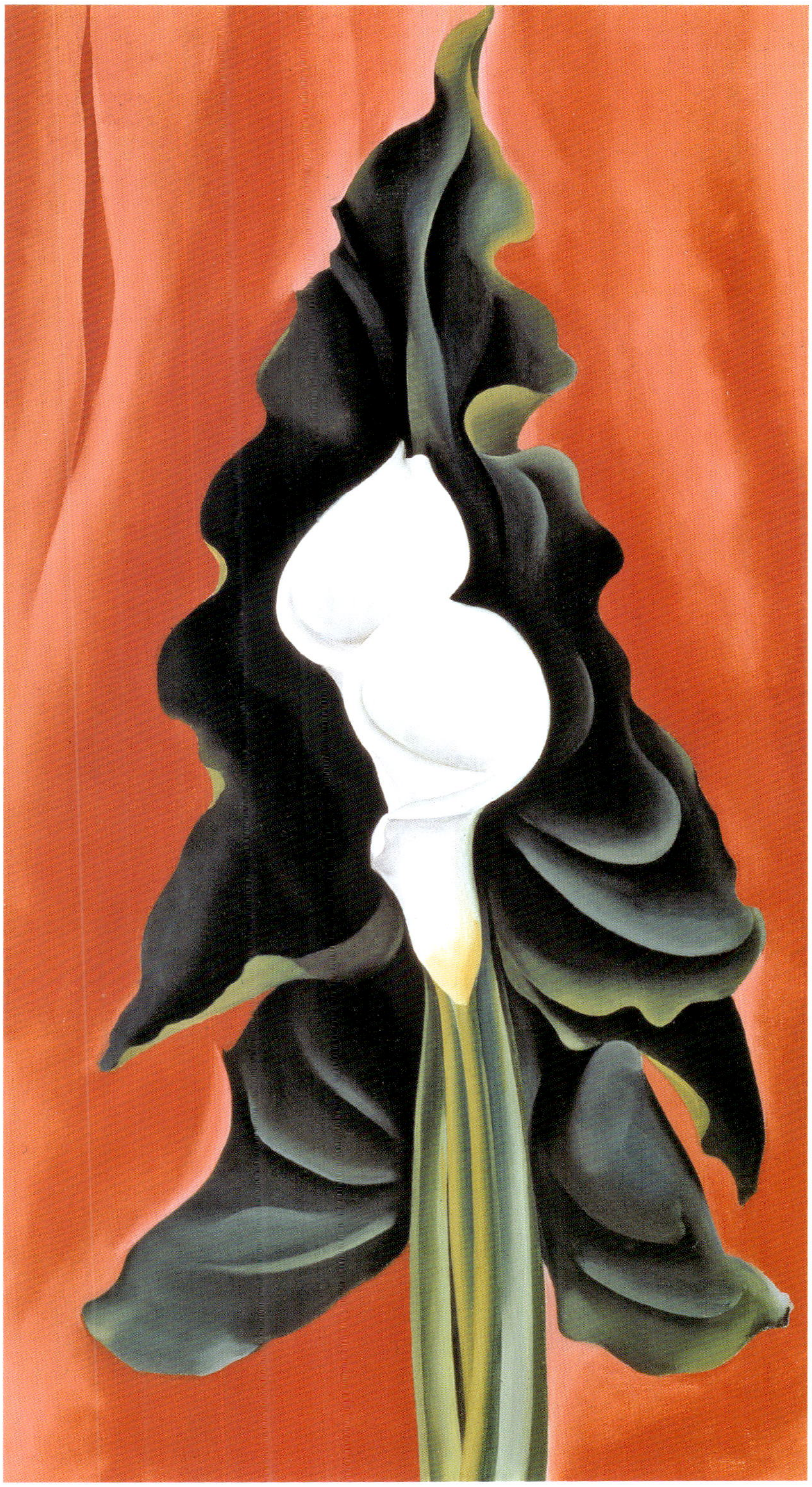

CALLA LILIES ON RED

1928

oil on canvas, 32 1/8" x 17 1/8"

Collection of Georgia O'Keeffe Museum, Santa Fe, New Mexico

Gift of Anne Windfohr Marion

1996.5.1

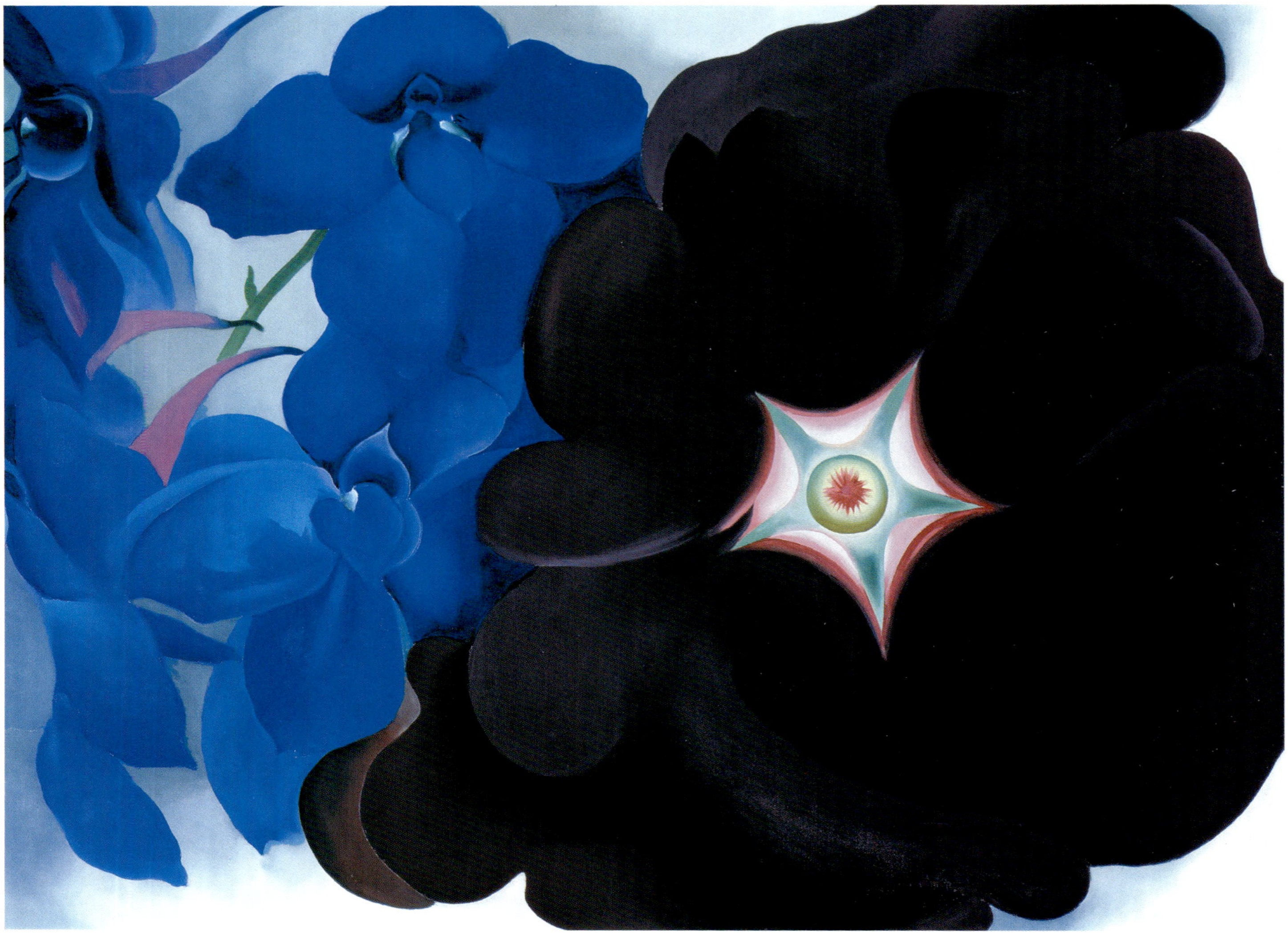

BLACK HOLLYHOCK BLUE LARKSPUR

1930

oil on canvas, 30 1/8" x 40"

Extended loan, private collection, Georgia O'Keeffe Museum, Santa Fe, New Mexico

L.1997.3.1

Georgia O'Keeffe Museum, Santa Fe, New Mexico, only

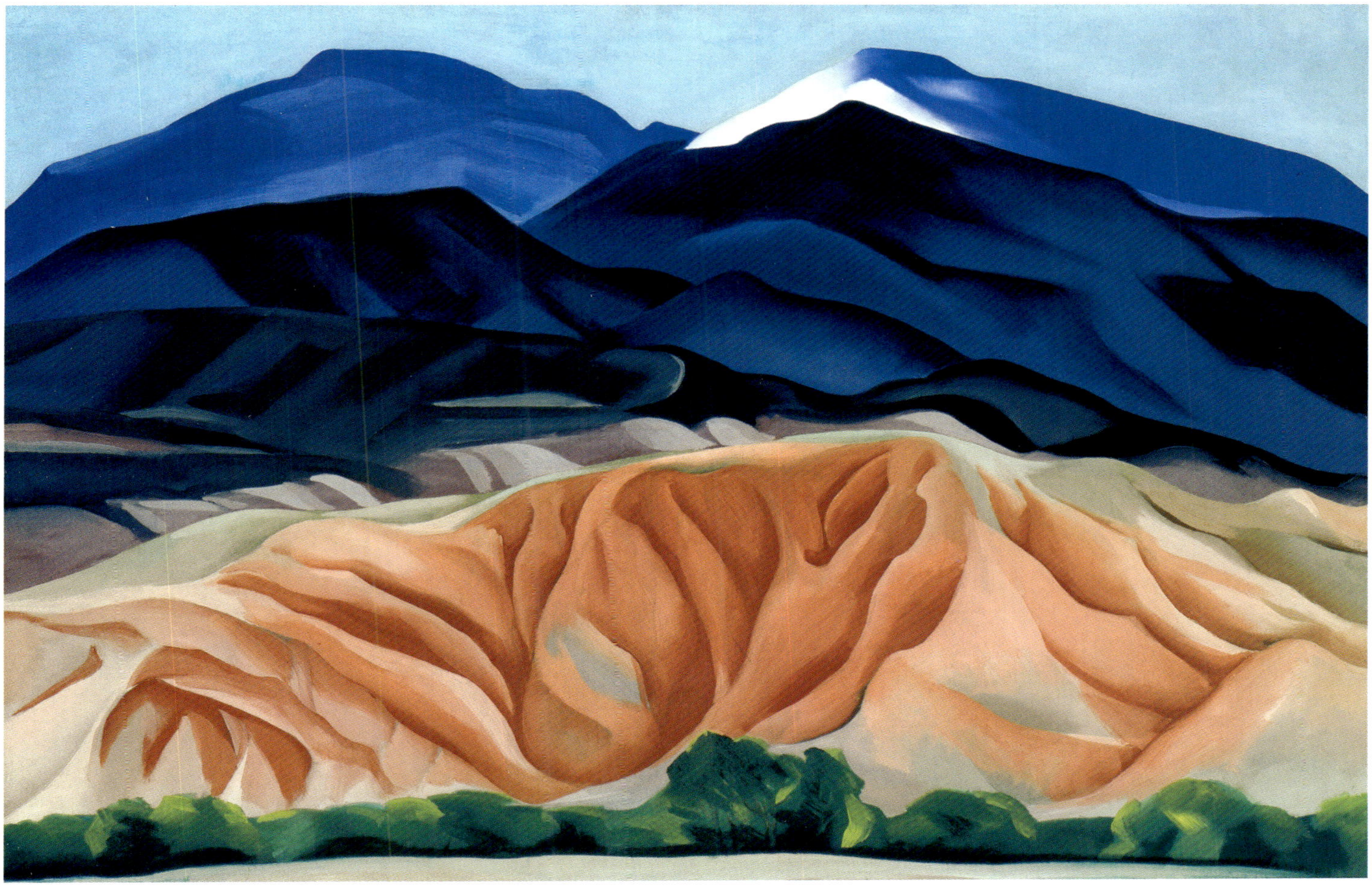

BLACK MESA LANDSCAPE, NEW MEXICO/OUT BACK OF MARIE'S II

1930

oil on canvas mounted on board, 24 1/4" x 36 1/4"

Collection of Georgia O'Keeffe Museum, Santa Fe, New Mexico

Gift of The Burnett Foundation

1997.06.15

Photograph: Malcolm Varon

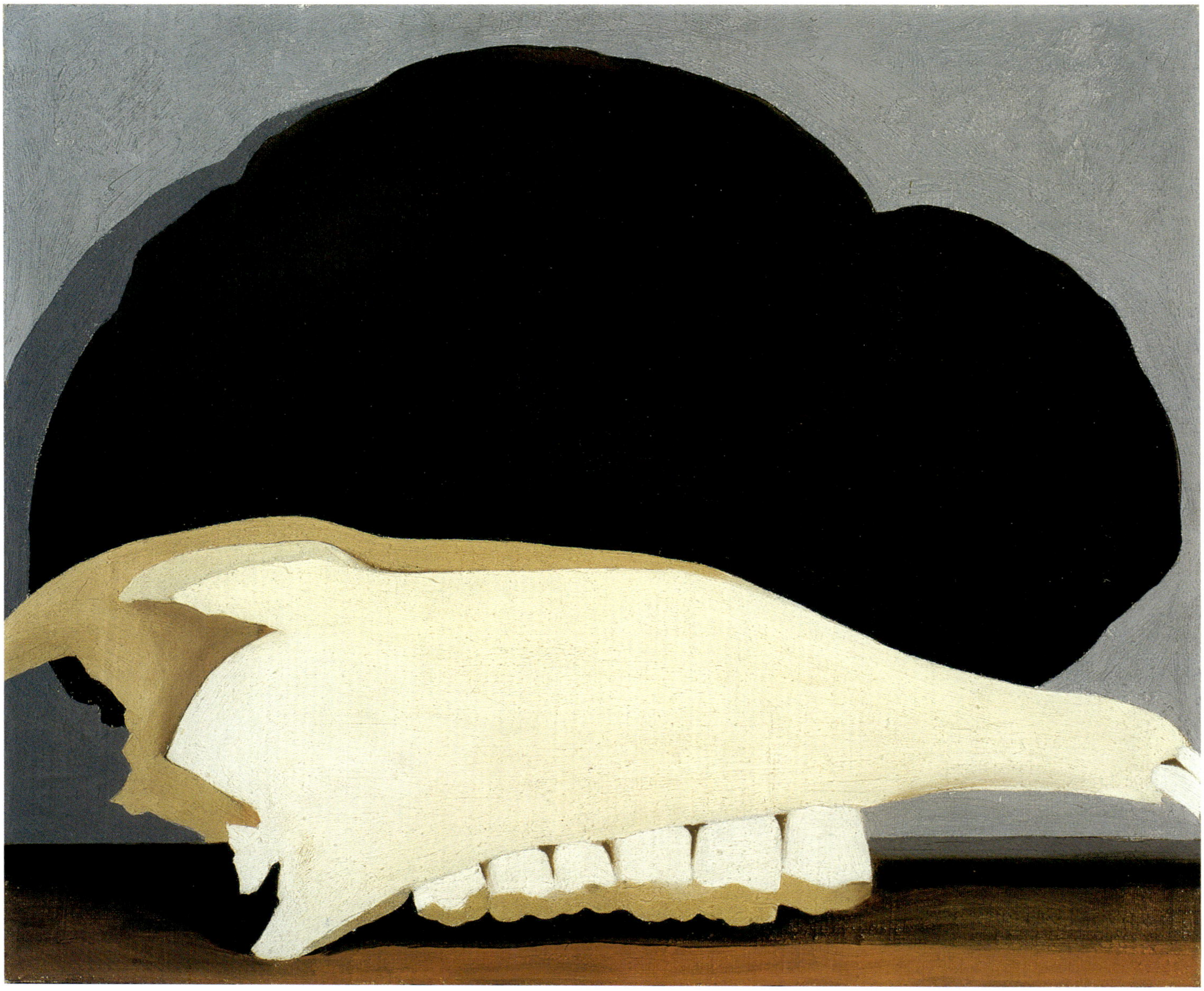

JAWBONE AND FUNGUS
1931
oil on canvas, 17" x 20"
Collection of Memorial Art Gallery of the University of Rochester, New York, Marion Stratton Gould Fund
51.11a
Photograph: James M. Via

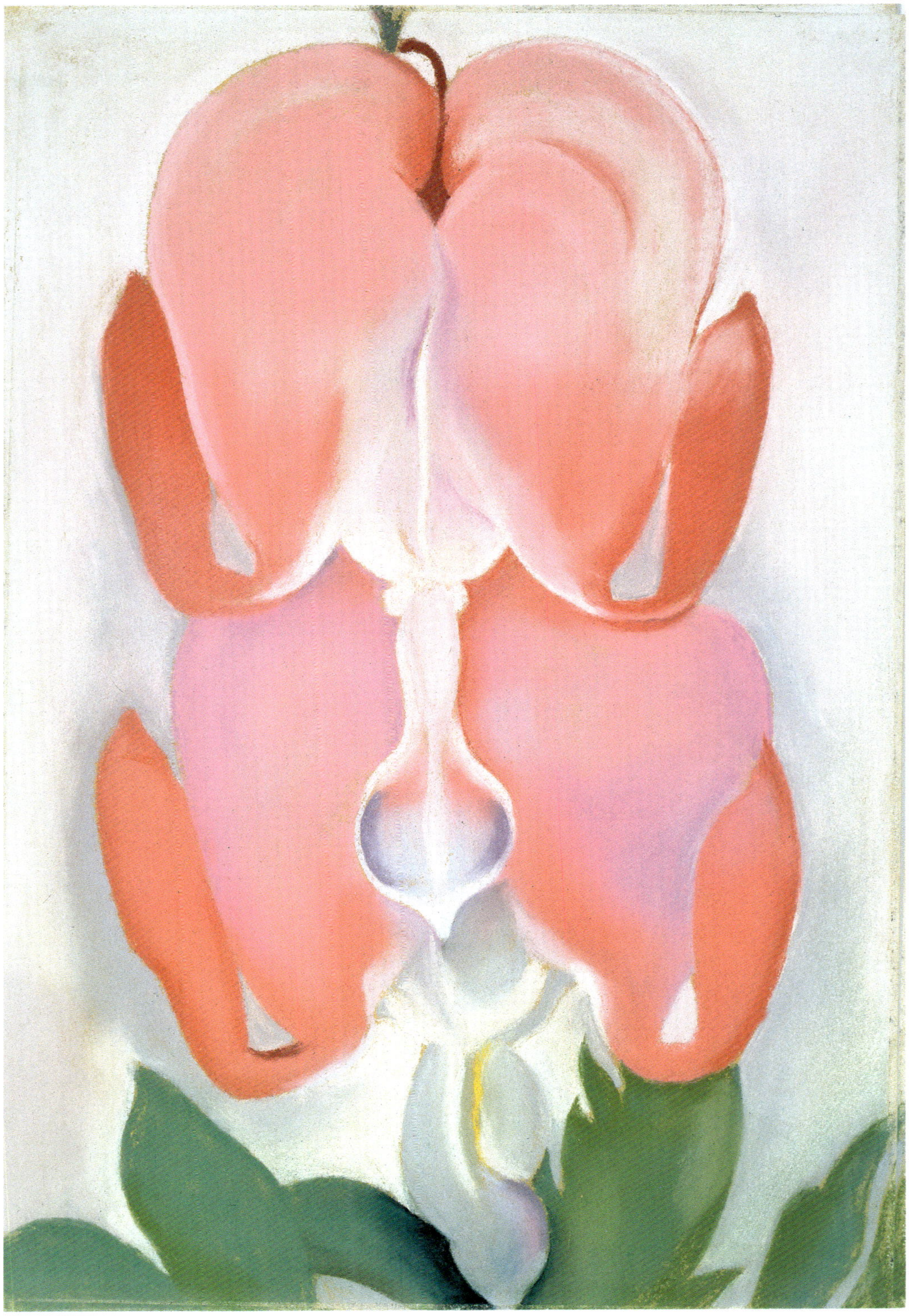

BLEEDING HEART

1932

pastel on cardboard, 15 1/8" x 10"

Collection of Georgia O'Keeffe Museum, Santa Fe, New Mexico

Gift of Anne Windfohr Marion and Anne Windfohr Grimes

1996.4.1

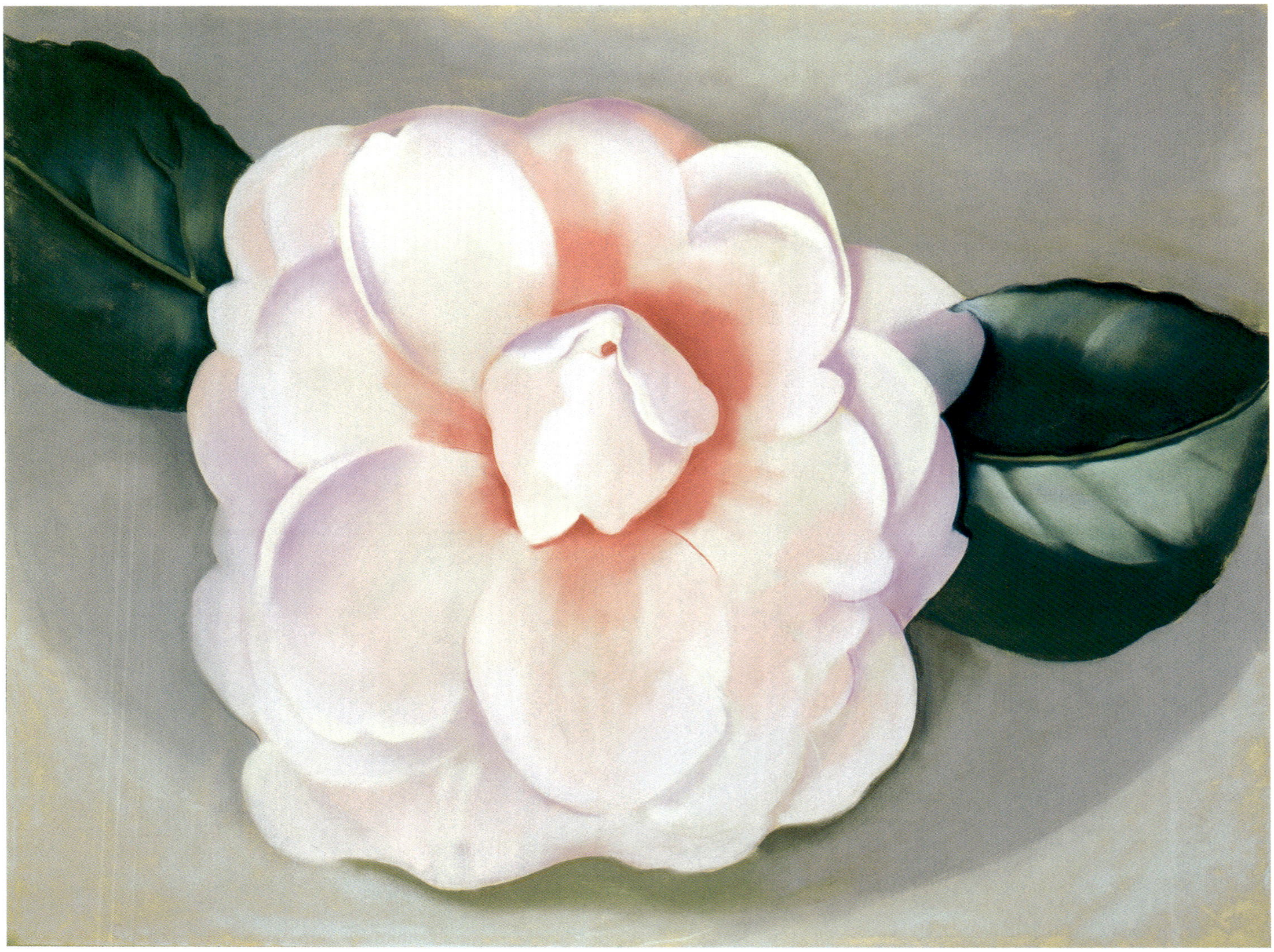

UNTITLED (PINK CAMELLIA)
1935
pastel on paper, 20 1/2" x 26 1/4"
Collection of Fitchburg Art Museum, Massachusetts
Gift of Margaret S. Sinon
1992.1
Photograph: Malcolm Varon
Mississippi Museum of Art, Jackson, only

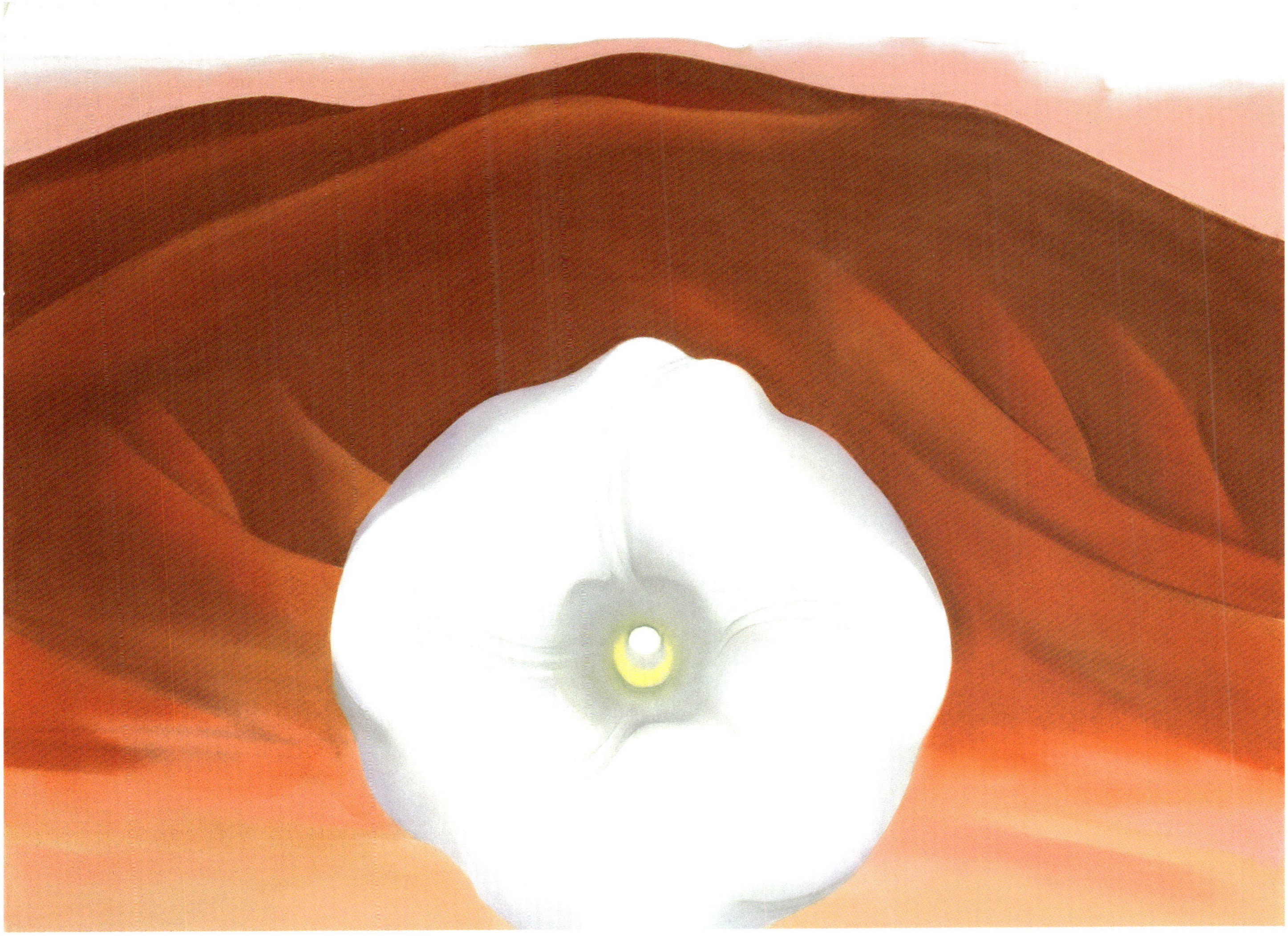

RED HILLS AND WHITE FLOWER

1937

pastel on paper mounted on cardboard, 19 3/8" x 25 5/8"

Collection of Georgia O'Keeffe Museum, Santa Fe, New Mexico

Gift of The Burnett Foundation

1997.06.02

Photograph: Malcolm Varon

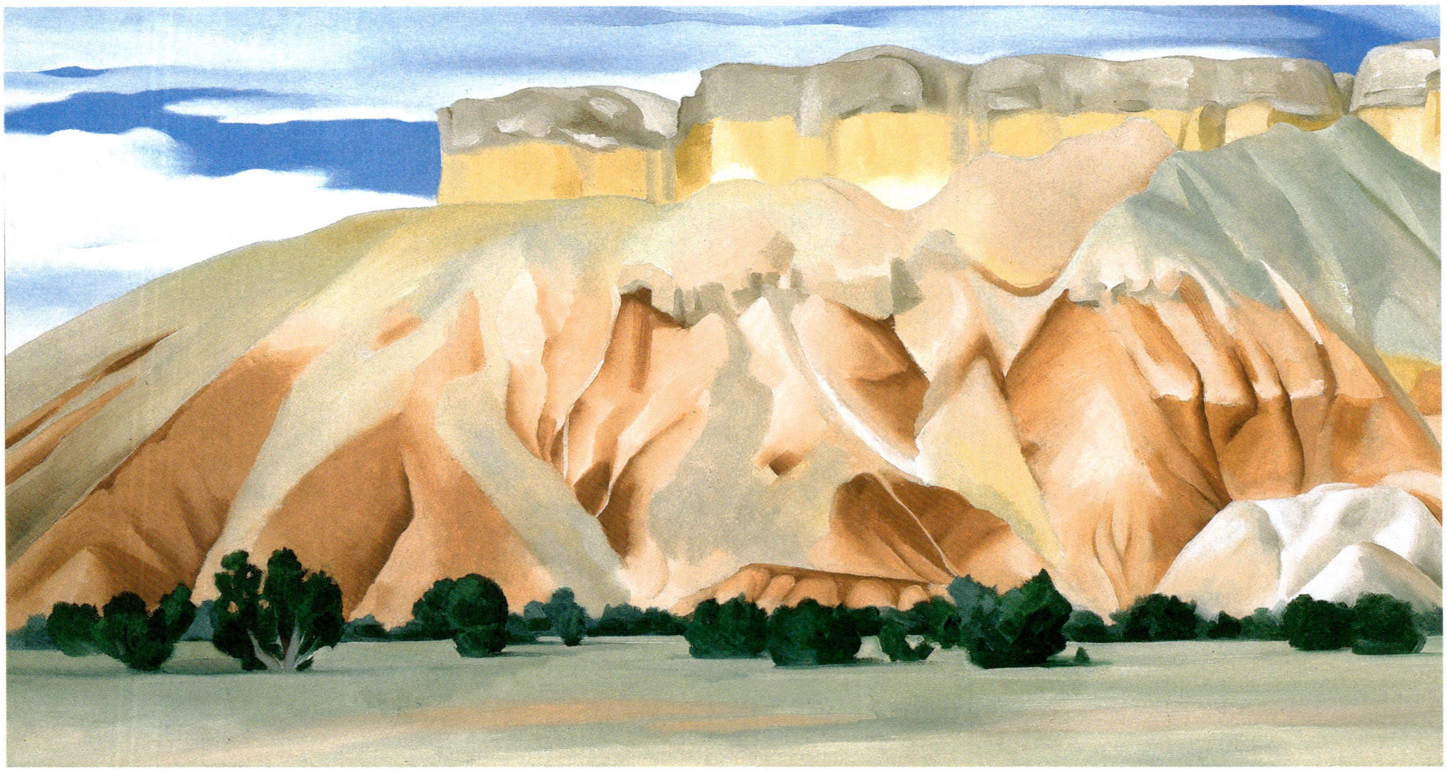

MY BACKYARD

1937

oil on canvas, 20" x 36"

Collection of New Orleans Museum of Art, Louisiana

Museum purchase, City of New Orleans Capital Funds

73.8

Mississippi Museum of Art, Jackson, only

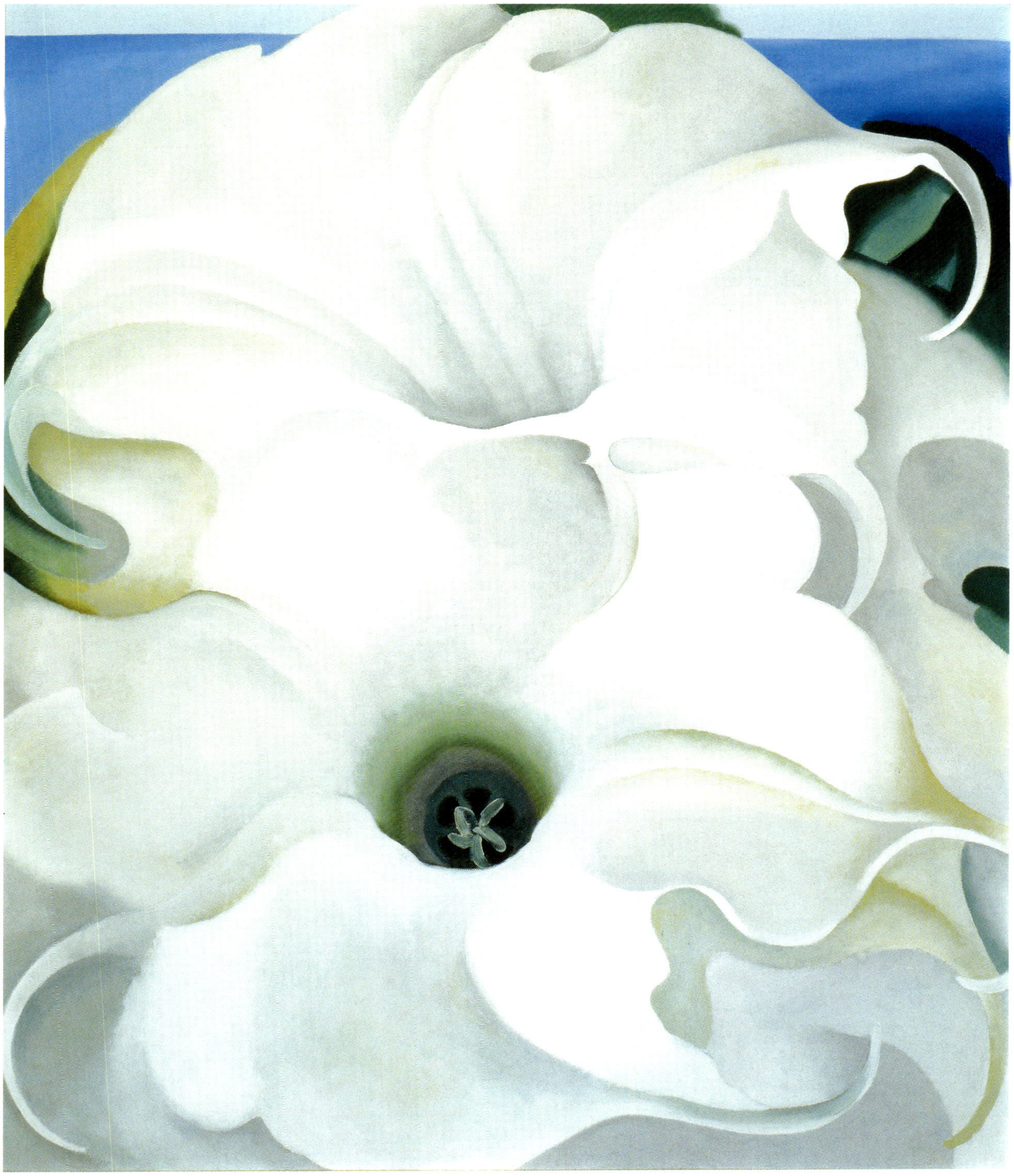

BELLA DONNA

1939

oil on canvas, 36 1/4" x 30 1/8"

Extended loan, private collection, Georgia O'Keeffe Museum, Santa Fe, New Mexico

L.1997.3.3

Georgia O'Keeffe Museum, Santa Fe, New Mexico, only

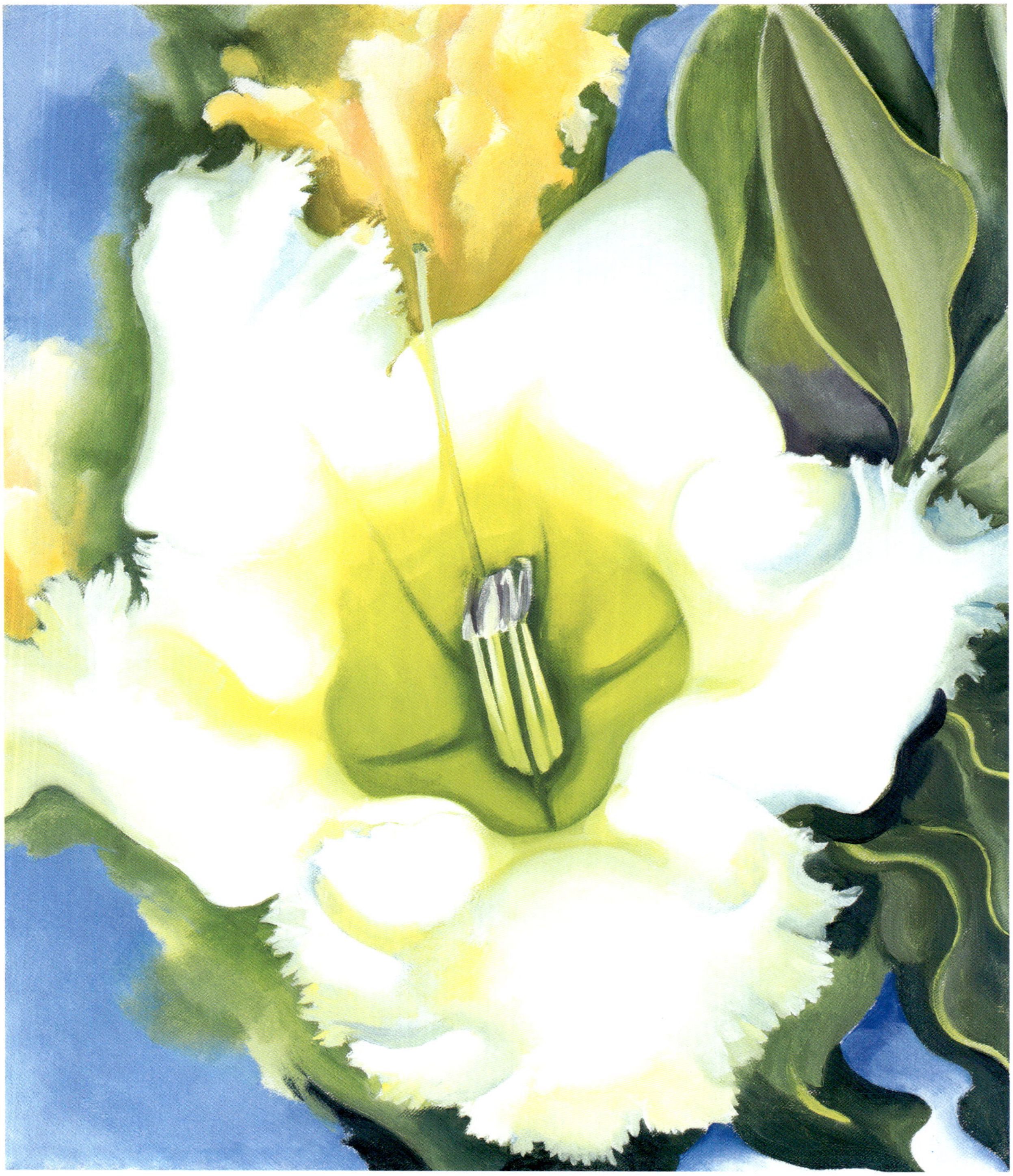

CUP OF SILVER GINGER
1939
oil on canvas, 19" x 16"
Collection of Baltimore Museum of Art, Maryland
Gift of Cary Ross
BMA 1940.122

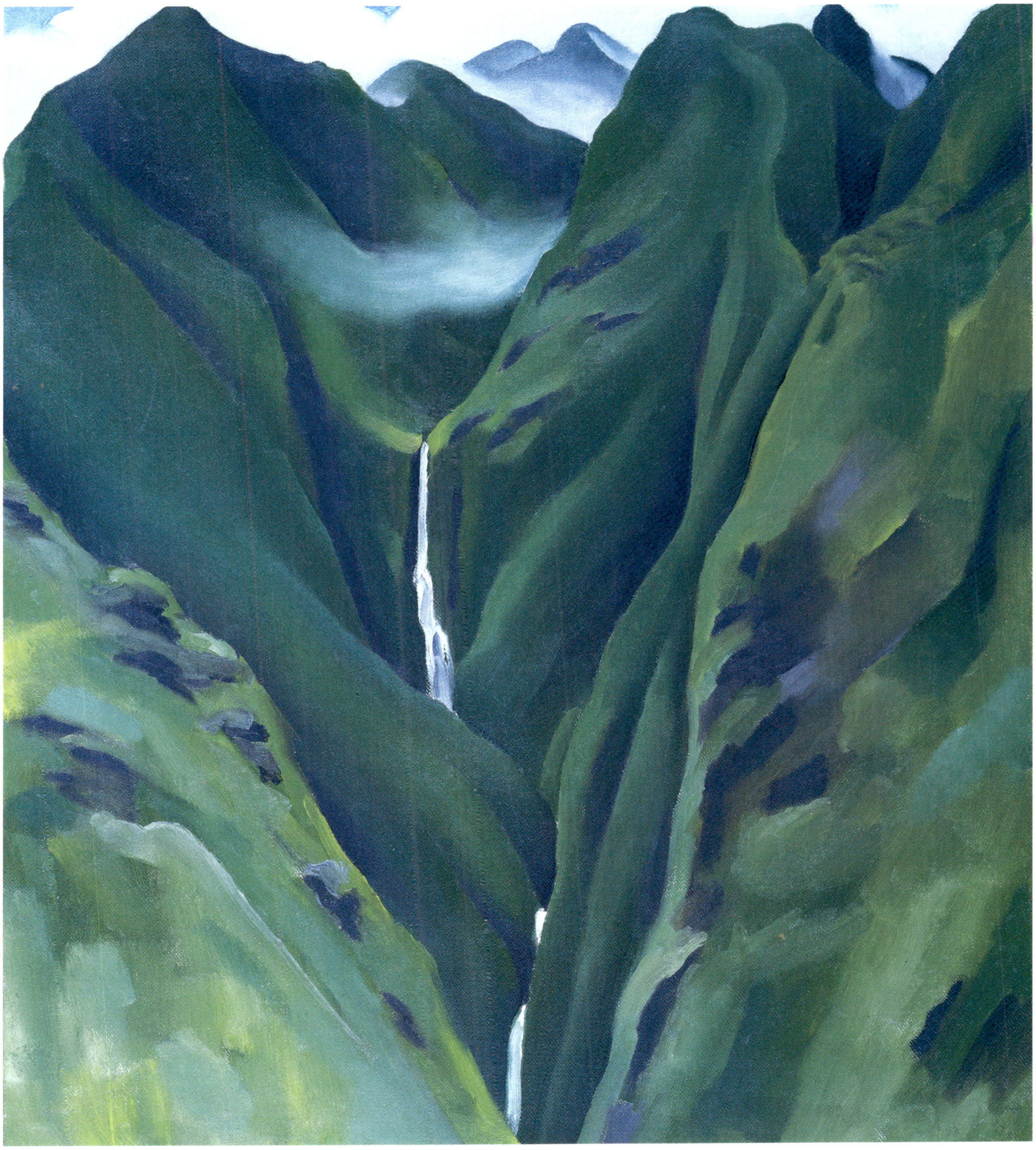

WATERFALL, NO. 1, ĪAO VALLEY, MAUI

1939

oil on canvas, 19" x 16"

Collection of Memphis Brooks Museum of Art, Tennessee

Gift of Art Today

76.7

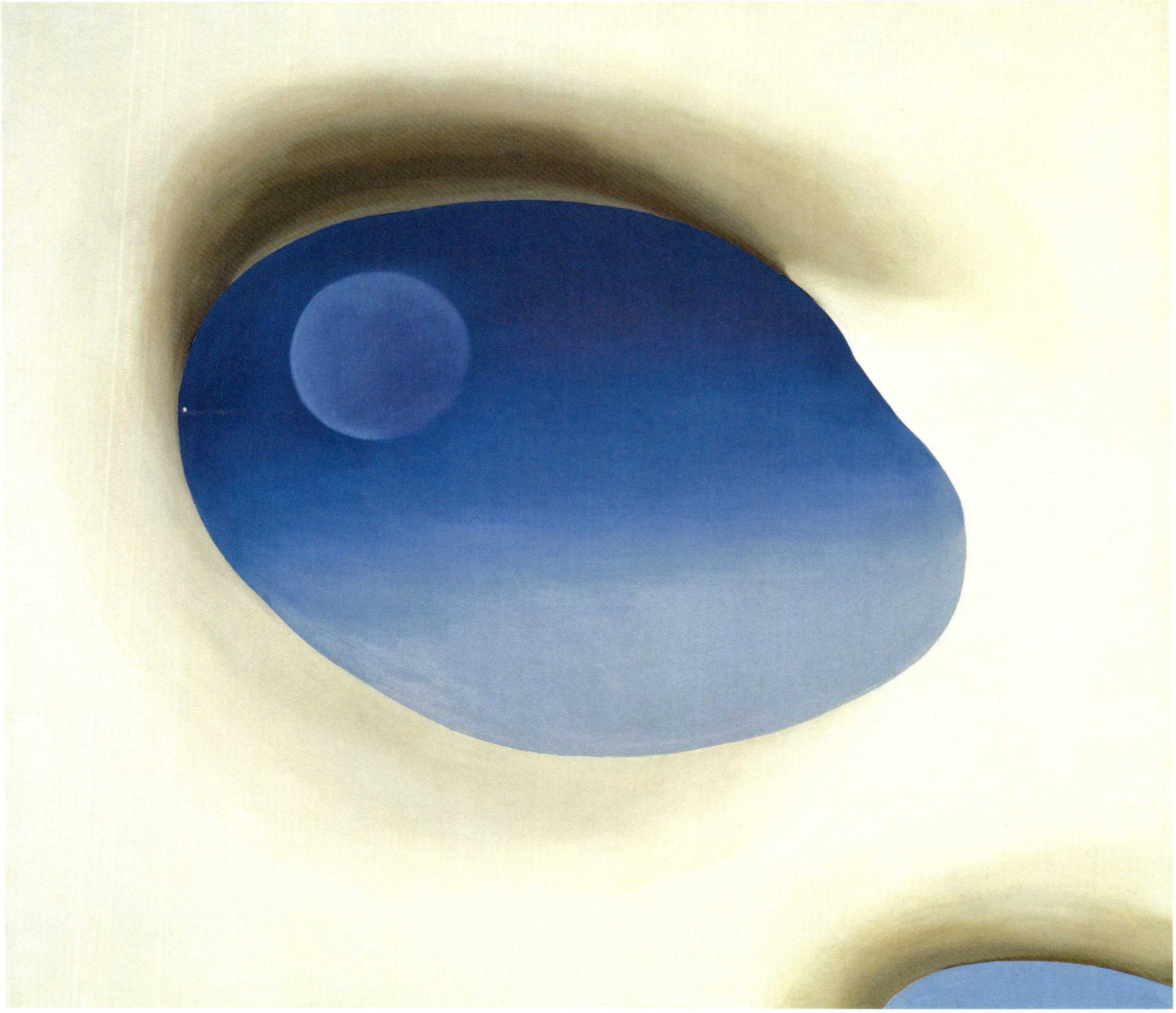

PELVIS IV
1944
oil on Masonite, 36" x 40"
Collection of Georgia O'Keeffe Museum, Santa Fe, New Mexico
Gift of The Burnett Foundation
1997.06.01
Photograph: Malcolm Varon

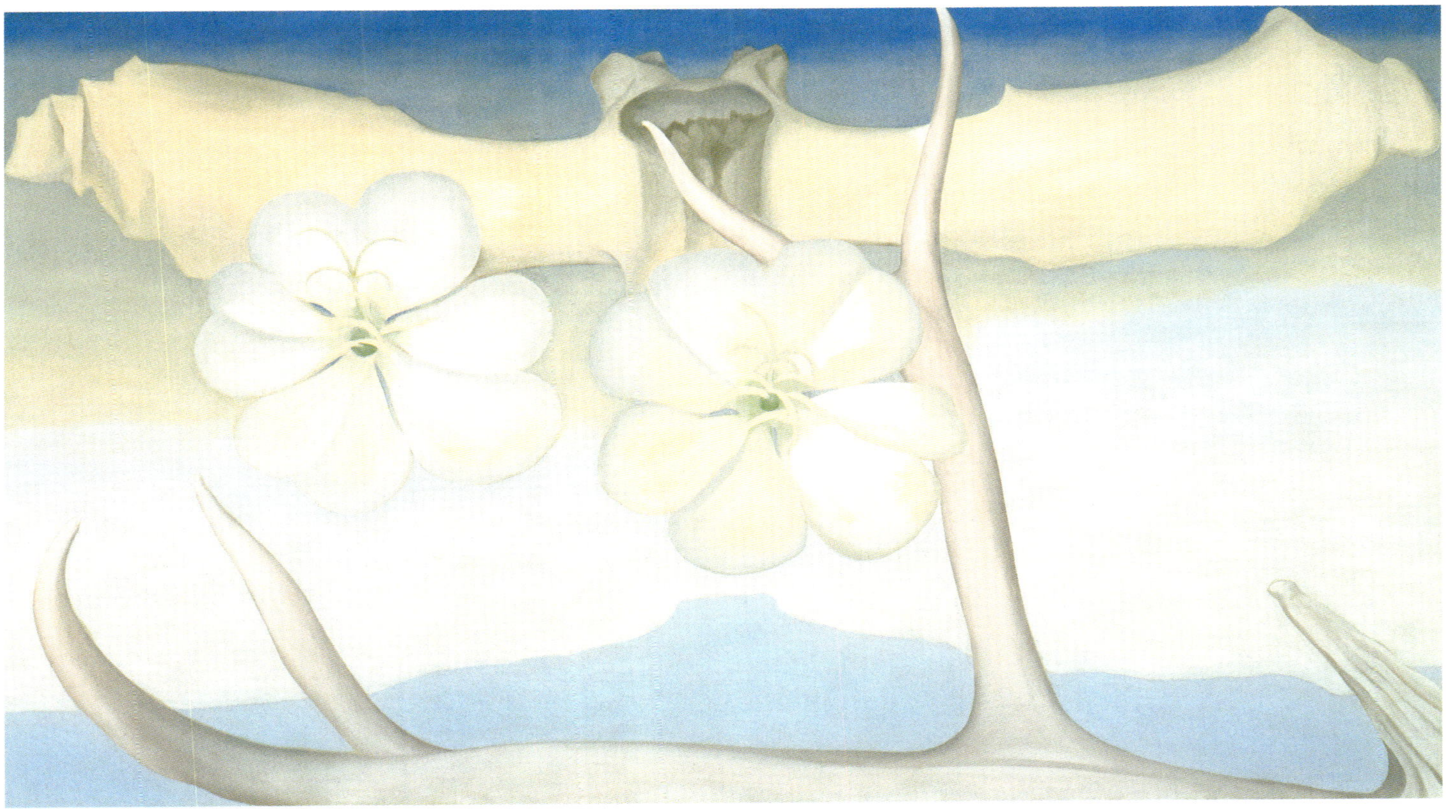

SPRING
1948
oil on canvas, 48 1/4" x 84 1/4"
Collection of Georgia O'Keeffe Museum, Santa Fe, New Mexico
Gift of The Burnett Foundation
1997.06.28
Photograph: Malcolm Varon

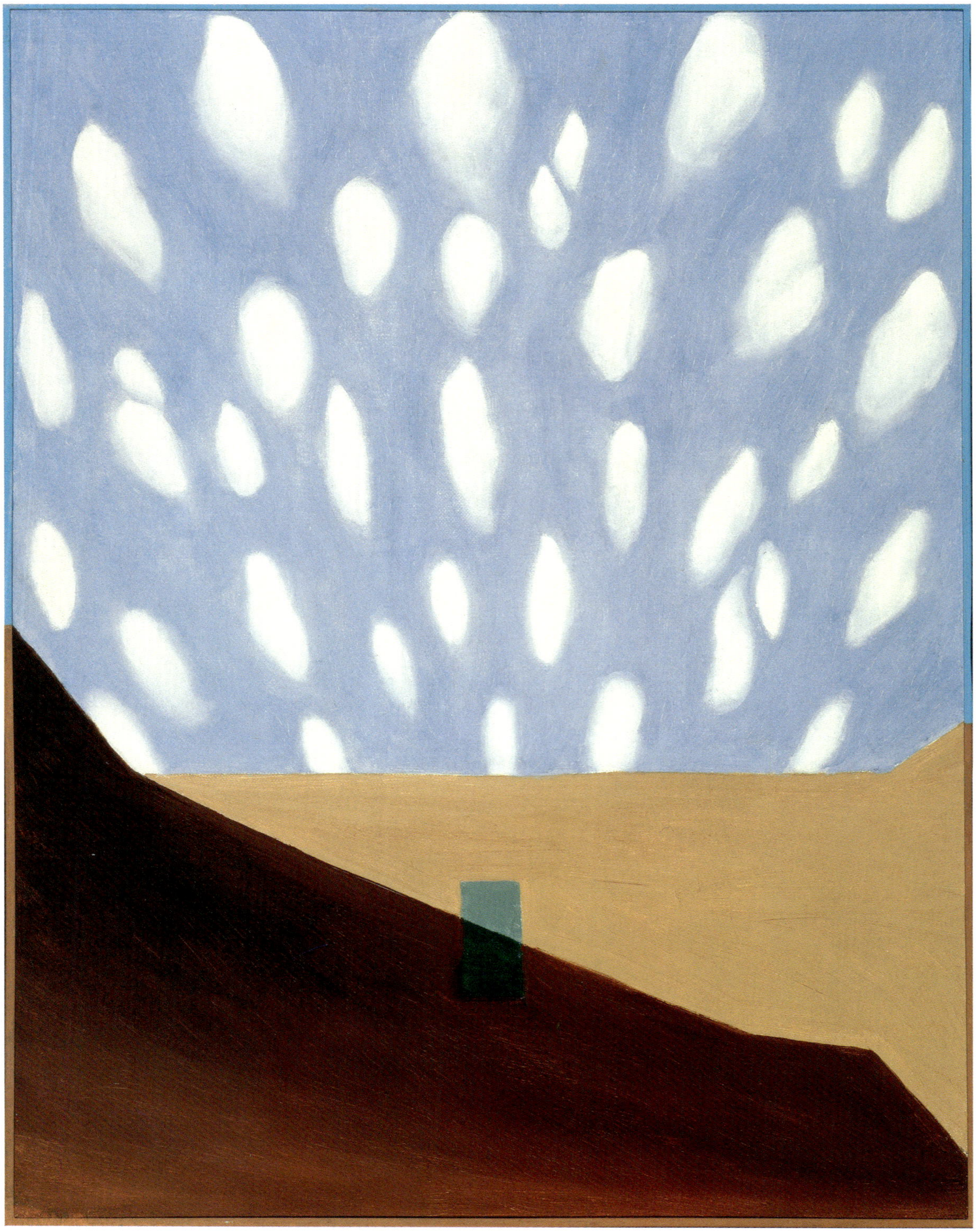

IN THE PATIO VIII
1950
oil on canvas, 26" x 20"
Collection of Georgia O'Keeffe Museum, Santa Fe, New Mexico
Gift of The Burnett Foundation and The Georgia O'Keeffe Foundation
1997.05.08
Photograph: Malcolm Varon

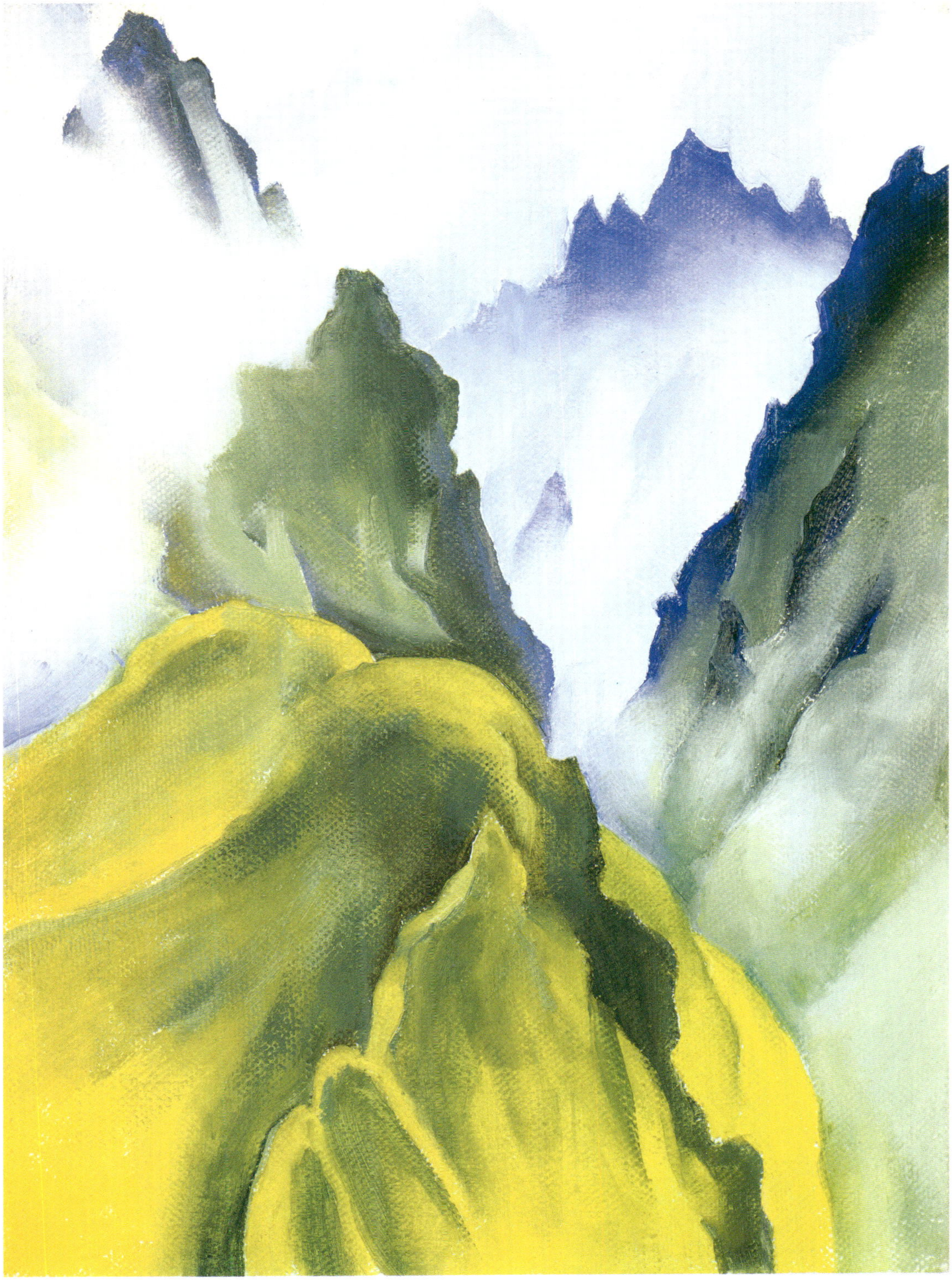

MACHU PICHU I
1957
oil on canvas, 11 1/8" x 8"
Collection of The Georgia O'Keeffe Foundation, Abiquiu, New Mexico

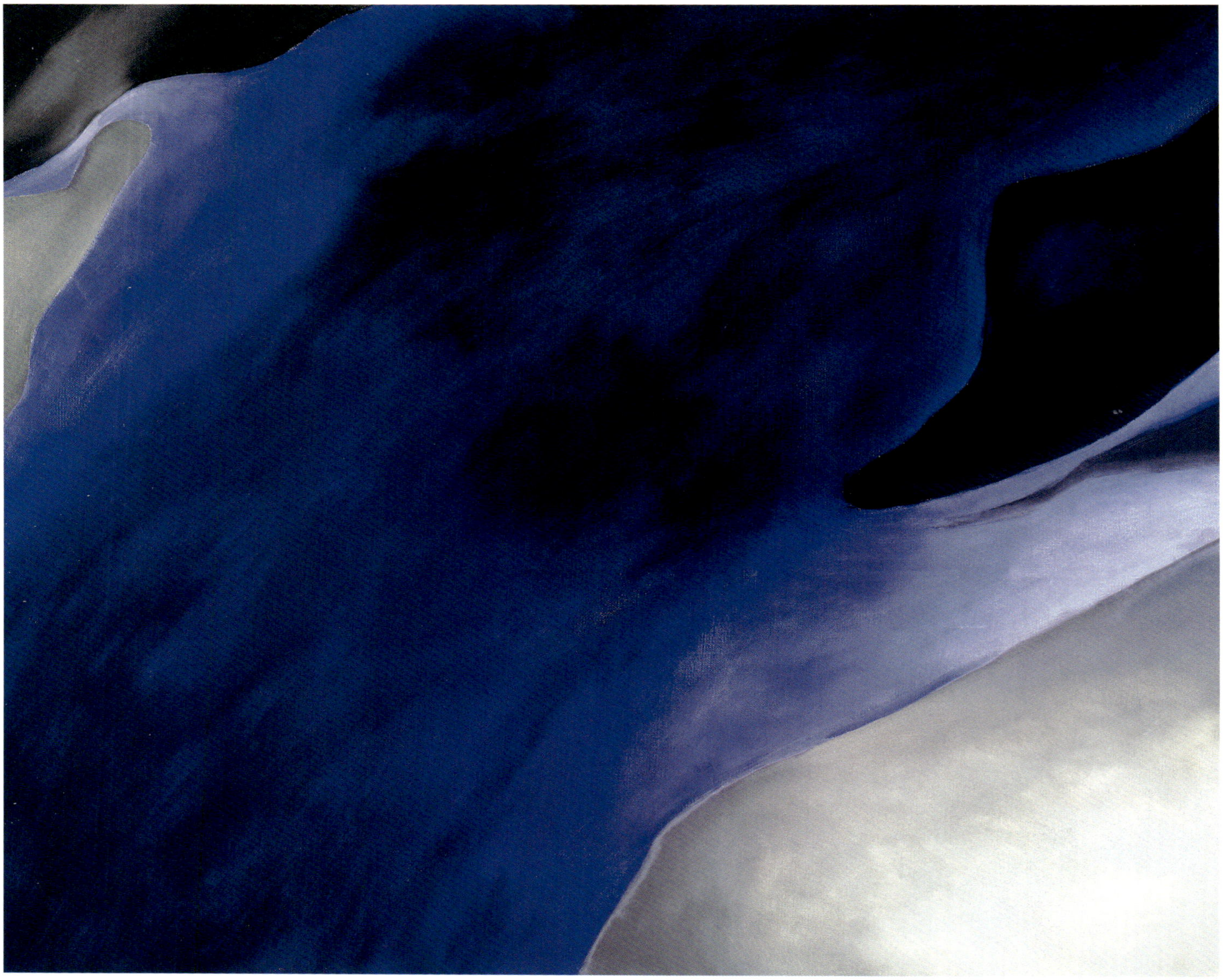

BLUE – A
1959
oil on canvas, 30" x 36"
Collection of The Georgia O'Keeffe Foundation, Abiquiu, New Mexico

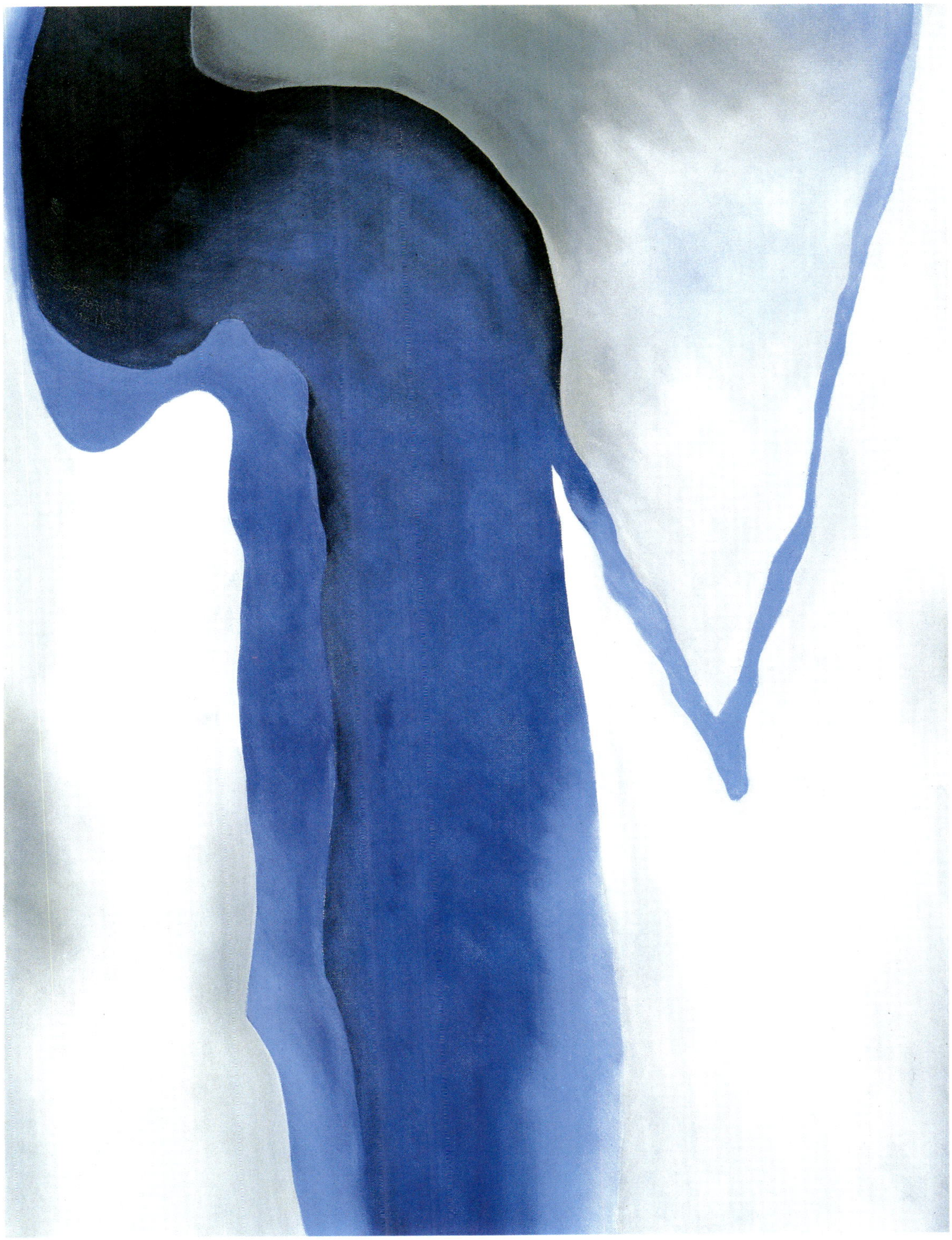

BLUE BLACK AND GREY

1960

oil on canvas, 40" x 30"

Promised gift, The Burnett Foundation, Georgia O'Keeffe Museum, Santa Fe, New Mexico

L.1998.2.7

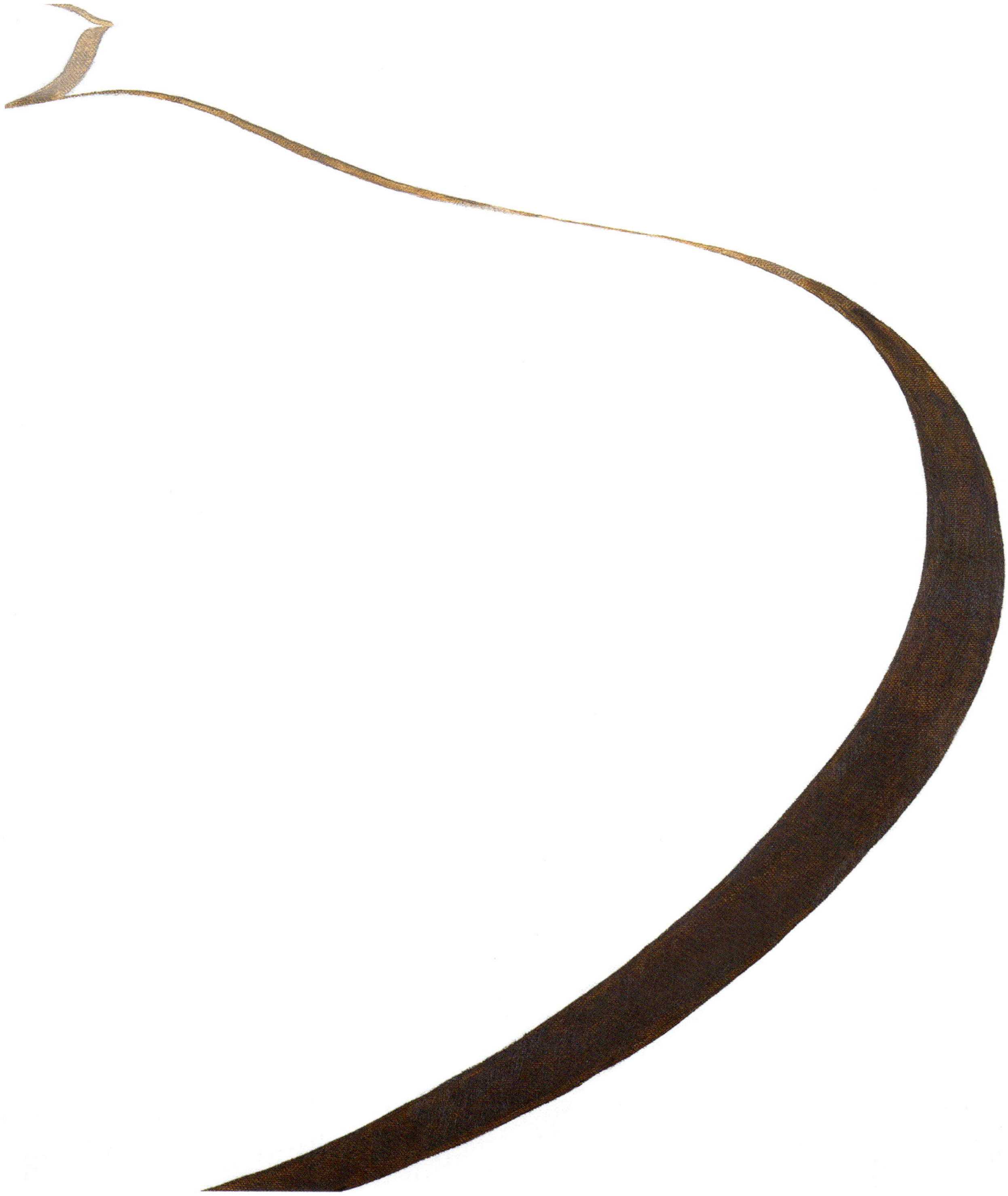

WINTER ROAD I
1963
oil on canvas, 22" x 18"
Collection of National Gallery of Art, Washington, D.C.
Gift of The Georgia O'Keeffe Foundation
1995.4.1
Courtesy of Board of Trustees, National Gallery of Art
Photograph: Bob Grove

COLOR AND CONSERVATION: EXHIBITION CHECKLIST

Untitled (Claudia O'Keeffe)
1907-8
oil on canvas
12" x 10"
Collection of Museum of Fine Arts, Museum of New Mexico, Santa Fe, Department of Cultural Affairs
Bequest of Claudia O'Keeffe, Museum of New Mexico Foundation, 1988

Red Landscape
1916-17
oil on board
24 1/2" x 18 1/2"
Collection of Panhandle-Plains Historical Museum, Canyon, Texas
Gift of The Georgia O'Keeffe Foundation
1995.86.1

Series 1 – No. 1
1918
oil on board
19 3/4" x 16"
Collection of Amon Carter Museum, Fort Worth, Texas
Purchase with assistance from the Anne Burnett Tandy Accessions Fund
1995.8

Over Blue
1918
pastel on paper
27 1/2" x 21 1/2"
Private Collection
Courtesy of Memorial Art Gallery of the University of Rochester, New York
Memorial Art Gallery of the University of Rochester, New York, only

Blue Flower
1918
pastel on paper mounted on cardboard
20" x 16"
Promised gift, The Burnett Foundation, Georgia O'Keeffe Museum, Santa Fe, New Mexico
L.1998.7.2
Georgia O'Keeffe Museum, Santa Fe, New Mexico, only

Untitled (Abstraction)
1918
oil on canvas board
19 1/4" x 14"
Collection of The University of Mississippi, University
Gift of Seymour Lawrence

Green Lines and Pink
1919
oil on canvas
18" x 10"
Collection of Georgia O'Keeffe Museum, Santa Fe, New Mexico
Gift of The Burnett Foundation and The Georgia O'Keeffe Foundation
1997.05.07

Series I – From the Plains
1919
oil on canvas
27" x 23"
Promised gift, The Burnett Foundation, Georgia O'Keeffe Museum, Santa Fe, New Mexico
L.1998.2.2
Georgia O'Keeffe Museum, Santa Fe, New Mexico, only

Lake George, Coat and Red
1919
oil on canvas
27 3/8" x 23 1/4"
Collection of The Museum of Modern Art, New York, New York
Gift of The Georgia O'Keeffe Foundation
65.1995

Apple Family A
1920
oil on canvas
10" x 8"
Collection of Gerald and Kathleen Peters, Santa Fe, New Mexico
Courtesy of Gerald Peters Gallery, Santa Fe, New Mexico

Apple Family – 2
1920
oil on canvas
8 1/8" x 10 1/8"
Collection of Georgia O'Keeffe Museum, Santa Fe, New Mexico
Gift of The Burnett Foundation and The Georgia O'Keeffe Foundation
1997.04.03

Abstraction, Seaweed and Water – Maine
1920
pastel on paper
20 1/4" x 17 3/4"
Collection of The Georgia O'Keeffe Foundation, Abiquiu, New Mexico

Water Lily
1921
pastel on paper
28 1/4" x 17 1/2"
Collection of The Georgia O'Keeffe Foundation, Abiquiu, New Mexico
Georgia O'Keeffe Museum, Santa Fe, New Mexico, only

The White Wave
1922
pastel on paper
19" x 25"
Extended loan, private collection, Georgia O'Keeffe Museum, Santa Fe, New Mexico
L.1998.03.01
Georgia O'Keeffe Museum, Santa Fe, New Mexico, only

Calla Lily Turned Away
1923
pastel on cardboard
14" x 10 7/8"
Collection of Georgia O'Keeffe Museum, Santa Fe, New Mexico
Gift of The Burnett Foundation
1997.18.2
Georgia O'Keeffe Museum, Santa Fe, New Mexico, only

Leaves
1923
oil on canvas mounted on board
12" x 9"
Collection of The Newark Museum, New Jersey
Bequest of Cora Louise Hartshorn
58.168

Corn, No. 2
1924
oil on canvas
27 1/4" x 10"
Collection of Georgia O'Keeffe Museum, Santa Fe, New Mexico
Gift of The Burnett Foundation and The Georgia O'Keeffe Foundation
1997.04.06

Petunia, No. 2
1924
oil on canvas
36" x 30"
Collection of Georgia O'Keeffe Museum, Santa Fe, New Mexico
Gift of The Burnett Foundation and Kathleen Peters
1996.3.2
Georgia O'Keeffe Museum, Santa Fe, New Mexico, only

Flagpole
1925
oil on canvas
35" x 18 1/8"
Collection of Georgia O'Keeffe Museum, Santa Fe, New Mexico
Gift of The Burnett Foundation and an anonymous donor
1997.02.01

New York – Night
1926
oil on canvas
32" x 12"
Collection of Museum of Fine Arts, St. Petersburg, Florida
Gift of Charles and Margaret Stevenson Henderson, in memory of Hunt Henderson
1971.31

Shell and Old Shingle IV
1926
oil on board
9 3/4" x 7"
Collection of Museum of Fine Arts, Boston, Massachusetts
Alfred Stieglitz Collection
Bequest of Georgia O'Keeffe
1987.538a

The Old Maple, Lake George
1926
oil on canvas
36" x 32"
Collection of Mississippi Museum of Art, Jackson
Purchase with funds from the Mississippi Arts Commission and Operation Snowball
1972.009

Dark Iris
1927
oil on canvas
32" x 12"
Collection of Colorado Springs Fine Arts Center, Taylor Museum, Colorado
Anonymous gift
FA 1954.4

Abstraction White Rose
1927
oil on canvas
36" x 30"
Collection of Georgia O'Keeffe Museum, Santa Fe, New Mexico
Gift of The Burnett Foundation and The Georgia O'Keeffe Foundation
1997.4.2
Georgia O'Keeffe Museum, Santa Fe, New Mexico, only

Calla Lilies on Red
1928
oil on canvas
32 1/8" x 17 1/8"
Collection of Georgia O'Keeffe Museum, Santa Fe, New Mexico
Gift of Anne Windfohr Marion
1996.5.1
Georgia O'Keeffe Museum, Santa Fe, New Mexico, only

Black Hollyhock Blue Larkspur
1930
oil on canvas
30 1/8" x 40"
Extended loan, private collection
Georgia O'Keeffe Museum, Santa Fe, New Mexico
L.1997.3.1
Georgia O'Keeffe Museum, Santa Fe, New Mexico, only

Black Mesa Landscape, New Mexico/Out Back of Marie's II
1930
oil on canvas mounted on board
24 1/4" x 36 1/4"
Collection of Georgia O'Keeffe Museum, Santa Fe, New Mexico
Gift of the Burnett Foundation
1997.06.15

Jawbone and Fungus
1931
oil on canvas
17" x 20"
Collection of Memorial Art Gallery of the University of Rochester, New York
Marion Stratton Gould Fund
51.11a

Bleeding Heart
1932
pastel on cardboard
15 1/8" x 10"
Collection of Georgia O'Keeffe Museum, Santa Fe, New Mexico
Gift of Anne Windfohr Marion and Anne Windfohr Grimes
1996.4.1
Georgia O'Keeffe Museum, Santa Fe, New Mexico, only

Untitled (Pink Camellia)
1935
pastel on paper
20 1/2" x 26 1/4"
Collection of Fitchburg Art Museum, Massachusetts
Gift of Margaret S. Sinon
1992.1
Mississippi Museum of Art, Jackson, only

Red Hills and White Flower
1937
pastel on paper mounted on cardboard
19 3/8" x 25 5/8"
Collection of Georgia O'Keeffe Museum, Santa Fe, New Mexico
Gift of The Burnett Foundation
1997.05.02
Georgia O'Keeffe Museum, Santa Fe, New Mexico, only

My Backyard
1937
oil on canvas
20" x 36"
Collection of New Orleans Museum of Art, Louisiana
Museum purchase, City of New Orleans Capital Funds
73.8
Mississippi Museum of Art, Jackson, only

Bella Donna
1939
oil on canvas
36 1/4" x 30 1/8"
Extended loan, private collection, Georgia O'Keeffe Museum, Santa Fe, New Mexico
L.1997.3.3
Georgia O'Keeffe Museum, Santa Fe, New Mexico, only

Cup of Silver Ginger
1939
oil on canvas
19" x 16"
Collection of Baltimore Museum of Art, Maryland
Gift of Cary Ross
BMA 1940.122

Waterfall, No. 1, Īao Valley, Maui
1939
oil on canvas
19" x 16"
Collection of Memphis Brooks Museum of Art, Tennessee
Gift of Art Today
76.7

Pelvis IV
1944
oil on Masonite
36" x 40"
Collection of Georgia O'Keeffe Museum, Santa Fe, New Mexico
Gift of The Burnett Foundation
1997.06.01

Spring
1948
oil on canvas
48 1/4" x 84 1/4"
Collection of Georgia O'Keeffe Museum, Santa Fe, New Mexico
Gift of The Burnett Foundation
1997.06.28
Georgia O'Keeffe Museum, Santa Fe, New Mexico, only

In the Patio VIII
1950
oil on canvas
26" x 20"
Collection of Georgia O'Keeffe Museum, Santa Fe, New Mexico
Gift of The Burnett Foundation and The Georgia O'Keeffe Foundation
1997.05.08

Machu Pichu I
1957
oil on canvas
11 1/8" x 8"
Collection of The Georgia O'Keeffe Foundation, Abiquiu, New Mexico

Blue – A
1959
oil on canvas
30" x 36"
Collection of The Georgia O'Keeffe Foundation, Abiquiu, New Mexico

Blue Black and Grey
1960
oil on canvas
40" x 30"
Promised gift, The Burnett Foundation, Georgia O'Keeffe Museum, Santa Fe, New Mexico
L.1998.2.7

Winter Road I
1963
oil on canvas
22" x 18"
Collection of National Gallery of Art, Washington, D.C.
Gift of The Georgia O'Keeffe Foundation
1995.4.1